ב"ה

The Art of
PARENTING

JEWISH WISDOM AND INSIGHTS
FOR RAISING CHILDREN

JLI

JEWISH LEARNING INSTITUTE

Lead Editor
Rabbi Naftali Silberberg

Course Consultants
Rabbi Shmuel Klatzkin, PhD
Casey Skvorc, PhD

Course Development
Rabbi Mordechai Dinerman
Rabbi Shmuel Lobenstein
Rabbi Eli Raksin
Rabbi Yanky Raskin
Rabbi Yanki Tauber

Editorial Board
Rabbi Avrohom Bergstein
Rabbi Yosef Hodakov
Mrs. Dina Kantor
Mrs. Chava Shapiro

Printed in the United States of America
© Published and Copyrighted 2014 by
The Rohr Jewish Learning Institute
822 Eastern Parkway, Brooklyn, NY 11213

(888) YOUR-JLI/718-221-6900
www.myJLI.com

The **Rohr Jewish Learning Institute**
gratefully acknowledges
the pioneering support of

George and Pamela Rohr

SINCE ITS INCEPTION,
the **Rohr JLI** has been
a beneficiary of the vision, generosity,
care, and concern
of the **Rohr family**

In the merit of
the tens of thousands of hours of Torah study
by **JLI** students worldwide,
may they be blessed with health,
Yiddishe nachas from all their loved ones,
and extraordinary success
in all their endeavors ✌

We acknowledge the

KOHELET FOUNDATION

OF PHILADELPHIA, PA

for providing the vision for this course
and inspiring its creation and development.

We salute

Mr. David Magerman

President and Founder of the Kohelet Foundation,

Holly Cohen, *Executive Director,*
and **Rebecca Goldberg,** *Program Officer,*

for their remarkable commitment to fostering
Jewish education and continuity.

ENDORSEMENTS

Parents constantly walk a tightrope, on the one hand keeping a firm handle on their children to maintain responsible behavior and instill strong values, and at the same time encouraging freedoms that are vital for the emergence of an independent adult. The Rohr Jewish Learning Institute's *The Art of Parenting* course provides solid footing for parents as they embark on this challenging endeavor. I laud their efforts and encourage parents everywhere to take advantage of this invaluable resource.

Marc N. Kramer, PhD
Executive Director, RAVSAK: The Jewish Community Day School Network

How families find a way to successfully parent is the cornerstone of my practice. Just because you are a parent does not mean you know how to develop confident, moral, and loving children. Finding the warm and authoritative parent zone is the key. *The Art of Parenting* offers families a way forward for children to grow into fully developed, moral adults.

Frank W. Gaskill, PhD
Founding Partner, Southeast Psych Licensed Psychologist

The Rohr Jewish Learning Institute is an exemplar of Jewish and general educational excellence. Their courses and learning materials are of the highest quality. We often complain that there is no manual on how to be an effective parent. The Rohr Jewish Learning Institute does it again. In a well-documented framework, *The Art of Parenting* is a necessary reading. It combines the wisdom of Biblical sages with the best in parenting. I urge you to participate in this remarkable learning adventure.

Dr. Steven Huberman
Dean, Touro College Graduate School of Social Work

JLI's newest course, *The Art of Parenting,* is really a masterwork of compiled wisdom. As a serious author of many parenting books and workshops, I am excited to see how practical and life changing this course will be for those who participate. We need to once again make parents the agents of change for our children and teenagers, and not the media and social psychologists. I have long believed that when you change the parents' reaction, you change the child's behavior.

Mark L. Brenner, MFT, PhD
Adjunct Professor, Pepperdine University
Founder, Parenting Without Therapy
Author of Raising an Adult *and*
The Best Parenting Book Ever!

We live in a time when we can read dozens of books on raising physically and emotionally healthy children. We can explore the internet sites, social networks, and blogs to discover ways to shape a healthy self-image and desire to succeed. We can summon Siri to tell us what to do with a child who bites her nails. JLI's *The Art of Parenting* offers parents an anchor and a light in a confusing sea of information. Based on the intersection of ancient text and modern theory, the course blends learning with the opportunity to apply lessons to one's life. In doing so, it creates an appreciation of what we have always known while helping us meet the challenges of parenting today.

Betsy Dolgin-Katz, PhD
Teacher of Adults, Florence Melton School of Adult Jewish Learning and Kol Isha Women's Study Center at the Board of Jewish Education of Metropolitan Chicago; Faculty, Spertus Institute of Jewish Studies; Author of The Adult Jewish Education Handbook *(Behrman House, 2005) and* Reinventing Adult Jewish Learning *(Ktav, 2012)*

Jewish life will not transmit through osmosis. For Judaism to continue to thrive, we as parents and educators must know and own the story of our families and the story of our nation. Through a methodical approach and expert educational materials, this Rohr Jewish Learning Institute course can train parents to teach their children to be passionate and knowing Jews, part of a purposeful people who partner with God.

Richard M. Joel
President and Bravmann Family University Professor Yeshiva University

Parenting at the beginning of the 21st century is very different from the first half of the 20th century. Over the past 100 years, the American family and the Jewish American family has transformed itself from a close knit group of parents, children, grandparents, aunts, uncles and cousins living in close proximity to independent family units. Parents today are very much on their own; they receive little guidance on how to raise their children. Children today have nowhere to turn other than to their parents for support, guidance and advice. For the first time in history, parents and children are left to their own devices to figure out how to make the experience meaningful and positive. By creating opportunities for parents to learn together and to share the experience of parenting with like-minded peers, the JLI is offering a much needed resource that meets the concerns of the 21st century. The real beneficiaries of such a program will be the children who will learn and grow in a stronger, more supportive community.

Paul A. Flexner, Ed.D.
Instructor, Department of Educational Psychology and Special Education Georgia State University, Atlanta, GA Co-Editor of What We NOW Know About Jewish Education

SPECIAL THANKS

The following individuals graciously agreed to be interviewed by the editorial team of the
Rohr Jewish Learning Institute. These interviews assisted us in developing the ideas and insights
of this course, and we thank them warmly for sharing their wisdom.

Rabbi Benjamin Blech, MA
Professor of Talmud, Yeshiva University
Rabbi Emeritus, Young Israel of Oceanside
Author, *Understanding Judaism: The Basics of
Deed and Creed* and 12 other titles
New York, NY

Rabbi Dr. Chaim Feuerman, Ed.D.
Golda Koschitzky Chair in Jewish Education
Chair, Mendheim Student Teaching and Administrative
Internship Program, Yeshiva University
Professor of Education at the Azrieli Graduate School
of Jewish Education and Administration
New York, NY

Rabbi Manis Friedman
Dean, Bais Chana Institute of Jewish Studies
Author, *Doesn't Anyone Blush Anymore?*
S. Paul, MN

Rabbi Nochem Kaplan
Director, Education Office of Merkos L'inyonei
Chinuch, Chabad-Lubavitch Headquarters
Vice President, National Council for Private School Accreditation
Author, *Principal's Administrative Manual*
Brooklyn, NY

Rabbi Shmuel Lew
Head of Education, Chabad-Lubavitch of the United Kingdom
Dean, Lubavitch Senior Girls' School
London, England

Dr. Bassya Pinson, Psy.D
Psychologist
Clinic Coordinator Supervisor at Aleinu Family Resource Center
Beverly Hills, CA

Sarah Chana Radcliffe, M.Ed., C.Psych.
Psychologist
Author, *Raise Your Kids without Raising Your Voice,
The Fear Fix, Make Yourself at Home* and 5 other
titles on family life and emotional well-being
Toronto, Ontario

Molly Resnick
Founder and Director, Mothers Against Teaching
Children To Kill and Hate (MATCKH)
New York, NY

Rabbi Yitzchak Schochet, M.A.
Rabbi, Mill Hill Synagogue
Honorary Principal, Rosh Pinah Primary School in Edgware
and Etz Chaim Jewish Primary School in Mill Hill
Member, Chief Rabbi's Cabinet
Chairman, Rabbinical Council of the United Synagogue
London, England

Rivkah Slonim
Education Director, Rohr Chabad Center for Jewish
Student Life at Binghamton University
Editor, *Bread and Fire; Jewish Women find God in the Everyday*
Binghamton, NY

Rabbi Adin Even-Israel Steinsaltz
Israel Prize laureate
Author, *Koren Talmud*
Jerusalem, Israel

ACCREDITATION

FOR MENTAL HEALTH
AND MEDICAL PRACTITIONERS

ACCREDITATION STATEMENT

*This activity has been planned and implemented through a joint sponsorship of **The Rohr Jewish Learning Institute (JLI)** and the **Washington School of Psychiatry (WSP)**. The Washington School of Psychiatry is approved by the **American Psychological Association (APA)** to sponsor continuing education for psychologists. Participants may earn up to **fifteen (15) CE credits** from the APA: nine (9) credits for participation in the live course, and up to (six) 6 additional credits for self-study of the Additional Readings.*

*The Washington School of Psychiatry is a **National Board for Certified Counselors**-Approved Continuing Education Provider, ACEP #6388, and may offer NBCC-approved clock hours for events that meet NBCC requirements. The School solely is responsible for all aspects of the program. Participants may earn **nine (9) credits** for participation in this course.*

*The School is accredited by MedChi, The Maryland State Medical Society, to provide continuing medical education for physicians. The School designates each session for 1.5 **AMA PRA Category I Credit(s)™** and an additional six (6) credits for the self-study of the Additional Readings for a total of up to **fifteen (15) credits**. Physicians should claim only the credit commensurate with the extent of their participation in the activity.*

*The School is approved by the **California Board of Behavioral Sciences** as provider #5691 of continuing education to Social Workers, Licensed Marriage and Family Therapists and Certified Counselors in California. Participants may earn up to **fifteen (15) CE credits**: nine (9) credits for participation in the live course and up to (six) 6 additional credits for self-study of the Additional Readings.*

*The School is approved by the **Social Work Board of the State of Maryland** as a provider of continuing education for social workers. The Maryland Social Work Board is an accredited member of the **Association of Social Work Boards**. Participants may earn up to **fifteen (15) CE credits**: nine (9) credits for participation in the live course and up to (six) 6 additional credits for self-study of the Additional Readings.*

DISCLOSURE OF COMMERCIAL SUPPORT AND THE UNLABELED USE OF A COMMERCIAL PRODUCT: No member of the planning committee and no member of the faculty for this event have a financial interest or other relationship with any commercial product.

TO CLAIM CREDIT *for attending the course (9 credits), professionals should submit their name, profession, e-mail, and mailing address to their instructor, or online at **www.MyJLI.com/continuingeducation**. To obtain credit for self-study of the Additional Readings (6 credits), professionals should take the brief online quiz at the above Web address.*

TABLE OF CONTENTS

the art of parenting

Lesson 1

The Parenting Principle

Every successful endeavor begins with a plan and vision. Being a successful parent is no different: we must know what our primary goals are in order to create a successful plan. Jewish tradition offers a parenting vision and definition that has trail-blazed the path for modern, enlightened parents.

JLI

JEWISH LEARNING INSTITUTE

Parenting's Mission Statement

A Right or a Responsibility?

LEARNING EXERCISE 1

Why do we choose to have children?

1. _____

   _____

   _____

2. _____

   _____

   _____

3. _____

   _____

   _____

Text 1

Encyclopædia Britannica Online, s. v. "patria potestas," accessed August 20, 2014

Patria potestas, (Latin: "power of a father"), in Roman family law, power that the male head of a family exercised over his children and his more remote descendants in the male line, whatever their age, as well as over those brought into the family by adoption. This power meant originally not only that he had control over the persons of his children, amounting even to a right to inflict capital punishment, but that he alone had any rights in private law. Thus, acquisitions of a child became the property of the father. The father might allow a child (as he might a slave) certain property to treat as his own, but in the eye of the law it continued to belong to the father.

Text 2a

Rabbi David ben Zimra, *Responsa* 1:123 📖

שָׁאַלְתָּ מִמֶּנִּי בִּרְאוּבֵן שֶׁמֵּתָה אִשְׁתּוֹ וְהִנִּיחָה לוֹ בֵּן קָטָן יוֹנֵק חוֹלֶה וְהוּא אֵצֶל אֵם אִמּוֹ, וְרָצָה רְאוּבֵן לָקַחַת אוֹתוֹ, וְהוּא לֹא נָשָׂא אִשָּׁה וְהוּא עָנִי, וּבִזְמַן שֶׁיּוֹצֵא לַחוּץ מַנִּיחַ אֶת הַבֵּן אֵצֶל הַשְּׁכֵנִים. אִם טוֹב שֶׁיַּעֲמוֹד הַבֵּן אֵצֶל אֵם אִמּוֹ אוֹ אֵצֶל אָבִיו?

תְּשׁוּבָה: הַדָּבָר בָּרוּר שֶׁ"הַבֵּן אֵצֶל אִמּוֹ" אָמְרוּ וְלֹא אֵצֶל אֵם אִמּוֹ, אֲבָל אִם רָאוּ בֵּית דִּין שֶׁתַּקָּנַת הַוָּלָד שֶׁיַּעֲמוֹד אֵצֶל אֵם אִמּוֹ לְפִי שֶׁהִיא מְרַחֶמֶת עָלָיו יוֹתֵר מֵאֲחֵרִים, מַנִּיחִים אוֹתוֹ אֵצֶל אֵם אִמּוֹ. וְאַף עַל פִּי שֶׁיֹּאמַר רְאוּבֵן "תְּנוּ לִי בְּנִי וַאֲנִי אֶעֱשֶׂה מַה שֶׁאֶרְצֶה, וְאִם יָמוּת יָמוּת", אֵין שׁוֹמְעִין לוֹ. וְלֹא מִבַּעְיָא אִם מַנִּיחוֹ בְּבֵית שְׁכֵנָיו אוֹ בְּבֵית אֲחֵרִים בִּזְמַן שֶׁהוּא יוֹצֵא לִמְלַאכְתּוֹ כַּאֲשֶׁר בָּא בַּשְּׁאֵלָה, דִּפְשִׁיטָא דְּאֵם אִמּוֹ קוֹדֶמֶת לַאֲחֵרִים, אֶלָּא אֲפִילוּ שֶׁרוֹצֶה הָאָב לַעֲמוֹד אֶצְלוֹ תָּמִיד אֵין שׁוֹמְעִין לוֹ, כֵּיוָן שֶׁנִּתְבָּרֵר לְבֵית דִּין שֶׁתַּקָּנָתוֹ שֶׁל וָלָד שֶׁיִּהְיֶה אֵצֶל אֵם אִמּוֹ . . .

כְּלָלָא דְמִלְתָא הַכֹּל תָּלוּי בִּרְאוֹת בֵּית דִּין בְּאֵי זֶה מָקוֹם יֵשׁ תַּקָּנָה לַוָּלָד יוֹתֵר.

Rabbi David ibn Zimra (Radvaz)
1479–1573

Noted halachist. Radvaz was born in Spain and immigrated to Safed, Israel upon the expulsion of the Jews from Spain in 1492. In 1513, he moved to Egypt and served as rabbi, judge, and head of the yeshivah in Cairo. He also ran many successful business ventures and was independently wealthy. In 1553, he returned to Safed where he would later be buried. He authored what would later become a classic commentary to Maimonides' code of law, and wrote many halachic responsa, of which more than ten thousand are still extant

Question: Reuven's wife died, leaving behind a sickly nursing infant. The infant is under the care of his maternal grandmother, but Reuven now wishes to take full custody. Reuven is a pauper and has not remarried. He intends to leave the infant in the care of neighbors when he will need to leave home. Should the child be placed in his father Reuven's custody or should he remain with his grandmother?

Response: It is clear that under normal circumstances, Jewish law grants custody of a young child to its mother, not its grandmother. Nevertheless, if the court determines that it is in the child's best interest to be placed in the care of his grandmother, for she will provide him with affectionate care more so than others, then the court should grant her custody. Even if Reuven shall say, "Give me my son and I will care for him as I see fit, and if he dies, so be it [that is no one's concern]," we pay no attention to this argument. Now, in this instance, it is clear that the grandmother takes precedence over the neighbors who will care for the baby while Reuven is at work. Moreover, even if the father expresses his wish to personally care for the child, the court should reject his claim, for it is in the child's interest that he remain under his grandmother's superior care. . . .

The guiding principle in such matters is that the child should be placed in the care of the party that will offer the child the best care possible.

Text 2b

Rabbi Eliezer Goldschmidt, *Ezer Mishpat*, p. 9

הַהֲלָכוֹת בְּדָבָר הַחֲזָקַת יְלָדִים אֵינָן הֲלָכוֹת בְּטוֹבַת הַהוֹרִים אֶלָא הֲלָכוֹת בְּטוֹבַת הַיְלָדִים. אֵין הַבֵּן אוֹ הַבַּת "חֵפֶץ" לְזְכֻיּוֹת אָב אוֹ אֵם. אֵין כַּאן זְכֻיּוֹת לָאָב אוֹ לָאֵם, רַק חוֹבוֹת יֶשְׁנָן כַּאן, שֶׁמְחֻיָּבִים הֵם לְגַדֵל וּלְחַנֵךְ אֶת יַלְדֵיהֶם.

The laws regarding child custody are not intended to benefit the parents, but the children. A son or daughter is not an "object" over which the father or mother has rights. The father and mother have no rights, only obligations, namely, the obligation to raise and educate their children.

Rabbi Eliezer Goldschmidt
1909–1992

Halachic authority and rabbinic judge. Born in Lithuania, at the age of 15 Goldschmidt moved with his family to the land of Israel and settled in Hebron. As a yeshiva student, he survived the Hebron massacre of 1929. Served as rabbinic judge, also on the Israeli Chief Rabbinate's highest court, during the years 1951–1979.

Text 3

Midrash, *Yalkut Shimoni*, Proverbs 964 📖

מַעֲשֶׂה הָיָה בְּרַבִּי מֵאִיר שֶׁהָיָה יוֹשֵׁב בְּמִנְחָה בְּשַׁבָּת וְדוֹרֵשׁ וּמֵתוּ שְׁנֵי בָנָיו.

מַה עָשְׂתָה אִמָּן? הִנִּיחָה שְׁנֵיהֶם עַל הַמִּטָּה וּפִירְשָׂה סָדִין עֲלֵיהֶם.

בְּמוֹצָאֵי שַׁבָּת בָּא רַבִּי מֵאִיר מִבֵּית הַמִּדְרָשׁ . . . אָמְרָה לוֹ, "רַבִּי, שְׁאֵלָה יֵשׁ לִי לִשְׁאוֹל . . . קוֹדֶם הַיּוֹם בָּא אֶחָד וְנָתַן לִי פִּקָּדוֹן, וְעַכְשָׁו בָּא לִיטוֹל, אַחֲזִיר לוֹ אוֹ לָאו?"

אָמַר לָהּ, "בִּתִּי מִי שֶׁיֵּשׁ לוֹ פִּקָּדוֹן, אֵינוֹ צָרִיךְ לְהַחֲזִיר לְרַבּוֹ?"

אָמְרָה לוֹ, "חוּץ מִדַּעְתְּךָ לֹא הָיִיתִי מַחֲזֶרֶת אוֹתוֹ" . . . תָּפְשָׂה אוֹתוֹ בְּיָדוֹ וְהֶעֱלֵהוּ לַחֶדֶר וְהִקְרִיבָה אוֹתוֹ לְמַטָּה. נָטְלָה הַסָּדִין מֵעֲלֵיהֶם וְרָאָה שְׁנֵיהֶם מֵתִים מוּנָחִים עַל הַמִּטָּה.

הִתְחִיל בּוֹכֶה וְאוֹמֵר, "בָּנַי בָּנַי! רַבִּי רַבִּי! בָּנַי בְּדֶרֶךְ אֶרֶץ וְרַבִּי שֶׁהָיוּ מְאִירִין עֵינַי בְּתוֹרָתָן!"

בְּאוֹתָהּ שָׁעָה אָמְרָה לֵיהּ, "רַבִּי, לֹא כַּךְ אָמַרְתָּ לִי שֶׁאָנוּ צְרִיכִין לְהַחֲזִיר פִּקָּדוֹן לְרַבּוֹ? כַּךְ 'ה' נָתַן וַה' לָקַח, יְהִי שֵׁם ה' מְבוֹרָךְ' (איוב א,כא)."

אָמַר רַבִּי חֲנִינָא, "בְּדָבָר זֶה נִחֲמַתּוֹ וְנִתְיַשְּׁבָה דַעְתּוֹ. לְכַךְ נֶאֱמַר (משלי לא,י), 'אֵשֶׁת חַיִל מִי יִמְצָא'."

Yalkut Shimoni

A Midrash that covers the entire Biblical text. Its material is collected from all over rabbinic literature, including the Babylonian and Jerusalem Talmuds and various ancient Midrashic texts. It contains several passages from Midrashim that have been lost, as well as different versions of existing Midrashim. It is unclear when and by whom this Midrash was redacted.

One Shabbat afternoon, while Rabbi Meir was lecturing [at the academy], his two sons died. What did their mother, Beruriah, do? She laid them on a bed and covered them with a sheet.

When Rabbi Meir arrived home after Shabbat . . . Beruriah asked him, "My teacher, I have a question to ask . . . Before today a man left an item with me for safekeeping and he has now come to collect it. Shall I return the item or not?"

"My dear," Rabbi Meir replied, "is not a custodian required to return a deposit to its owner?"

"My teacher," she replied, "If not for your words I could not [have brought myself to] return it." . . .

Beruriah took Rabbi Meir's hand and led him to the bedroom. She approached the bed, drew back the sheet, and he saw his two children lying dead. "My sons, my sons, my teachers, my teachers!" he cried. "My sons in the ways of the world, but my teachers who enlightened my eyes with words of Torah."

At that moment Beruriah interjected, "My teacher, did you not tell me that we are required to return our deposit to its master? 'God has given and God has taken. May His name be blessed for eternity'" (Job 1:21).

Said Rabbi Chanina, "With these words she offered him solace and relief [from the intensity of his grief]. Of her it is written 'A woman of valor who can find'" (Proverbs 31:10).

In Whose Interest?

Text 4

Rabbi Adin Even-Israel Steinsaltz, Interview with the JLI
Curriculum Development Team, August 7, 2014

Rabbi Adin Even-Israel Steinsaltz
1937–

Talmudist, author, and philosopher. Rabbi Even-Israel Steinsaltz is considered one of the foremost Jewish thinkers of the 20th century. Praised by *Time* magazine as a "once-in-a-millennium scholar," he has been awarded the Israel Prize for his contributions to Jewish study. He lives in Jerusalem and is the founder of the Israel Institute for Talmudic Publications, a society dedicated to the translation and elucidation of the Talmud.

First and foremost, parenting is about love. It is about truly loving our children. And true love means doing what is good for my beloved; not doing what is good for me.

Some parents make big plans for their children, but they forget to ask: "Are those plans really good for my children? Maybe those plans are just good for me and my image as a parent?"

LEARNING EXERCISE 2

(a) One day, your four-year-old son insists on wearing his favorite outfit to school. The problem: The pants are frayed and too small, and garishly clash with the shirt he has chosen.

What is your natural response and why?

_____

_____

If different from above, what *ought* to be your response and why?

_____

_____

(b) Your two-year-old daughter has a meltdown in the supermarket. You are getting "the look" from annoyed (or condescending) fellow shoppers.

What is your natural response and why?

_____

_____

If different from above, what *ought* to be your response and why?

_____

_____

Don't "Peer-ant"

Text 5

Anne Frank, *Diary*, January 6, 1944

Anne Frank
1929–1945

A German-Jewish teenager who spent over two years with her family in hiding during World War II before being arrested by the Nazis and deported to a concentration camp. Frank died of typhus at Bergen-Belsen at the age of fifteen. Her diary, first published in 1947, has been translated into 67 languages, and is one of the most widely-read books about the Holocaust.

As you know, I've frequently complained about [Mother] and then tried my best to be nice. I've suddenly realized what's wrong with her. Mother has said that she sees us more as friends than as daughters. That's all very nice, of course, except that a friend can't take the place of a mother. I need my mother to set a good example and be a person I can respect.

Text 6

Genesis 18:19

כִּי יְדַעְתִּיו לְמַעַן אֲשֶׁר יְצַוֶּה אֶת בָּנָיו וְאֶת בֵּיתוֹ אַחֲרָיו
וְשָׁמְרוּ דֶּרֶךְ ה' לַעֲשׂוֹת צְדָקָה וּמִשְׁפָּט.

I love Abraham, because he instructs his children and his household after him to follow the path of God by doing righteousness (charity) and justice.

Text 7

Thomas Gordon, PhD, *Parent Effectiveness Training: The Proven Program for Raising Responsible Children* [New York: Three Rivers Press, 2000], p. 330

A Credo for My Relationships

You and I are in a relationship that I value and want to keep. Yet each of us is a separate person with our own unique needs and the right to try to meet those needs. I will try to be genuinely accepting of your behavior when you are trying to meet your needs or when you are having problems meeting your needs.

When you share your problems, I will try to listen acceptingly and understandingly in a way that will facilitate your finding your own solutions rather than depending upon mine. When you have a problem because my behavior is interfering with your meeting your needs, I encourage you to tell me openly and honestly how you are feeling. At those times, I will listen and then try to modify my behavior, if I can.

However, when your behavior interferes with my meeting my own needs, thus causing me to feel unaccepting of you, I will share my problem with you and tell you as openly and honestly as I can exactly how I am feeling, trusting that you respect my needs enough to listen and then try to modify your behavior.

At those times when either of us cannot modify our behavior to meet the needs of the other and find that we have a conflict-of-needs in our relationship, let us commit ourselves to resolve each such conflict without ever resorting to the use of either my power or yours to win at the

Thomas Gordon, PhD
1918–2002

Professor of psychology, clinical psychologist, and author. Founder of Gordon Training International and developer of what came to be known as the Gordon Model or the Gordon Method, a system for building and maintaining effective relationships.

expense of the other losing. I respect your needs, but I also must respect my own. Consequently, let us strive always to search for solutions to our inevitable conflicts that will be acceptable to both of us. In this way, your needs will be met, but so will mine—no one will lose, both will win.

A Healthy Family Structure

Text 8

Exodus 20:12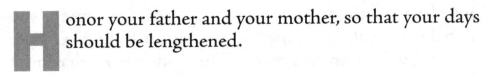

כַּבֵּד אֶת אָבִיךָ וְאֶת אִמֶּךָ לְמַעַן יַאֲרִכוּן יָמֶיךָ.

Honor your father and your mother, so that your days should be lengthened.

Text 9a

Leviticus 19:3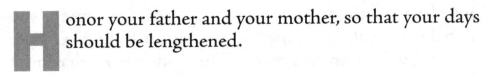

אִישׁ אִמּוֹ וְאָבִיו תִּירָאוּ.

Each person shall revere his mother and father.

Text 9b

Talmud, Kidushin 31b

מוֹרָא: לֹא עוֹמֵד בִּמְקוֹמוֹ, וְלֹא יוֹשֵׁב בִּמְקוֹמוֹ, וְלֹא סוֹתֵר אֶת דְּבָרָיו, וְלֹא מַכְרִיעוֹ.

Reverence implies that one may not stand in a place designated for one's parent to stand or sit in a place designated for one's parent to sit. One may not contradict a parent nor express a view [in an instance where others disagree with a parent's opinion].

Babylonian Talmud

A literary work of monumental proportions that draws upon the legal, spiritual, intellectual, ethical, and historical traditions of Judaism. The 37 tractates of the Babylonian Talmud contain the teachings of the Jewish sages from the period after the destruction of the 2nd Temple through the 5th century CE. It has served as the primary vehicle for the transmission of the Oral Law and the education of Jews over the centuries; it is the entry point for all subsequent legal, ethical, and theological Jewish scholarship.

Text 10

Rabbi Shlomo Ganzfried, *Kitzur Shulchan Aruch*, Laws of Honoring Parents 10

רָאָה לְאָבִיו שֶׁעוֹבֵר עַל דִּבְרֵי תּוֹרָה, לֹא יֹאמַר לוֹ, "עָבַרְתָּ עַל דִּבְרֵי תּוֹרָה!" אֶלָּא יֹאמַר לוֹ, "אַבָּא, כְּתִיב בַּתּוֹרָה כַּךְ וְכַךְ?" כְּאִלּוּ הוּא שׁוֹאֵל מִמֶּנּוּ וְלֹא כְּמַזְהִירוֹ, וְהָאָב יָבִין מֵעַצְמוֹ וְלֹא יִתְבַּיֵּשׁ.

If one sees his father transgressing, he must not say, "You have violated a Torah commandment!" Rather, he should say, "Father, does not the Torah say such-and-such?" The tone should be that of a question, not of an admonishment. The father will thus understand [that he erred], but will not be humiliated.

Rabbi Shlomo Ganzfried
1804–1886

Rabbi and halachic authority. Rabbi Ganzfried was born in Uzhhorod (today part of Ukraine), and after being orphaned at a very young age was adopted by Uzhhorod's chief rabbi, Rabbi Tzvi Hirsh Heller. Rabbi Ganzfried is best known for his *Kitsur Shulchan Aruch*, a user-friendly summary of the Shulchan Aruch (Code of Jewish Law) and the observations of subsequent halachic commentators. This highly acclaimed work quickly became a classic, a mainstay in every Jewish home.

EXERCISES FOR THE WEEK

1. SELFLESS PARENTING

Identify one way that you can modify your parenting approach to better accommodate your child's interests.

2. ESTABLISH PARENTAL STATUS

Identify one area in your and/or your child's behavior that can be modified to improve your standing as your child's parent and guide.

Key Points

1. Judaism has a proven successful parenting track record in the sphere of the religious and ethical as well as the social-moral and academic domains. Also, Judaism offers a time-tested parenting formula that does not go out of style upon the arrival of the next popular parenting theory.

2. Historically, Judaism has viewed parenting as a responsibility rather than a right. In past times, this view distinguished the Jews in various important areas of family law. Today, secular family law has largely come to reflect Jewish values in this area.

3. At times, we make parenting choices while (consciously or subconsciously) considering our own benefit and comfort rather than our children's. A cardinal rule in parenting is to question our every parenting decision: "Is this good for me? Or is this good for my child?"

4. Parents are, first and foremost, their children's role models and moral guides. A child needs and wants parents who behave like parents. Kids don't need their parents to be their friends. A parent's desire to be his or her child's friend does not result from considering the child's interests.

5. Parents need to establish their parental status and teach their children the proper way to respect them. This is done not (only) for the benefit of the parents, but for the benefit of the children.

Appendix A

Text 1a

Genesis 21:15–17

וַיִּכְלוּ הַמַּיִם מִן הַחֵמֶת, וַתַּשְׁלֵךְ אֶת הַיֶּלֶד תַּחַת אַחַד הַשִּׂיחִם,
וַתֵּלֶךְ וַתֵּשֶׁב לָהּ מִנֶּגֶד הַרְחֵק כִּמְטַחֲוֵי קֶשֶׁת, כִּי אָמְרָה, "אַל
אֶרְאֶה בְּמוֹת הַיָּלֶד", וַתֵּשֶׁב מִנֶּגֶד וַתִּשָּׂא אֶת קֹלָהּ וַתֵּבְךְּ.

וַיִּשְׁמַע אֱלֹקִים אֶת קוֹל הַנַּעַר, וַיִּקְרָא מַלְאַךְ אֱלֹקִים אֶל הָגָר מִן הַשָּׁמַיִם
וַיֹּאמֶר לָהּ, "מַה לָּךְ הָגָר? אַל תִּירְאִי! כִּי שָׁמַע אֱלֹקִים אֶל קוֹל הַנַּעַר".

The water was depleted from the canteen. Hagar cast the child under one of the bushes, and she went and sat down from afar, at about the distance of two bowshots, for she said, "Let me not see the child's death." She sat from a distance and raised her voice and wept.

God heard the lad's voice. An angel of God called to Hagar from heaven and said to her, "What is troubling you, Hagar? Fear not, for God has heard the lad's voice."

Text 1b

Rabbi Samson Raphael Hirsch, *Commentary*, ad loc. 📖

כָּל הִתְנַהֲגוּתָהּ שֶׁל הָגָר אוֹפְיָינִית בְּיוֹתֵר וּמְצַיֶּינֶת אֶת הַטֶּבַע שֶׁל בַּת-
חָם שֶׁלֹּא נִתְעַדֵּן. אֵם יִשְׂרְאֵלִית לֹא תִּטּוֹשׁ אֶת יַלְדָּהּ, וְלוּ רַק כְּדֵי לְדַבֵּר
עַל לִבּוֹ, וְלוּ רַק כְּדֵי לְהָקֵל עָלָיו כְּדֵי חֵלֶק אֶחָד בְּמִילְיוֹן שֶׁל שִׁנְיָה.

הַנּוֹטֵשׁ יֶלֶד בְּאֶפֶס מַעֲשֶׂה, מִפְּנֵי "שֶׁאֵין בְּכוֹחוֹ לִרְאוֹת בְּיִיסּוּרוֹ", אֵינוֹ פּוֹעֵל מִתּוֹךְ
רַחֲמִים; זוֹהִי אָנֹכִיּוּת אַכְזָרִית שֶׁל נֶפֶשׁ-אָדָם שֶׁנֶּעֶצְרָה בְּטִבְעָהּ הַגַּס. אָדָם בַּעַל
שִׁעוּר-קוֹמָה אֱנוֹשִׁי יוֹדֵעַ לְהַשְׁלִיט אֶת הַכָּרַת חוֹבָתוֹ עַל רִגְשׁוֹתָיו הָעַזִּים בְּיוֹתֵר.

Hagar's behavior is characteristic of an unrefined heathen. A Jewish mother would never abandon her child in such a situation; she would remain at his side to soothe and comfort, to alleviate his pain—if only a millionth part of it!

One who abandons a child, instead of taking action, while claiming "I can't bear to see my child's pain," is *not* acting out of compassion. Rather, this is the *cruel selfishness* of an unrefined individual. A truly humane individual would, in such an instance, utilize his sense of duty to overcome even his strongest emotions.

Rabbi Samson Raphael Hirsch
1808–1888

Born in Hamburg, Germany; rabbi and educator; intellectual founder of the *Torah Im Derech Eretz* school of Orthodox Judaism, which advocates combining Torah with secular education. Beginning in 1830, Hirsch served as chief rabbi in several prominent German cities. During this period he wrote his *Nineteen Letters on Judaism*, under the pseudonym of Ben Uziel. His work helped preserve traditional Judaism during the era of the German Enlightenment. He is buried in Frankfurt am Main.

ADDITIONAL READINGS

WHAT IS THE GOAL?

BY RABBI ABRAHAM J. TWERSKI, MD, AND URSULA SCHWARTZ, PhD

At the risk of appearing absurd, I must ask prospective parents the question, "Why do you want to have children?"

In every other venture in life, our methodology is generally determined by the goal we desire. For example, my goal is to build a house, I must then decide on a plan. Do I have enough money? Can I obtain a mortgage? How do I go about finding a reliable contractor? How do I wish the house furnished? Many questions may arise, and they will all be dealt within the light of my ultimate goal for this particular project. There should thus be a tripartite composition to our behavior: (A) a goal; (B) a plan; and (C), action. If we begin to act without a goal or plan, we will end up with a chaotic situation. Just a bit of thought will reveal that we go through a similar process for every undertaking even though we may not be conscious of this.

The nature of the plan and the action may well be different according to our reason for the end product. If I wish to build a house for commercial purposes, to lease to tenants rather than as a personal dwelling, I may well choose a different design, different building materials, and different furnishings. To look for a plan before one has a clear understanding of the goal is both unwise and totally confusing.

It is therefore not quite as absurd as it may seem at first in discussing techniques of parenting to ask. "Why do you wish to be a parent?" This is one time where the stakes are too great to accept the answer, "Because."

I have had the occasion to talk with young women who are distressed because after two years of marriage they have not yet conceived. While their concern is easily understandable, they invariably mention how distressed they are that all their peers are pushing baby carriages, and they have nothing to display. While I truly feel for them and can identify with their distress, there is no escaping the conclusion that while this is by far not the major factor, nonetheless, for them having a child is at least partially an "ego" thing. The child's fulfilling an ego need of the parent is perfectly normal, but this must be recognized and considered in the parenting process. Having a child to satisfy an ego need may still be operative when the child is 8, 12, or 16, as well as when he is an infant in the carriage. Thus, while perfectly normal, it can affect parenting.

There is a very enlightening episode in the Torah, where the matriarch Rachel, who was childless, was envious of her sister Leah, and in desperation cried out to Jacob, "If I cannot have children, then I might as well be dead." Jacob, who loved Rachel intensely, responds to her angrily (Genesis 30: 1–2). A bit later, the Torah states that G-d remembered Rachel and she conceived Joseph (ibid. 30:22). Rashi comments that Rachel merited a child because she had selflessly yielded her beloved Jacob to her sister Leah, and although the Divine wisdom had deprived her of children until now, it was this virtue that was her salvation. We may not be capable of achieving the great spirituality of the patriarchs and matriarchs, yet they are meant to serve as models of the idea.

What the Torah is teaching us is that the saintly matriarch Rachel had momentarily been overcome by a personal interest to have a child, and this is why Jacob replied with rebuke, that one must submit to the supreme will of G-d. Rachel quickly recovered her lofty spiritual status of total selflessness as had been characterized by her willingness to yield her beloved Jacob to her sister rather than to allow Leah to be publicly humiliated. Having shed her personal interest and having returned to her lofty spiritual level, she was then given a child, who indeed became Joseph the *tzaddik*. The average mother cannot be Rachel, and does have an ego interest in being a parent. Again I must stress, this is perfectly normal, yet should be reckoned with.

It is too simplistic to say that language determines thought, but on the other hand, language certainly influences thought or, at the very least, gives us clues to levels of meanings that may not be obvious or points out assumptions that are not immediately evident.

The phrase "to have children" is a very interesting one. Let's take some time to listen closely. How many children do you "have"? Do you want to "have" children? When do you plan to "have" a child? Do you want to "have" a boy or a girl? "Having" implies a possession, something that we own, something that we acquire out of our own volition. In and of itself, "having" something implies a state. To "have" a house implies that I own it, that it is mine to do as I please, that a transaction has taken place, and that I am in full control over this acquisition. Since I chose to make this acquisition it enhances me, and if it does not, my goal may be to exchange this acquisition for something that suits me better. In addition, the relationship between an owner and his possession is a simple two-way relationship, the owner and the object owned.

From a Jewish perspective, having children is first of all not a matter of a possession and secondly it is not a matter of a two-way relationship between parent and child. The Talmud says that there are three partners in every child: G-d, the father, and the mother (*Kiddushin* 30b). The same way that G-d is involved in a Jewish marriage, in our kitchens, in our sleeping and awakening, so is He also involved in the enterprise of parenting. This means that there needs to be space in our child-rearing equation for G-d.

With G-d as an intimate partner in parenting, we can no longer talk of "having" a child in the simple pos-

sessive fashion implied by ordinary language. Rather, having a child means to be entrusted with a responsibility. A child is a gift of G-d chosen for us specifically and entrusted to us for safekeeping to be raised and treasured. As a gift from G-d, a child—any child—cannot be looked upon at as an accident or a mistake. Rather, we need to believe—hard as this may be at times—that our children are a perfect match for us and we for them. The same way that a marriage holds in it potential for growth for each partner, it is precisely in the affirmation of this match that there is the potential for good and for growth.

The task for parents is not simply to teach children manners to get them to behave properly. This is not at all minimizing good manners and civilized ways. On the contrary, *middos* and *derech eretz* (decency) are extremely important, but these are qualities that become lasting attributes of a child's character and personality or if they are embedded in a vision of the world that is imbued with Torah values. In *Ethics of the Fathers* (3:17) we read "If there is no Torah there is no *derech eretz*, and if there is no *derech eretz* there is no Torah." The two are interdependent.

The job of the parent involves much more than simply "training" the child to do things the right way. Training is merely a method teaching that does not require understanding and simply rests on an association between a stimulus and a response that has been reinforced. Raising Jewish children means that the parents instill them a view of the world where events and actions are seen through Torah eyes; where words are heard with Torah ears; where words are spoken with Torah thoughts in mind. In a sense, then, is our job to construct the world for them as one of Torah and build up with them and for them a map of life and the world that will guide them for the rest of their lives. It is a task that transcends our own existence on earth. The Torah is indeed a "map." It is the master plan whereby G-d created the universe, as stated in the Zohar, "G-d looked into the Torah, and created the universe according to it" *(Zohar Terumah* 161a).

But giving our children a map of the world does not ensure that their actions will be appropriate at all times. A map is a guide. It tells us when we are on track and when we are off track. Most importantly, it allows us to move closer to our destination. If we get lost, it allows us to turn around and to redirect ourselves. So too, raising a child is to transmit to him our map of the world so that at some point in time he can embark on the journey by himself. The parent who transmits a map gives the child tools that transcend by far any automatic conditioning of good behavior.

For the Torah-observant couple, the *mitzvah* of procreating is important, and bringing a child into the world should be the fulfillment of an important *mitzvah*. Yet we would be wise not to deceive ourselves, because self-deception never has positive results. If an ego element is present, one should not deny it and try to conceal it under some other factors.

Again, it is certainly not wrong to have an ego investment in a child, and common sense tells us that it cannot be otherwise. We are, after all, human beings, and not spiritual angels. But the ego investment in a child can be either positive or negative, and if we recognize its presence, we are in a position to direct it positively.

Raising children is a goal-directed and purposeful task and demands a concentrated sustained effort on the parents' part. It really is hard work.

Parenting may also be said to be "absorbing," which means that this task can be successfully accomplished only if we connect to it and to the child in a deep and lasting fashion, overcoming immediate frustrations, setbacks, disappointments, and fatigue. In this sense, parenting is quite similar to the study of Torah, which is an encounter with the word of G-d, and it, too, is often fraught with frustrations, questions, and difficulties. At the same time, learning opens up to the student delights that only a fellow learner can understand. Similarly, when a child says a first word, takes a first step, has a first recognition of the *aleph-beis,* makes the first moral decision based on Torah law, these are the delights that only a parent can truly savor.

G-d gave us a head start with the *mitzvah* of parenting by giving us the capability of feeling a deep bond with our children right from birth, and by embellishing the newborn with capabilities that allow him to connect with us immediately. We know that optimal vision for newborns and young infants is at approximately 12 inches, just about the distance to his mother's face when he is nursing or being held. Studies indicate that a baby is indeed "wired" for speech: For example, even newborns can distinguish between "B" and "P" sounds, which shows that they are particularly attuned to human voices. Research has also shown that as early as a few weeks, the infant gazes longer at his mother's face than that of a stranger, and is also capable of differentiating between the voice of his mother and that of a stranger. Given the challenges that young children pose from infancy throughout childhood, including the sleepless or interrupted nights, and their seemingly irrational behavior, crying, "I want the blue cup and not the yellow cup!," the stability of this bond is just short of amazing, and is due only to the *chesed* which G-d has granted to parents.

The commitment to a child can indeed bring out the best in a parent. By investing themselves completely in their child, parents are capable of acting purely in the service of the child, and for the moment their own selves become subsumed to the needs of the child. We might say that at such a moment the parent loses his self and his resources in the service of the child.

An example from clinical practice comes to mind. A couple who could not have children was finally able to adopt a healthy little baby boy, just a few weeks old. As the child grew older, he became increasingly more difficult to manage and seemed to have great difficulty communicating and socializing. This progressed to the point where he became a threat to their second child, a son born to them about two years after they had adopted their first child. The painful diagnosis was finally made that their adopted child was autistic. These parents have continued to amaze me in their dedication to this child and their lack of regrets at having adopted him, and their firm belief that G-d gave them this child and that he was meant to be their own. The child's progress in therapy is no doubt due to a great degree to their attitude which allows them to give freely of themselves and to meet his needs.

Let us avoid a possible major pitfall. Putting oneself at a child's disposal by no means implies that the parent is asked to become a shadow-like presence, catering to every whim of the child. Rather, it means that the parent puts all of his inner resources in the service of raising this child. Looking at it this way resolves a paradox. A parent needs to be strong, determined, caring, focused—hardly a doormat or a menial worker. The role of the Jewish mother has been aptly likened to that of a *rosh yeshivah*. Just as the *rosh yeshivah* guides his pupils and watches over them for their own benefit, the parents' investment in their children is not for the sake of the parent, but a means to bring their children to reach their fullest potential as individuals and as Jews, and to bring them closer to G-d. Both with a parent and the *rosh yeshivah,* it is a determination that does not have as its goal the celebration of one's ego. This analogy is clearly stated in the Talmud. "Whoever teaches a child Torah is as though he has given birth to him" *(Sanhedrin* 19b).

Let us therefore draw a distinction between "ego involvement" and "self-investment." Ego involvement in a child's upbringing views the child primarily as a source of parental enhancement. The *nachas* that children, G-d willing, bring to the parents, are experienced as tributes to parental competence, or are indicators of social status and personal superiority. The parent feels entitled to these gifts from the child and needs them to preserve his own self-esteem. In contrast, the parent who has little "ego involvement" but high "self-investment" can experience the *nachas* that a child brings as expressions of the child's growth as a Jew and as feedback that he is on the right track as a parent. The result is enjoyment of the child for his own sake, and gratitude to G-d for His blessings.

The parent who is primarily driven by ego involvement interprets the same experience very differently than the parent who has invested himself in the parental task. When parental expectations and needs correspond to the child's natural inclinations, talents, and capabilities, this relationship, although flawed, can work. But the ego boost that one gets from "My son the Talmud whiz" or "My daughter the well-known educator" are but fortuitous coincidences and in constant need of reaffirmation. One patient complained to his therapist. "I am sick and tired of being a *nachas* machine." The wise Solomon cautioned, "Train the child according to *his* way" *(Proverbs* 22:6). The child's makeup and needs must be understood.

Children are often very much aware of their parents' needs and their role in fulfilling them. As adults, they pose a challenge in therapy of having to work through a sense of alienation of themselves and their identity. When the parents are primarily ego driven, this house of cards tends to fall apart if the child does not correspond to the parents' image and is "different" or truly makes mistakes. Since the parental ego is so tied to the child's success, it becomes extremely difficult for such parents to acknowledge a problem, to get help, and to disclose the extent of their difficulties. Often this results in denial, covering up, and blaming everyone else. The child, unfortunately, gets lost in all of this.

Given our frailties as human beings, it is not astonishing that all of us, perhaps with the exception of a few saintly persons, are involved with our children at some level of ego involvement. This should not cause us to feel guilty. Rather, the task is for us to become aware of our particular weaknesses and blind spots, our ego-driven goals and expectations for the child, and our difficulties in accepting even positive traits in our children when they do not correspond to our wishes and needs.

Self-awareness results in self-knowledge. This allows a parent to change a destructive ego-driven wish and helps to overcome selfish needs that can be detrimental to the child. If this does not happen, parents and children can get stuck in a destructive circle of fear, disappointment, resentment, and misunderstanding. We need to be clear in our minds that *our task as parents is to invest ourselves in our children without entangling ourselves in a self-centered way.* Sometimes our ego involvement is easily evident; other times it is covered up and hidden.

Ego involvement does not necessarily refer to a drive for feeling superior to others, as when we say, "He has a huge ego." Rather, it may refer to certain needs of our own which are not necessarily those of the child, and may conceivably even be contrary to the child's interests.

One mother was driven to distraction by one of her sons, who from the earliest days was fiercely independent, insisting on doing things by himself and learning by his own mistakes. He would not accept help or guidance, and his most famous words were "Don't worry, Ima," which was precisely when she began worrying. She was extremely frustrated by having to restrain herself from offering any help unless he asked for it. This should not have posed so severe a problem, since many children are highly individualistic in every sense of the word, and prefer self-sufficiency with all its drawbacks rather than being helped.

In therapy it emerged that this woman's father was a self-made man, eminently practical, an organizer, and a leader. He was domineering, and lectured to his children who had to be a passive, receptive audience. As a child, this woman was frustrated by her father's lack of receptivity to her juvenile ideas and wishes, and her child's attitude of fierce independence triggered an association to her frustration with her father. She was essentially carrying over to her child her own early childhood attitudes toward her father. When she realized this, she was able to think through her reactions toward him, and the parenting process was greatly facilitated.

This, too, is ego involvement; i.e., not reacting to the child's independence objectively, but being affected by a personal attitude, a remnant from her own feelings of frustration that had never been completely resolved.

A fairly reliable sign of ego involvement is the degree of hurt, upset, or anger we feel toward a child. When our feelings are out of proportion to the offense or the problem at hand, we can be pretty sure that we are dealing with a considerable degree of ego involvement. Even when a problem is really significant and a child has gotten himself into actual trouble, we can become aware of our ego involvement when we notice that we are more concerned with what this means for us ("I won't be able to show my face in *shul!*"), and when our own reaction prevents us from constructive problem solving and getting help to a child in trouble. Self-reflection and self-awareness are the prerequisites for putting our ego in the background. Being aware of our own foibles allows us to bracket our own issues and keep them separate. This enables us as parents to deal with the issue constructively and in the child's best interest. Self-awareness allows a parent to invest his self into the child for the child's good.

This description of parenting is no doubt daunting and formidable. It is a task that demands the best in us and at its best becomes for the parent a stepping stone toward self-growth and increased closeness to G-d.

Positive Parenting: Developing Your Child's Potential [New York: Mesorah Publications Ltd., 1996], pp. 21–30.

Reproduced from *Positive Parenting*, by Rabbi Abraham J. Twerski, MD, with permission of ArtScroll/Mesorah Publications, Ltd.

ADOPTION AS A MITZVAH

BY RABBI SHMUEL KLATZKIN, PhD

In clear and ringing words, the Talmud endorses adoption:

> For all who raise an orphan child, whether boy or girl, in their home, Scripture accounts it as if they have given birth to that child. (*Megilah* 13a)

The Midrash too adds its praise:

> G-d showed Moses all the treasures in which the rewards of the righteous are stored away. Moses asked: "To whom does all this treasure belong?" and He replied, "To those who fulfill My commandments." "And to whom does this next treasure belong?" "To those who bring up orphans." (*Shemot Rabba* 45:6)

The Midrash cites another text shortly afterwards:

> There was an orphan who was brought up by a good and trustworthy man, who raised her and looked after her very carefully and saw her through to marriage. When the scribe came to write the *ketuba* (marriage contract), he asked her, "What is your name?" She replied, "So-and-so"; but when he asked her what her father's name was, she was silent.

> Her guardian asked her, "Why are you silent?" She replied, "I know of no other father than you, for he that brings up a child is called a father, not he who causes the birth."

> Similarly, Israel is the orphan . . . and the good and faithful guardian is the blessed Holy One. (*Ibid.* 46:5)

Adoption has been present in Jewish life since its earliest days. For whatever reason it may be, sometimes a child is raised by others as their own. In the first instance mentioned in the Bible, Moses must be given away, for otherwise he would have been killed by Pharaoh's decree. A contemporary of Moses, Caleb, was understood by tradition to be adopted as well (see Talmud, *Temurah* 16a).

A different misfortune struck Esther, and because of it, she was raised by her cousin, Mordecai.

> There was a Judean man in Shushan the capital, whose name was Mordecai the son of Jair the son of Shimei the son of Kish, a Benjamite, who had been exiled from Jerusalem with the exile that was exiled with Jeconiah, king of Judah, which Nebuchadnezzar, king of Babylon, had exiled. And he had brought up Hadassah, that is Esther, his uncle's daughter, for she had neither father nor mother, and the maiden was of comely form and of comely appearance, and when her father and mother died, Mordecai took her to himself for a daughter. (Esther 2:5–7)

Esther is described as an orphan, a member of a class to whom G-d forcefully directs our concern in the Torah:

> Do not oppress any widow or orphan. (Exodus 22:21)

Rashi (Rabbi Shlomo Yitzchaki; 1040–1105) notes in his commentary on this verse that this particular caution of the Torah would seem to be unnecessary, as we are forbidden to oppress anyone. Why mention the widow and the orphan specifically if the general law against oppression already protects them?

But this is not a redundancy, Rashi asserts. Rather, the Torah is hinting to us by this repetition that the widow and the orphan are those people who are least able to protect themselves from oppression, and thus we must take special care to see that they not be oppressed.

Sensitive to this idea, Rabbi Yaakov ben Asher (Baal Haturim), basing himself on the following verse ("If someone will oppress him, then if he cries out to Me,

I will certainly hear him"), states explicitly that this special care really applies to all of Israel.

> This teaches us that all Israel are guarantors for each other, for if even one person were to oppress him, it would be as if all Israel were doing so.

Baal Haturim is noting that the verse uses the singular when referring both to an oppressor and one who is oppressed. He sees this as teaching that even one case of oppression is too much. Even if the oppression is normal, as in the case of those who lack power (whom the widow and the orphan epitomize), we must not accept it.

The situation of people being helpless and subject to exploitation calls upon all of Israel to accept the responsibility to remedy the situation. We are all guarantors of each other. When the stability established by life's most basic relationships breaks down, we must find a way to help restore that stability. And of the two emblematic examples given here, the widow and the orphan, the one most in need of stability and least able to fend for himself is the orphan.

Thus, Mordecai's adoption of his niece was not something novel, but rather the fulfillment in action of an obligation already understood as binding the entire community. It is that long-held understanding that the Rabbis expressed.

Adoption, though, raises many challenges. Sages point out that the relation between parent and child is fundamental and unchanging. Distinct from the spousal relationship, which is established by choice and dissolvable by choice as well, the parent-child relationship begins with the beginning of the child's being and endures for better or for worse, even if estranged. The relation may become troubled, but it cannot be dissolved.

But adoption is a chosen relationship, at least on the side of the adoptive parents. Can a chosen relationship ever serve the same as the relationship of birth parents? If it can, it must be primarily because of the choice of the adoptive parents to make it so. They assume the burden of supplying that same kind of stable life-foundation that natural parents are meant to do.

In making those kinds of choices, some have felt that the child must never suspect that his adoptive parents were not the ones who actually brought her into the world. The knowledge of their being adopted will act counter to all they are trying to do, will destabilize them emotionally. Though not necessarily for the same reason, many American states sealed the records of adoption, and even upon becoming an adult, an adopted child could not learn the identities of his birth parents.

Regarding this common urge, a great rabbinic authority of the last generation wrote:

> There are those who don't want to reveal anything at all about the adoption, but that is prohibited by Jewish law. (Rabbi Moshe Feinstein, *Igrot Moshe, Even Ha'ezer*, Part 4, 64:2)

He cites the compelling reason of avoiding an unwitting incestuous relation, and rules then that, at least before the child is grown, the adoptive parents must reveal the name of the biological mother and father, if known, and other things about them, such as where they may live. A consensus of modern decisors rule the same way.

Implicit in these rulings is that such knowledge will not destabilize the child's life at all. As the Midrash had stated earlier, there is something about the adoptive relationship that uniquely defines parenthood in its highest: people devoted entirely and selflessly to a child they chose to love and take for their own.

How appropriate that the Midrash sees this as a vivid example of how G-d Himself chooses to love and care for us as His own.

the art of parenting

Lesson 2

Parent: The Noun and the Verb

What are our specific parenting goals? Where do we set the bar for expectations and rules? And how can we encourage our children to do things that are outside of their comfort zone? An understanding of the ultimate goal of all child rearing will help us answer these important questions.

JLI

JEWISH LEARNING INSTITUTE

Introduction

A Boy and a Melon

Text 1

Rabbi Yosef Yitschak Schneersohn, *Sefer Hasichot* 5705, pp. 10–11

Rabbi Yosef Yitschak Schneersohn
(Rayats, Frierdiker Rebbe, Previous Rebbe)
1880–1950

Chasidic rebbe, prolific writer, and Jewish activist. Rabbi Yosef Yitschak, the 6th leader of the Chabad movement, actively promoted Jewish religious practice in Soviet Russia and was arrested for these activities. After his release from prison and exile, he settled in Warsaw, Poland, from where he fled Nazi occupation, and arrived in New York in 1940. Settling in Brooklyn, Rabbi Schneersohn worked to revitalize American Jewish life. His son-in law, Rabbi Menachem Mendel Schneerson, succeeded him as the leader of the Chabad movement.

אִין יָאר תרמ"ח רֹאשׁ הַשָּׁנָה, אִיך בִּין דאן אַלְט גֶעוֶוען זִיבְּן יָאר מִיט עֶטְלֶעכֶע חֳדָשִׁים, בִּין אִיך אַרֵיינְגֶעגאַנְגֶען צוּ כְּבוֹד אִמִּי זְקָנָתִי הָרַבָּנִית אוּן זִי הָאט מִיר מְכַבֵּד גֶעוֶוען מִיט אַ "קאַווֶען". אִיך בִּין אַרוֹיס אוֹיפֶן הוֹיף אוּן זִיך גֶעזֶעצְט מִיט מַיינֶע חַבֵרִים אוֹיף אַ בֶּאנְק וואָס אִיז גֶעוֶוען פּוּנְקְט אַנְטְקֶעגֶן אִיבֶּער דֶעם פֶענְסְטֶער פוּן הוֹד כְּבוֹד קְדוּשַׁת אאמו"ר הרה"ק, אוּן הָאָב גֶעגֶעבְּן פוּן דֶעם קאַווֶען אוֹיך צוּ מַיינֶע חַבֵרִים.

הָאָט מִיר הוֹד כְּבוֹד קְדוּשַׁת אאמו"ר הרה"ק אַרֵיינְגֶערוּפֶן צוּ זִיך אוּן הָאָט מִיר גֶעזאָגְט: אִיך הָאָב בַּאמעֶרְקְט אַז דוּ הָאסְט טאַקֶע גֶעגֶעבְּן צוּ דַיינֶע חַבֵרִים אָבֶּער נִיט מִיטְן גאַנְצְן הָארְצְן. אוּן הוֹד כְּבוֹד קְדוּשַׁת אאמו"ר הרה"ק הָאָט מִיט מִיר פִיל גֶערֶעדְט וֶוגֶען דֶעם עִנְיָן טוֹב עַיִן אוּן רַע עַיִן.

אִיך בִּין פוּן דִי רֵייד פוּן הוֹד כְּבוֹד קְדוּשַׁת אאמו"ר הרה"ק אַזוֹי נִתְעוֹרֵר גֶעוואָרֶן, אִיך הָאָב זִיך שְׁטאַרְק צֶעווֵיינְט, אִיך הָאָב נִיט גֶעקֶענְט קוּמֶען צוּ זִיך בְּמֶשֶׁךְ אַ הַאלְבֶּע שְׁטוּנְדֶע אוּן אִיך הָאָב צוּרִיק אָפְּגֶעגֶעבְּן וואָס אִיך הָאָב גֶעגֶעסְן פוּן דֶעם קאַווֶען.

כְּבוֹד אִמִּי הָרַבָּנִית הָאָט גֶעפְרֶעגְט הוֹד כְּבוֹד קְדוּשַׁת אאמו"ר הרה"ק: וואָס ווִילְסְטוּ פוּן דֶעם קִינְד? הָאָט עֶר גֶעעֶנְטְפֶערְט: גוּט אַזוֹי, זאָל אִין אִים נִקְנֶה וֶוערֶן.

אָט דאָס אִיז חִינוּך.

On Rosh Hashanah of 5648 [1887], when I was a child of seven years and several months, I visited my grandmother and she treated me to a melon. I went out to the yard and sat with my friends on a bench directly opposite the window of my father [Rabbi Shalom

DovBer, the fifth rebbe of Chabad-Lubavitch], and shared the melon with my friends.

Father called me in and said to me: "I noticed that you did indeed share with your friends, but you did not do it with a whole heart." He then explained to me at length the idea of a "generous eye" and a "begrudging eye."

I was so deeply affected by Father's words that I was unable to recover for half an hour. I wept bitterly and threw up what I had eaten of the melon.

"What do you want from the child?" asked my mother. Father replied: "It is good this way. Now the trait [of generosity] will be ingrained in his character."

This is education.

QUESTIONS FOR DISCUSSION

1. Does Rabbi Yosef Yitschak's concluding statement, "This is education," resonate with you?

2. Do you think that the situation described in the memoir (a seven-year-old child sharing a treat with his friends but doing so grudgingly) warranted parental intervention?

LEARNING EXERCISE 1

My primary goals as a parent are to see my child grow up to be

1. Confident ~~but~~ not defensive

2. a good friend,

3. not over-critical of others. & self

4. values herself, & her worth.

Show and (Then) Tell

The Power of Role Modeling

LEARNING EXERCISE 2

What are the most important things you learned from your parent(s)?

1. nothing more important than family

2. fiscal responsibility
   - don't spend what you don't have
   - pay cc bills in full each mo.

3. work ethic.
   joy of ~~knowing~~ doing projects at home.

Text 2

Rabbi Moshe Sofer, *Chidushei Chatam Sofer*, Bava Batra 21a

וְנִרְאֶה בְּתַקָּנַת הַמְלַמְּדִים נַמִי הוּא שֶׁיִּהְיֶה יְרֵא שָׁמַיִם יוֹתֵר . . . כִּי דְּבָרִים
הַיּוֹצְאִים מִן לֵב יָרֵא וְחָרֵד נִכְנָסִים לְלֵב וּמַלְהִיבִים כְּאֵשׁ בּוֹעֵר בְּיִרְאַת
ה' וְאַהֲבָתוֹ בְּלֵב הַנַּעַר. וְעַל דֶּרֶךְ זֶה יִתְפָּרֵשׁ, "וְהָיוּ הַדְּבָרִים הָאֵלֶּה אֲשֶׁר
אָנֹכִי מְצַוְּךָ הַיּוֹם עַל לְבָבֶךָ" וְאָז "וְשִׁנַּנְתָּם לְבָנֶיךָ" (דְּבָרִים ו, ו–ז).

וְהַהֵיפוּךְ, אֲפִילוּ דַּיֵּיק וְגָרִיס וְאֵין לְבָבוֹ נָכוֹן עִם ה', מְלַאכְתּוֹ רְמִיָּה וּמַחֲרִיב הַנַּעַר.

Rabbi Moshe Sofer
(*Chatam Sofer*)
1762–1839

A leading rabbinical authority of the 19th century. Born in Frankfurt am Main, *Chatam Sofer* ultimately accepted the rabbinate of Pressburg (now Bratislava), Slovakia. Serving as rabbi and head of the yeshivah that he established, Rabbi Sofer maintained a strong traditionalist perspective, opposing deviation from Jewish tradition. *Chatam Sofer* is the title of his collection of halachic responsa and his commentary to the Talmud.

Those who teach Torah to children should be exceedingly devout and God-fearing . . . because words that emanate from a reverent heart penetrate the hearts of the young listeners and instill in them love and awe of God. The opposite is also true: If the teacher's heart is not true to God, even if he is a scholar and pedagogue, his work is fraudulent and he destroys his charges.

With this principle in mind, we can understand the sequence of verses [in the *Shema* prayer]: "These words that I command you this day shall be upon your heart," and then "and you shall teach them to your children" (Deuteronomy 6:6–7).

Text 3

Midrash, *Bereishit Rabah* 98:20

Bereishit Rabah

An early rabbinic commentary on the Book of Genesis. This Midrash bears the name of Rabbi Oshiya Rabah (Rabbi Oshiya "the Great") whose teaching opens this work. This Midrash provides textual exegeses and stories, expounds upon the biblical narrative, and develops and illustrates moral principles. Produced by the sages of the Talmud in the Land of Israel, its use of Aramaic closely resembles that of the Jerusalem Talmud. It was first published in Constantinople in 1512 together with four other Midrashic works on the other four books of the Pentateuch.

רַב הוּנָא בְּשֵׁם רַב מַתְנָה, אִיקוּנִין שֶׁל אָבִיו רָאָה וְצִיּנֵן דָּמוֹ.

רַבִּי מְנַחֲמָא בְּשֵׁם רַבִּי אַמִי, אִיקוּנִין שֶׁל אִמּוֹ רָאָה וְצִיּנֵן דָּמוֹ.

Rav Huna said in the name of Rav Matneh: He saw the visage of his father Jacob and it cooled his blood.

We can't control outcomes, just moral character & traits

Rabbi Menachema said in the name of Rabbi Ami: He saw the visage of his mother Rachel and it cooled his blood.

Text 4

Talmud, Sukah 46b

לֹא לֵימָא אִינִישׁ לְיָנוּקָא דְיַהֲבִינָא לָךְ מִידִי וְלֹא יָהִיב
לֵיהּ מִשּׁוּם דְּאָתֵי לְאַגְמוּרֵיהּ שִׁיקְרָא.

o not tell a child that you will give him or her something and then not give it. For the child will thus be taught to say falsehood.

Babylonian Talmud

A literary work of monumental proportions that draws upon the legal, spiritual, intellectual, ethical, and historical traditions of Judaism. The 37 tractates of the Babylonian Talmud contain the teachings of the Jewish sages from the period after the destruction of the 2nd Temple through the 5th century CE. It has served as the primary vehicle for the transmission of the Oral Law and the education of Jews over the centuries; it is the entry point for all subsequent legal, ethical, and theological Jewish scholarship.

Text 5

Rashi, Genesis 29:11

לְפִי שֶׁרָדַף אֱלִיפַז בֶּן עֵשָׂו בְּמִצְוַת אָבִיו אַחֲרָיו לְהוֹרְגוֹ וְהִשִּׂיגוֹ,
וּלְפִי שֶׁגָּדַל אֱלִיפַז בְּחֵיקוֹ שֶׁל יִצְחָק מָשַׁךְ יָדוֹ.

אָמַר לוֹ, "מָה אֶעֱשֶׂה לְצִיוּוּי שֶׁל אַבָּא?"

אָמַר לוֹ יַעֲקֹב, "טוֹל מַה שֶּׁבְּיָדִי, וְהֶעָנִי חָשׁוּב כַּמֵּת".

Esau commanded his son Eliphaz to pursue Jacob and kill him. But because Eliphaz had grown up in Isaac's lap, he was reluctant to kill Jacob.

Eliphaz said to Jacob: "What shall I do about my father's command?"

Said Jacob: "Take everything I own, and a pauper is like a dead man."

Rabbi Shlomo Yitschaki (Rashi)
1040–1105

Most noted biblical and Talmudic commentator. Born in Troyes, France, Rashi studied in the famed *yeshivot* of Mainz and Worms. His commentaries on the Pentateuch and the Talmud, which focus on the straightforward meaning of the text, have appeared in virtually every edition of the Talmud and Bible.

Expanding the Role

Text 6

Proverbs 22:6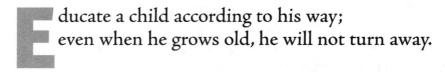

חֲנֹךְ לַנַּעַר עַל פִּי דַרְכּוֹ, גַּם כִּי יַזְקִין לֹא יָסוּר מִמֶּנָּה.

Educate a child according to his way;
even when he grows old, he will not turn away.

Text 7

Rabbi Yosef Yitschak Schneersohn, cited in *Hayom Yom*, 22 Tevet

הַכְרָזַת אאמו"ר בְּאַחַת הַהִתְוַעֲדוּת: אָט אַזוֹי וִוי הַנָחַת תְּפִילִין בְּכָל יוֹם אִיז אַ מִצְוָה דְאוֹרַיְיתָא אוֹיף יֶעדֶן אִידֶען, אָהן אַ חִילוּק צִי אַ גָדוֹל שֶׁבַּתּוֹרָה, צִי אַ אִיש פָּשׁוּט, אַזוֹי אִיז אַ חוּב גָמוּר אוֹיף יֶעדֶן אִידֶען צוּ טְרַאכְטֶען יֶעדֶען טָאג אַ הַאלְבֶּע שָׁעָה וֵוגֶן דֶעם חִנּוּךְ פוּן קִינְדֶערֶע, אוּן טָאן אַלְץ, וָואס עֶס אִיז בְּכֹחוֹ צוּ טָאן אוּן יֶתֶר מִכְּפִי כֹחוֹ, זֶעהֶן פּוֹעֵל זַיִן בַּיי דִי קִינְדֶערֶע, אַז זֵיי זָאלֶען גֶעהֶן אִין דֶעם דֶרֶךְ וָואס מֶען אִיז זֵיי מַדְרִיךְ.

My father [Rabbi Shalom DovBer of Lubavitch] once proclaimed: Just as wearing *tefilin* every day is a biblical mitzvah that applies to every Jewish man regardless of his standing in Torah, whether a great scholar or a simple person, so too it is an absolute duty for every person to spend a half hour every day thinking about the education of children. We must do everything within our power and even that which is [seemingly] beyond our power to inspire children to follow the path we envision for them.

QUESTION FOR DISCUSSION

Why isn't role modeling enough to transmit values to our children?

It must be in a way that child learns best. eg. w/Amanda not in heat of moment, in a calm, quiet place. Not "to parent"

The Ultimate Makeover

Transformational Education

LEARNING EXERCISE 3

When a child is born, he/she is most comparable to a

- a) Beautiful rose
- b) Delicate crystal
- c) Holy angel
- d) Moldable clay
- e) Wild donkey
- f) All of the above with the exception of (e)

Text 8

Job 11:12 ▐▌

וְעַיִר פֶּרֶא אָדָם יִוָּלֵד.

A human is born a wild donkey.

Children are SELFISH

QUESTIONS FOR DISCUSSION

1. **What is the primary attribute that distinguishes human from animal?**

2. **What is the implication of a "wild donkey"? (I.e., what makes the wild donkey unique among animals?)**

Text 9

The Rebbe, Rabbi Menachem M. Schneerson, *Sefer Hasichot* 5747, 1:74

דֶער גאַנצֶער עִנְיָן פוּן חִינוּךְ אִיז – בִּכְדֵי מְשַׁנֶּה זַיין טֶבַע הָרְגִילוּת: אַ קִינְד בְּטֶבַע
טוּט וְוִי בַּיי אִים קוּמְט אוֹיס, בְּלִי שׁוּם הַגְבָּלוֹת. וּבִלְשׁוֹן הַכָּתוּב – "יֵצֶר לֵב הָאָדָם
רַע מִנְּעוּרָיו" (בראשית ח,כא). דֶעְרִיבֶּער דאַרְף מֶען אִים מְחַנֵךְ זַיין – בִּכְדֵי מַגְבִּיל
זַיין אוּן מְשַׁנֶּה זַיין טֶבַע הָרְגִילוּת שֶׁלוֹ, בִּיז אַז בַּיי אִים זאָל זַיין מוֹחַ שַׁלִיט עַל הַלֵּב.

The whole point of education is to change the child's habitual nature. Children, by nature, do whatever they see fit, without any restraints; in the words of the verse (Genesis 8:21), "The impulse of the heart of man is evil from his youth." Children must therefore be trained to set boundaries and change their habitual natures, until they attain sovereignty of mind over heart.

Rabbi Menachem Mendel Schneerson
1902–1994

The towering Jewish leader of the 20th century, known as "the Lubavitcher Rebbe," or simply as "the Rebbe." Born in southern Ukraine, the Rebbe escaped Nazi-occupied Europe, arriving in the U.S. in June 1941. The Rebbe inspired and guided the revival of traditional Judaism after the European devastation, impacting virtually every Jewish community the world over. The Rebbe often emphasized that the performance of just one additional good deed could usher in the era of Mashiach. The Rebbe's scholarly talks and writings have been printed in more than 200 volumes.

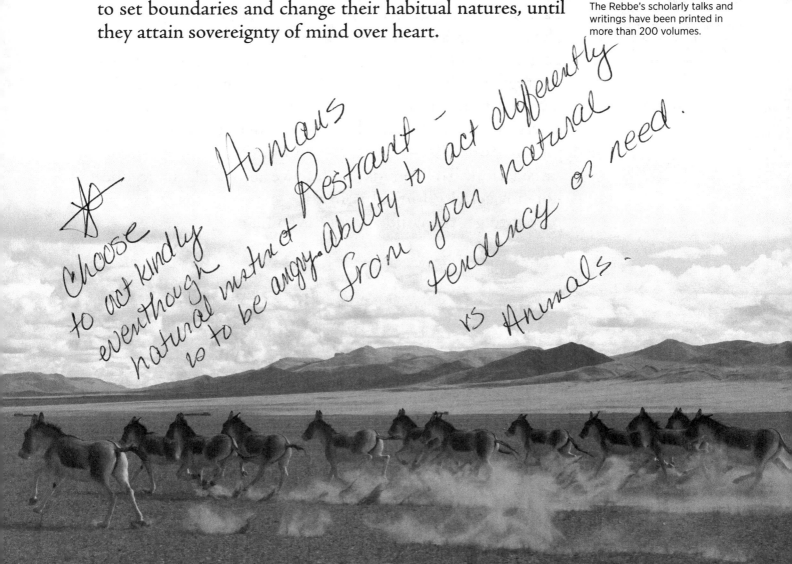

[Handwritten notes:] Humans — Choose to act kindly eventhough natural instinct is to be angry — Restraint — Ability to act differently from your natural tendency or need. vs Animals.

Application Time

Pushing, Prodding, and Nudging

Text 10

Amy Chua, *Battle Hymn of the Tiger Mother* [New York: Penguin Press, 2011], p. 29

Amy Chua

Chinese-American lawyer, legal scholar, and author. Chua is the John M. Duff Jr. Professor of Law at Yale Law School. She specializes in the study of international business transactions, law and development, ethnic conflict, and globalization and the law. She wrote two books on law, *World on Fire* and *Day of Empire*, but is most known for her bestselling provocative parenting memoir, *Battle Hymn of the Tiger Mother.*

What Chinese parents understand is that nothing is fun until you're good at it. To get good at anything you have to work, and children on their own never want to work, which is why it is crucial to override their preferences. This often requires fortitude on the part of the parents because the child will resist; things are always hardest at the beginning, which is where Western parents tend to give up. But if done properly, the Chinese strategy produces a virtuous circle. Tenacious practice, practice, practice is crucial for excellence. . . . Once a child starts to excel at something—whether it's math, piano, pitching or ballet—he or she gets praise, admiration and satisfaction. This builds confidence and makes the once not-fun activity fun. This in turn makes it easier for the parent to get the child to work even more.

Socialization, [handwritten annotation with arrows pointing to text]

So, when you are uncomfortable in a situation, fight your urge to run away.
Watch, work at it and eventually you will master it and enjoy it, too. [handwritten note]

Text 11

Rabbi Manis Friedman, Interview with the JLI Curriculum Development Team, May 29, 2014 ▮

Discipline is usually seen as a necessary evil. You're young, you're irresponsible, you're ignorant, so you have to obey your parents. If you don't follow instruction, you might get hit by a truck or you might burn down the house.

If that's what discipline means, then naturally, as soon as kids get a little smarter, they start scheming: How do I get out of this?

Chasidic teaching sees it very differently. Obedience is not a yoke that you don't want; it is a talent that you never outgrow.

Every human being has limitations and handicaps. Some people can't function before they have their morning coffee. Some people can't function after eight o'clock at night: "It's past my bedtime, I can't!" When it's cold outside or wet—"I can't." "I'm not in the mood—I can't." There are a hundred different things that keep me from functioning.

All that changes when you have discipline. Look at a soldier. Soldiers are trained to follow orders. But more importantly, soldiers are trained to be free from all sorts of petty restrictions so that they *can* follow an order. Whether it's hot or cold outside—irrelevant. Uphill, downhill—irrelevant. How much does the pack weigh? Forty pounds, sixty pounds, eighty pounds—irrelevant. If it needs to happen, a soldier makes it happen.

Rabbi Manis Friedman
1946–

Renowned author, lecturer, and philosopher. More than 150,000 copies of Rabbi Friedman's thought-provoking and entertaining video and audio tapes have been sold. He is the author of *Doesn't Anyone Blush Anymore?* and the founder and dean of Bais Chana Institute of Jewish Studies in Minnesota.

True discipline means freeing yourself, getting beyond the petty restrictions that limit average human beings and cause them to under-function and under-perform.

Training a child through discipline doesn't mean, "I'm going to impose my will on you because you're not intelligent enough to know what's right or wrong." Yes, there are things the parent knows that the child doesn't; but there is much more to discipline than that.

Let's consider the following scenario: You say to your child, "Put away your books." The child says, "I don't want to." So you say, "Okay, but you still have to put away your books." What are you teaching your child? You're saying: "You don't want to, but that is not a crippling thing—do it anyway!" You're training the child to go beyond his or her limitations.

The Objective of Incentive

Text 12

Midrash Mishlei (Buber), 22:6 🔊

"חֲנוֹךְ לַנַּעַר עַל פִּי דַרְכּוֹ גַּם כִּי יַזְקִין לֹא יָסוּר מִמֶּנָּה" . . .

כְּהֲדָא תוֹרְתָּא דְּלָא יְלִיפָא רַדְיָא וּמִתְקַשְׁיָא עֲלָה בְּסוֹפָא.

וּכְהֲדָא עוּבַּרְתָּא דְּכַרְמָא דְּאִית לָהּ אֲתָר כִּי אֲתָא עַד
דְּהִיא רְטִיבָא, וְכִדְקַשְׁיָא לֵיהּ אִי אַתְּ יָכִיל לָהּ.

> **"E**ducate a child according to his way; even when he grows old, he will not turn away from it." . . .
>
> Like an ox that was not trained to plow [when young] that finds it difficult to do so later.
>
> Like a sapling in the vineyard that can be fixed when [young and] moist, but cannot be remedied once it hardens.

Midrash Mishlei

A rabbinic commentary on the Book of Proverbs. Midrash is the designation of a particular genre of rabbinic literature. The term "Midrash" is derived from the root d-r-sh, which means "to search," "to examine," and "to investigate." This particular Midrash provides textual exegeses and develops and illustrates the principles of the Book of Proverbs.

Text 13

Maimonides, Commentary on the Mishnah, Introduction to *Chelek* 📖

שִׂים בְּדַעְתְּךָ כִּי נַעַר קָטָן הֱבִיאוּהוּ אֵצֶל הַמְלַמֵּד לְלַמְּדוֹ תּוֹרָה. וְזֶהוּ
הַטּוֹב הַגָּדוֹל לוֹ . . . אֶלָּא שֶׁהוּא, לְמִיעוּט שְׁנוֹתָיו וְחוּלְשַׁת שִׂכְלוֹ, אֵינוֹ
מֵבִין מַעֲלַת אוֹתוֹ הַטּוֹב . . . וּלְפִיכָךְ בְּהֶכְרֵחַ יִצְטָרֵךְ הַמְלַמֵּד . . . שֶׁיְזָרֵז
אוֹתוֹ עַל הַלִּמּוּד בִּדְבָרִים שֶׁהֵם אֲהוּבִים אֶצְלוֹ לְקַטְנוּת שְׁנוֹתָיו. וְיֹאמַר
לוֹ: "קְרָא וְאֶתֵּן לְךָ אֱגוֹזִים אוֹ תְאֵנִים, וְאֶתֵּן לְךָ מְעַט דְּבַשׁ" . . .

וּכְשֶׁיַּגְדִּיל וְיֶחֱזַק שִׂכְלוֹ וְיֵקַל בְּעֵינָיו אוֹתוֹ הַדָּבָר שֶׁהָיָה אֶצְלוֹ נִכְבָּד
מִלְּפָנִים, וְחָזַר לֶאֱהוֹב זוּלָתוֹ . . . יֹאמַר לוֹ מְלַמְּדוֹ: "קְרָא וְאֶקַּח לְךָ מִנְעָלִים
יָפִים אוֹ בְּגָדִים חֲמוּדִים" . . . וּכְשֶׁיִּהְיֶה דַעְתּוֹ שְׁלֵמָה . . . יֹאמַר לוֹ רַבּוֹ:
"לְמוֹד כְּדֵי שֶׁתִּהְיֶה רֹאשׁ וְדַיָּין, וִיכַבְּדוּךְ בְּנֵי אָדָם וְיָקוּמוּ מִפָּנֶיךָ" . . .

וְכָל זֶה מְגוּנֶּה . . . שֶׁאֵין לְשׁוּם תַּכְלִית הַחַכְמָה לֹא לְקַבֵּל כָּבוֹד מִבְּנֵי אָדָם,
וְלֹא לְהַרְוִיחַ מָמוֹן . . . וְלֹא תִהְיֶה אֶצְלוֹ תַּכְלִית לִמּוּד הַחַכְמָה אֶלָּא לָדַעַת
אוֹתָהּ בִּלְבַד . . . וְאוּלָם זֶה טוֹב לָהֶם, עַד שֶׁיִּהְיֶה לָהֶם כֹּחַ וְהֶרְגֵּל וְהִשְׁתַּדְּלוּת
בַּעֲשִׂיַּית הַתּוֹרָה, וּמִזֶּה יִתְעוֹרְרוּ לָדַעַת הָאֱמֶת וְיַחְזְרוּ עוֹבְדִים מֵאַהֲבָה.

וְזֶה הוּא מַה שֶּׁאָמְרוּ ז"ל (פסחים נ,א) "לְעוֹלָם יַעֲסוֹק אָדָם בַּתּוֹרָה
וַאֲפִילוּ שֶׁלֹּא לִשְׁמָהּ, שֶׁמִּתּוֹךְ שֶׁלֹּא לִשְׁמָהּ בָּא לִשְׁמָהּ."

Rabbi Moshe ben Maimon
(Maimonides, Rambam)
1135–1204

Halachist, philosopher, author, and physician. Maimonides was born in Cordoba, Spain. After the conquest of Cordoba by the Almohads, he fled Spain and eventually settled in Cairo, Egypt. There, he became the leader of the Jewish community and served as court physician to the vizier of Egypt. He is most noted for authoring the Mishneh Torah, an encyclopedic arrangement of Jewish law, and for his philosophical work, Guide for the Perplexed. His rulings on Jewish law are integral to the formation of halachic consensus.

magine a young child who is brought to a teacher to learn Torah, which is the child's greatest good . . . but due to youth and immaturity, the child does not appreciate this. . . . So the teacher needs to motivate the child with age-appropriate incentives. So the teacher should say, "Read your lesson, and I will give you nuts, figs, or honey." . . .

When the child grows older, and the sweets are no longer attractive . . . the teacher should say, "Read your lesson, and I will buy you nice shoes or attractive clothes." . . . Then, as the child's mind reaches full maturity, the teacher should say, "Study, and you will become a leader and scholar, and people will respect you and rise in your honor." . . .

Now all this is shameful. . . . For the purpose of wisdom is not to receive honor from people, nor to bring monetary profit. . . . We should study wisdom for no purpose other than to know it. . . . Yet this is for the children's good, for it gives them the motivation and gets them in the habit of studying and observing the Torah, and from this they will be roused to know the truth and to do it out of love.

Thus our sages have said (Talmud, Pesachim 50b): "We should study and observe the Torah even if not for its own sake; because doing it for ulterior motives will bring us to do it for its own sake."

Role Modeling v. Proactive Parenting

QUESTION FOR DISCUSSION (REPRISE)

Why isn't role modeling enough to transmit values to our children?

EXERCISES FOR THE WEEK

a) Identify one habit, value, or character trait that you would like to see your child develop and/or improve.

b) Design an action plan for how *you* can improve *yourself* in that area.

c) Identify a benchmark (in the same character area) that you want your child to reach. Sit down with your child and calmly explain the goal and, if necessary, describe the associated rewards and/or consequences.

Sample Answers:

a) *Anger. My five-year-old son has great difficulty controlling his behavior when he is angered.*

b) *I will read a book on anger management and learn how to reduce some of the anger in my life. I will schedule weekly discussions with my spouse to discuss my (or our) progress in this area and brainstorm how we can further improve.*

c) *I will start with focusing on my child's tendency to throw things when angered. I will explain to him that such behavior is not appropriate for a big boy and will no longer be tolerated—regardless of what provokes his anger. I will also tell him that if a week passes and he has not thrown anything, I will take him on a trip to the mall. If he does throw things, he will need to pick up and clean up whatever he threw, and he will have a five-minute break in his room to contemplate what he has done.*

Key Points

1. "Parenting" isn't (primarily) something we do, but something we are. Parents are always parenting, no matter what they are doing; children are always watching and taking note.

2. Children tend to absorb their parents' values—both good and bad—and emulate their behaviors. Therefore, if we see our child struggling in a certain area, one of the most effective things we can do to help is to work on improving *ourselves* in that area.

3. A child is born naturally selfish and lazy and without the capacity for mindful self-control. The primary goal of child rearing is to wean children off their default nature and help them acquire self-mastery and a new, adult personality.

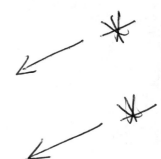

4. Self-mastery is crucial to success in every area of life: material, social, intellectual, moral, and spiritual. Self-mastery means freeing oneself from the petty restrictions that limit many people and cause them to under-function and under-perform.

5. We train our children to be disciplined by pushing them beyond their comfort zones, setting a high standard for them and insisting that they reach it.

6. When instructions alone will not suffice, parents should employ incentives to get their children to achieve important goals. Reward and/or negative consequence can be driving forces behind the greater goal of self-mastery.

7. Role modeling fosters proper values and aspirations. Proactive parenting and careful planning are required, however, to give children the gifts of self-discipline and self-mastery necessary for them to live up to these values and aspirations.

Appendix A

LEARNING EXERCISE

Near each trait, fill in whether it is primarily a "childish" trait or an "adult" trait. Also note whether it is a positive or negative trait.

Trait	Childish or Adult?	Positive or Negative?
Responsibility	A	✓
Self-Control	A	✓
Laziness	A	
Selfishness	C	
Greed	C	
Impulsiveness	C	
Optimism	C ✓	✓
Enthusiasm	C ✓	✓
Faith	A A	✓
Trust	C ✓	✓

ADDITIONAL READINGS

INSTILLING VALUES

BY RABBI RAPHAEL PELCOVITZ AND DAVID PELCOVITZ, PhD

Children are not born with a natural sense of what is right and what is wrong. Transmitting values takes effort, thought and an awareness of what standards we want to set (and impart) for respectful and proper behavior in our children. Among the most basic values that parents must instill in their children is gratitude *(hakaras ha'tov)*. In fact, gratefulness is such a central value of Judaism that the very name *Yehudi*, "Jew," has as its source the Hebrew word *hodaah*, thankfulness. Regarding the birth of Leah's fourth child, the Torah teaches us that *She conceived again, and bore a son and declared, "This time let me gratefully praise Hashem"; therefore she called his name Judah; then she stopped giving birth (Genesis 29:35).*

Rashi explains: "I took more than my share so I must be thankful." Leah knew through prophecy that Jacob would have twelve sons. As one of four wives, her fair share would have been three sons. The verse, "This time let me gratefully praise Hashem," reflects Leah's recognition that she received more than her portion. This is why Jews are called *Yehudim*—to be Jewish is to express gratitude.

Yet many children take for granted what their parents do for them. They are not even aware of the debt of gratitude that they owe to their parents. In turn, parents are often uncomfortable with asking for recognition for the countless acts of kindness they do for their children. Instilling in children the habit of thanking their parents is an important component of teaching them this central value of being a Jew.

Another component that parents should attend to in the moral education of their children is the lesson that children should be helpful and considerate. They should pitch in and help out with the family's everyday chores and tasks. Once upon a time, a universal requirement of children was to be helpful and share in family chores and responsibilities. Today, this makes some parents uncomfortable. Interesting insights on the benefits of requiring children to assume their fair share in helping with family chores comes from research into what factors are associated with children who are successfully raised in families facing chronic hardships such as poverty or violence. Children who are required to help out and take an active role in assisting their parents face adversity are more resilient and better adjusted as adults than children who are not required to play this active role. Requiring active contributions by children gives them a sense of mastery and control and teaches them to go beyond their own selfish needs.

In addition to *directly* teaching our children what is expected of them, the transmission of proper values is often a subtle process. It is important to be aware of the many indirect forces that shape our children's values, since raising a *mentch* is so much more complicated than only telling a child what to do. Longitudinal studies that identify the core ingredients associated with raising an empathic child identify a subtle process that is typically present in such families. Parents who raise children who are kind and charitable as adults expose them to discussions that show respect for those with whom they disagree. Imagine a family sitting around a Shabbos table discussing an issue about which they feel passionately. Parents who show contempt or disrespect regarding those with whom they disagree are conveying a very powerful message to their children. They are modeling an approach to conflict that includes disdain and contempt for those who view the world differently. Whether the discussion is about family members, friends, or the leadership of the local shul or yeshivah, showing respect for those with whom we disagree is a very powerful lesson for children. A crucial facet of this process is parental promotion of perspective-taking in their children. It is common sense that when children are encouraged to see things respectfully through the eyes of others—even those with whom we disagree—they are getting an important lesson in one of the basic building blocks of empathy. Parents whose discussion style is associated with instilling the proper values in their children are also more likely to actively encourage their children's participation in family discussions. These parents draw their children into discussions with adults and supportively challenge their children's thinking in an atmosphere that is marked by respect and tolerance for the views of others, as well as that of their children.

> *After I gave a lecture that included a discussion about the importance of showing respect to others in conversations we have in front of our children, a rabbi in the audience told me the following story. He had just taken a position as the leader of a shul that had had a rocky relationship with the previous rabbi. He was shocked to hear that the son of one of his congregants had just become engaged to a non-Jewish girl. He met with the young man to try to understand how this happened and to attempt to dissuade him from his decision to intermarry. The young man explained that, all of his life, the conversations he heard around the Shabbos table were dominated by his parents bitterly complaining about the previous rabbi. When company came over, this, too, was a major topic of conversation. He asked the rabbi, "How do you expect me to view this religion? I was a young, impressionable boy and my view of Judaism was mainly informed by the bitter anger my parents and their friends felt toward their spiritual leader. I see no reason to continue to belong to a religion that was so devalued by my parents and their friends."*

Another indirect force that shapes a child's acquisition of the proper values is having an actively involved father. The role of mothers in shaping a child's moral development is obvious. Less intuitive is the finding in a number of research studies that active involvement of fathers in their young children's moral education is the strongest predictor of their children's moral reasoning and empathy in adolescence and young adulthood. Conversely, in homes with absentee fathers, children are at increased risk for behavioral difficulties. This finding is in keeping with what we are taught in *Proverbs* 1:8: *Hear, my child, the discipline of your father, and do not forsake the teaching of your mother.* King Solomon is telling us that when it comes to *mussar*—the limit-setting component of parenting—fathers play a particularly central role. Although there are many forces that may be pulling a father away from active involvement with his children, it is important for him to remember that, especially when his children are young, he has a pivotal role to play in their moral development. Young children living in homes where their fathers are largely absent experience what psychologists call *father hunger.* They have an almost physical thirst for active interaction with their father. Once children reach adolescence, they have much less interest in spending time with either parent than they did when they were younger. While a father continues to play a central role in shaping his child's values into adulthood, he needs to actively prioritize his role as moral educator of his young child during the critical window of opportunity that fades all too quickly.

Research in neuropsychology has uncovered two types of learning that are part of the moral education process. Didactic learning, for example, teaching a child *Hilchos Derech Eretz* (the laws of proper conduct) predominantly involves the brain's left hemisphere. When the left side of the brain dominates, learning consists of logical, factual thinking. This type of learning is characterized by abstract, context-independent ideas. Right-hemisphere learning consists primarily of concrete human and interpersonal situations. The focus of this part of the brain is on people and the cause of their actions.

Right-hemisphere learning is what takes place when children learn through stories or by absorbing the moral behavior they see in admired adults. Such learning is integrated in a more pervasive way than its more scientific, left-hemisphere counterpart. It becomes part of the person, rather than disconnected pieces of knowledge. Although parents may be concerned that stories or *chessed* (acts of kindness) projects take their children away from *real* learning, *softer* approaches such as telling stories that contain moral lessons or affording children opportunities to perform *chessed* are the most powerful methods we have for effectively transmitting our values to our children.

The powerful impact of role models on the behavior pattern of the child is perhaps the most potent type of right-hemisphere learning. Seeing *tzaddikim* (righteous people) in action helps our children internalize proper values in a particularly meaningful manner, as the verse *(Isaiah* 30:20) teaches us, *And your eyes will behold your teacher.* According to the *Radak,* a Scriptural commentator, this teaches us how important "seeing" a teacher in action can be in imparting values. Judaism has always taught that exposure to a *tzaddik's* day-to-day behavior is a valued mode of absorbing practical lessons about how to lead a proper life.

There is a major difference between moral knowledge and moral action—*knowing* what is right and *acting* on this knowledge. A child can *know* exactly what is expected of him in a given situation, yet not *act* on this knowledge when actually faced with a moral dilemma. The Chofetz Chaim told the following story to illustrate this concept: There was a landowner who had to leave town for an extended period of time. Before embarking on his trip he left the responsibility for supervising his properties to his trusted overseer who was given a detailed "to do" list that described a series of tasks that were to be done during the landowner's absence. Upon the latter's return everything was in a state of chaos. The landowner severely chastised the overseer for neglecting his duties, reminding him that he had left him a detailed list of his duties. The overseer defensively protested, "But I read the list every morning!" The Chofetz Chaim explained that the same is true of Jews who are meticulous in their study of Torah, but not as careful in putting their Torah knowledge into practice. Teaching our children the *Shulchan Aruch* (The Code of Law), without providing active guidance regarding the actual implementation of this knowledge in the real world, is analogous to the overseer reading and not implementing his *to do* list.

Robert Coles, a Harvard child psychiatrist, who is a leading expert on instilling values in children, relates a very powerful story in his book on this topic: A young woman who had taken several courses he taught on moral development came to his office to inform him that she was leaving Harvard. Dr. Coles was surprised to hear this, since the woman came from a small town that took great pride in sending one of its own to such a prestigious college. She explained that she had to put herself through college by cleaning rooms in the university's dormitories. One of those rooms was occupied by the student who consistently received the highest grade in Dr. Cole's classes on morality, a young man who came from a wealthy home. She bitterly related to Dr. Coles how, when she came to clean this student's room, he did everything he could to demean her and taunt her for being a cleaning lady. She left Harvard, telling Dr. Coles that she could not be part of an institution that could reward such an immoral individual with top grades in the very area in which he was so deficient. As a university professor once said regarding a top student, "He always got an A in my course, but ultimately he got an F in life."

Mental health professionals and educators who work with "at-risk" children have noted the unexpected healing powers of giving alienated adolescents a chance to do *chessed.* I have repeatedly seen the transforming effects of giving such children a chance to find meaning by affording them an opportunity to achieve success and recognition by helping others.

A 17-year-old boy was becoming increasingly defiant of his parents and teachers. He stayed out practically all night, associating with friends who had dropped out of school and who were experimenting with drugs. He was on the verge of being expelled from his school because he slept late, missed most of his classes and completed none of his assignments. The boy's principal had a "hunch" that he could kill two birds with one stone. The principal assigned the youngster to work with a neurologically impaired special education student who attended the lower school. This student had frequent explosive tantrums and even the most experienced special education teachers were having difficulty controlling him. The rebellious adolescent was able to reach the young child in a manner that was unprecedented. He was patient with him and seemed to be able to get him to cooperate with his teachers in a way that short-circuited the boy's explosive outburst. He was ultimately given a job as a paid aide for this child and received so much praise and recognition for his role in turning the child around that he once again felt connected to his family and school. No longer feeling marginalized, he gave up his street friends and an arrangement was worked out for him to finish high school by taking courses that were built around his job.

The positive impact of requiring our children to perform acts of *chessed* is also evident with mainstream children. Several summers ago a fascinating event took place in a large summer camp. As an experiment, this camp added some bunks populated with children who had special needs. These children, who were diagnosed with mental retardation, mild autism and various other developmental disabilities, took part in the camp's activities together with the other children. A totally unintended outcome emerged. It was expected that the children with special needs would benefit from being included in activities with the mainstream. What was totally unexpected, however, was the way this experience transformed the manner in which the mainstream children interacted with one another. After several weeks, the children and staff noticed that the whole atmosphere of the camp had changed. Children started to be kinder to each other. The cliques and competitiveness that often characterize interaction between children had vanished. It seems that once these children had been required to go beyond themselves and perform *chessed* with children less fortunate than themselves, their acts of kindness became contagious, and they were more kind and tolerant in all their interactions.

The most obvious subtle transmitter of values occurs when we unconsciously model proper behavior for our children. Every time a husband and wife resolve a disagreement with calm, respectful discussion they are modeling how to deal with disagreements with others in a respectful way. Each time parents enter a museum or amusement park and tell the truth about their children's age, even though they could easily lie and get less expensive children's tickets, a powerful lesson about honesty is transmitted. In countless ways parental interaction with others conveys messages that shape impressionable children's sense of what is right and wrong. Transmitting values to children is a constant process that is formed by the climate of values that pervades our homes. When parents set a tone of honesty, guidance, kindness and genuine respect for others, children absorb these values and grow into adults who, in turn, take part in the intergenerational transmission of what it means to be a Jew.

Instilling Honesty/Integrity

The *Midrash (Midrash Rabbah, Parshah* 8) teaches us that when God was about to create man there was a difference of opinion among the angels. *Tzedek,* the attribute of Righteousness, and *Chessed,* the attribute of Kindness, argued in favor of the creation of man, since he is "inherently righteous and kind." The attributes of *Shalom,* Peace, and *Emes,* Truth, argued against man's creation, since man is "thoroughly contentious and thoroughly false." God responded by taking Truth and hurling it to the ground. Thus, God made room for the creation of man by temporarily setting aside Truth.

The Kotzker Rebbe asks an obvious question. Why did God choose to cast down Truth and not Peace? Didn't Peace also argue against man's creation? The Rebbe answers that when something is cast down to the ground it fragments. When God threw down Truth it broke into pieces and is thus, by definition, no longer Truth. It had been shattered, and since Truth brooks no compromise it was neutralized and was no longer a factor in deciding for or against the creation of man. On the other hand, if God had thrown down Peace it too would have broken into pieces as well. However, as the Kotzker said, *"A shtikel shalom iz oych shalom"*— "A little Peace is also Peace." In contrast to Truth, Peace is not an all-or-nothing concept. Even a little bit of Peace between husband and wife, or parent and child, is better than no Peace at all. Alternatively, there is no compromise with Truth, it demands total integrity and completeness.

It is of note, that the ally of Truth in the *Midrash* was *"Shalom,"* a word that not only means Peace but is also related to the word *sheleimus*—completeness or integrity. The word *integrity* is defined in the dictionary as "the quality of being whole or undivided, completeness."[1] The root of the word is from the Latin word *integritas*, which is based on the word *integer* meaning *whole* or *complete*.

This concept is further reflected in the Hebrew word for Truth (*Emes*), which is spelled *aleph, mem, tuf*—the first, middle and last letters of the Hebrew alphabet. The very word *Emes* implies integrity—something that is whole and all-encompassing from the start, through the middle and until the very end. In contrast, the Hebrew word for falsehood (*Sheker)* is spelled with letters that are close to one another alphabetically, and out of order—*shin, kuf, reish*. The lesson is clear. The forces of *Sheker* find it easy to unite, while those of Truth find the quest for integrity and unity to be more elusive, requiring a longer haul (from *aleph* through *tuf*).

The *Maharal* in *Avos* (1:18) further highlights the lessons to be learned from the physical attributes of the letters spelling *Emes* and *Sheker*. The letters of *Emes* symbolize solidity and stability, as signified by the two legs that form the foundation of both the letter *aleph* and *tuf*, and the long base of the *mem*. In contrast, the expression "Falsehood has no feet" (*Tikunei Zohar* 425) is graphically portrayed by the three letters of *Sheker* that sit shakily on a point: *Shin*, in Torah script (unlike the printed form in today's books), comes to a point, as do *kuf* and *reish* . From the standpoint of parenting, the wisdom inherent in these two words carries a powerful lesson. To imbue our children with the sense of stability that honesty and integrity engender requires much diligence and effort. Conversely, in a society rampant with *Sheker*, the draw toward deceit and falsehood can easily pull our children toward an unstable and slippery slope.

The central role of Truth is described by King David in *Psalms* (85:12), *Truth grows from the earth*. The

Kotzker Rebbe asks, "Since everything that grows needs a seed, what seed must be planted to yield a crop of *Emes?"* He answered. "If you bury falsehood, then truth will grow." The seed of *Emes* begins by uprooting and burying dishonesty. If we live in a society where *Sheker* is rampant, then Truth can only be cultivated by training ourselves and our children to recognize and reject an atmosphere of dishonesty that can be so pervasive that we are not even aware of it.

The pervasive pull of the forces of *Sheker* is well illustrated by a national survey of 12,000 high school students conducted in 2002 by the Josephson Institute of Ethics. The percentage of adolescents admitting they cheated on an exam at least once in the past year jumped by 13 percent compared to the previous decade (61 percent in 1992 vs. 74 percent in 2002.). Similar trends were found in the percentage of high school students who acknowledged lying to parents or teachers. In just two years (2000–2002), there was an 11 percent increase in the number of secondary school students who reported that they would be willing to lie to get a good job (28 percent to 39 percent).

The 2002 report also reported an alarming finding. Common sense would dictate that adolescents attending religious schools would demonstrate higher levels of honesty than public school students. The survey found that students who attend private religious schools relative to their public school counterparts were marginally more likely to cheat on exams (78 percent vs. 72 percent) than their public school counterparts. They were also somewhat more likely to lie to their teachers (86 percent vs. 81 percent).

In contrast to their behavior and attitudes, adolescents clearly *know* the difference between right and wrong. Their parents have communicated a message that has led to an intellectual message that their child should do the right thing regardless of negative consequences. In the survey, 84 percent agree with the statement, "My parents want me to do the ethically right thing, no matter what the cost." Similarly, 93 percent said that their parents would prefer that they get bad grades rather than cheat on tests. As in so many other areas of life there is a difference between

---

[1] *American Heritage Dictionary of the English Language,* Fourth edition, Houghton Mifflin, 2000.

moral knowledge and moral action. Knowing that honesty is the right approach is very different from acting honestly when having to face the unpleasantness of doing poorly on a test or assignment. Taking the easy way out by cheating appears to have reached epidemic proportions.

The increase in cheating is also evident in the college-age population. The Center for Academic Integrity at Duke University reports that approximately 70 percent of college students admit to cheating, and 95 percent of them claim that they have never been caught. Likewise, Donald McCabe of Rutgers University conducted a survey in 1999 of thousands of students on 21 campuses across the country. Approximately one-third admitted to serious test cheating and half acknowledged at least one episode of serious cheating on written assignments. When asked to explain how they rationalize their dishonesty, most of the students attributed their actions to what they view as the unrealistic pressures they face. For example, they say that they feel compelled to cheat because of the demands placed on them to excel academically for the purposes of getting into the "right" graduate school or job. These studies also document a pervasive attitude on the part of faculty at the secondary and university level that makes them reluctant to take action against suspected cheaters. In spite of the pervasiveness of cheating, less than half of 800 faculty surveyed on 16 campuses in 1992 say they have ever reported a student for cheating. In a 1999 survey of over 1,000 faculty members on 21 campuses, one-third of those who were aware of student cheating in their course in the last two years, did nothing to address it. It should come as no surprise that students report that academic dishonesty is higher in courses where it is well known that faculty members are likely to ignore their cheating.

Unfortunately, our community is not immune to this problem. As noted earlier, parents typically teach their children how to arrive at an intellectual awareness of the importance of acting truthfully and honestly. The parental role of teaching children not to cheat in school requires an increased awareness of the multiple ways that indirect messages, in this area, are transmitted to our children. For the segment of our community that places great value on having their children attend highly selective colleges, intense parental focus on grades and SAT scores at the expense of developing high levels of integrity and moral behavior transmits a powerful lesson as to what *really* matters. Of course, equally powerful lessons are transmitted to our children if they are exposed to parental dishonesty in business or paying taxes. Even more subtle but, perhaps, equally important messages are conveyed to children, for example, every time they are told to falsely tell a telemarketer or *meshulach* (collector for charity) that the parent is not home, when parents exaggerate about their achievements to a friend, or lie to a police officer to avoid getting a ticket. Such behavior can provide powerful, albeit unintended lessons regarding honesty.

In Tractate *Shabbos* (55a), Rav Chanina teaches us: "The signature of Hashem is Truth." Artists are often known by their signature piece—the song or piece of art that defines them. *L'havdil* (to distinguish), God's signature piece is *Emes*. The teachers of ethical values teach us that since man is created "*b'tzelem Elokim,*" in God's image, engaging in falsehood violates one's own *tzelem Elokim*. In essence, our Rabbis teach us that cheating, deceit and lying are akin to negating the part of us that is Godlike. Like a counterfeiter who forges another's signature, *Sheker* makes us guilty of forging Hashem's signature. The role of parents is to help their children understand that cheating goes beyond the obvious costs of dishonesty. By cheating they are impairing their human dignity, the essence of their connectedness to Hashem.

Instilling Values Regarding Money

For more than four decades the American Council on Education, and UCLA have together surveyed nearly one quarter of a million entering college freshmen in the United States, asking them to rank their primary life goals. In 1965, 82 percent said that developing a meaningful philosophy of life was essential, while only 42 percent said that earning a good living was essential. In contrast, in 1998, only 35 percent endorsed the finding of meaning as a core goal, while 74 percent ranked being very well off financially at the top of their list.

In what is termed by psychologists "The American Paradox," researchers have found that while (corrected for inflation) Americans are twice as rich, there has been no corresponding rise in levels of happiness and satisfaction with life. In fact, during the same period of time that real income has doubled in the United States there has been a doubling of the divorce rate and the rates of adolescent suicide have tripled. In what some mental health experts term "affluenza," the rate of depression in affluent adolescents has increased substantially. It appears that when children are taught to value money instead of more enduring sources of meaning, such as religion, family and friends, their risk for leading empty, unfulfilling lives increases significantly.

While an excessive emphasis on the importance of money risks a focus on superficial materialism, it is also important to teach children about the value of earning money through their own efforts rather than consistently feeling entitled to receive money from their parents for whatever they want or need. There are numerous ways that overindulgence can negatively impact on a child. Not only can possessions come to lose their value, but children are at risk of failing to learn the crucial benefits of self-discipline. A powerful indicator of this dynamic is the difference many educators observe in the lost and found sections of yeshivas in affluent communities as compared to those in communities that are financially less fortunate. Electronic games, toys and expensive coats worth hundreds of dollars often go unclaimed in the lost and founds of the wealthy schools, while very little of value goes unclaimed in the yeshivas in the less affluent neighborhoods. When possessions are so easily replaced that they have little value to children, we are in danger of producing spoiled and overindulged children.

Psychologists emphasize the crucial importance of teaching children how to learn the connection between effort and reward. When a child demands possessions with no corresponding requirement to earn it, he or she is deprived of learning self-discipline—a skill that is essential to leading a successful life. The Jewish attitude toward money clearly emphasizes the importance of understanding the value of earning money through one's own efforts rather than receiving it as a gift. The *Talmud Yerushalmi (Orah* 1:3) speaks of *"nehama d'kesufa,"* "bread of shame," regarding the psychological discomfort that individuals feel when their basic needs are met without any effort on their part. The Talmud explains that one who eats the food of another is ashamed to look at his benefactor's face. A corollary of this psychological truth can be found in the words of Rav Kahana: "An individual prefers one portion of his own over nine belonging to his friend" *(Bava Metzia* 38a). Finally, in an insight that helps explain the high rate of depression in affluent adolescents who have everything handed to them on a silver platter, the Talmud teaches us: "The world looks dark to somebody who depends on the sustenance of others" *(Beitzah* 32b).

The *Midrash* teaches us that when the Third *Beis Ha-Mikdash* (The Holy Temple) will be established it will come down from heaven fully built except for the gates and doors, which we will have to add ourselves. As the *Midrash* explains, the gates of the Temple were consumed and, at the time of the third Temple, will be excavated and put in place through our own efforts *(Bamidbar Rabbah, Parshah* 15). The obvious question is if God is ready to give us the Third *Beis HaMikdash,* why not give it to us complete? The valuable lesson learned from this is that it is important to always take an active role. Even at the time of redemption, when we are so fully in God's hands, we must do our share by taking an active role in reestablishing the Temple. Otherwise, our rejoicing in the redemption will have an element of overdependence—of *nehama d'kesufa.*

Recent research in psychology has consistently documented the benefits of requiring that children actively pitch in and help out with the tasks that busy families need in order to function efficiently. Several studies have found that in families going through chronic stresses, such as financial pressures or illness, it is protective to require that children go beyond themselves by pitching in and helping the family. Obligating children to help out with everyday chores and tasks can give such children a sense of control and fulfillment. Obviously, it is important that these children not be overburdened by being assigned an unreasonable load that can rob them of their childhood. Researchers suggest that the following ingredients are characteristic of appropriate required helpfulness:

- Age-appropriate responsibility that the child can handle.

- Responsibilities that do not interfere with the age-appropriate tasks of childhood.

- Responsibilities accompanied by clear and consistent expectations of what is required of the child.

While the Jewish and psychological perspectives on the importance of not indulging one's children are clear, many parents find it difficult not to be overindulgent. To counter these tendencies it is important to examine some of the internal and external forces that may serve to feed this potentially destructive force. Parents should engage in a *cheshbon hanefesh* (mental and spiritual self-examination) regarding why they have difficulty not giving their children everything they want. Some common reasons include trying to keep up with friends, a misguided attempt to be *fair* by giving children what their friends have, or discomfort with our children's tantrums when they are denied what they are asking for. Another increasing contributor to overindulgence occurs in families where both parents work and are often unable to spend enough time with their children. At times, in these families, parents give their children material possessions in an attempt to replace themselves. Another subtle, perhaps unconscious force feeding this tendency is found in parents, who might have grown up with very little, who give too much to their children as a means of vicariously enjoying that which they were themselves unable to enjoy in their own childhood.

Psychologists suggest that the first step in developing an approach that transmits healthy values about money to our children is increased awareness of our own attitudes toward money. Lee Hausner, a psychologist who specializes in this area, suggests that parents should ask themselves the following questions:

- What was the attitude of each of your parents toward money and how did this affect you?

- What did you learn about money from watching other family members and friends?

- What does money mean to you now? What do you see as its greatest value/its greatest danger?

- What attitudes about money would you like to teach your children? What changes would you like to make?[2]

Recommendations:

- Children should be reminded to thank parents for what they may take for granted—for help with homework, for a lift to a friend's house, or even for preparing dinner. Parents should resist any tendency to inadvertently sabotage this lesson by responding with phrases like, "Don't mention it." Instead, children should be praised for expressing gratitude. Acting as a role model by expressing gratitude to others, in front of your children, is another powerful lesson in instilling this core Jewish value.

- Monitor children's exposure to angry discussions about others. Parents often underestimate the degree to which children are tuned in to marital disputes or criticism of friends, family, or educators. If such discussions must take place, make sure that children are not eavesdropping.

- Deal with a child's disrespect calmly and firmly. Parents may have no immediate control over a child's inappropriate statements, but they do have ultimate control over consequences for such disrespect. Logical consequences that directly flow from the child's lack of respect are often the most effective. For example, a parent may respond to a child's *chutzpah* by refusing to do something that he or she normally does for that child, such as providing a lift to a friend's house. Consequences that are of a shorter du-

---

[2] Hausner, Lee (1990), *Children of Paradise: Successful Parenting for Prosperous Families*, Archer, Los Angeles.

ration tend to be more effective than drawn out punishments or those that are not time-limited.

- Children should be actively encouraged to become involved in *Chessed* projects. Many opportunities abound, ranging from organizations like *Tomchei Shabbos,* to working with ill children, or those with special needs. Projects should be suited to children's interest and temperament and should **never** be forced on children.

Parental Interventions Regarding Cheating

If a child is found to be cheating at school, a frank, planned, unemotional discussion is called for. This is a perfect time to share your view about how seriously you value honesty. Arriving at an understanding of the underlying forces that led to your child's cheating is an essential component of preventing future incidents. Try to elicit your child's view as to how he justified the cheating to himself. Creating an atmosphere that allows for such a discussion will entail a combination of finding the balance between parental calmness while conveying how seriously you value honesty. To insure that your child does not become overly defensive, make clear that whatever consequence you will deliver for this serious infraction will be tempered by the child's willingness to honestly discuss how he or she can try to avoid the temptation to cheat in the future.

Examine how competition is handled in the family. How does your child handle competition on the playground, in playing board games with siblings or peers? These venues can provide valuable lessons that can teach healthy competition while avoiding internal pressure to cheat.

Examine your expectations—particularly how you handle situations where your child disappoints you with poor academic performance. You may need to work on yourself by adjusting your expectations regarding your child's ability to achieve. Let your child know that much as you value his or her performing well in school, you place a higher value on honesty in the face of pressure. You can say, "I understand the temptation to cheat, particularly when you feel that you are under a lot of pressure, but I'm disappointed

when you aren't honest. Telling the truth is far more important to me than your grades."

If the underlying issue is your child's difficulty to keep up with unrealistic academic demands, work with your child's teacher and principal to modify the curriculum in a manner that creates more realistic academic goals. Parents are often pleasantly surprised by the willingness of the school to accommodate their academic demands to a child's specific needs.

As in other areas of parenting, logical consequences that make sense to your child work best. If the child was caught cheating, help him or do proper *teshuvah* (here, make reparation) by having him or her make up for the action. If he or she was caught copying a term paper, supervise the writing and resubmitting of an alternative assignment. If your child was caught cheating on a test, try to work as a team with the school in arriving at a logical punishment. It makes sense, however, to work with the teacher in arranging a retest after offering your child support in mastering the work being tested.

Instilling Proper Values Regarding Money

It can be helpful for parents to monitor the content of the conversations that their children are exposed to around the home. How much talking is there about goods and possessions? Is the focus of adult conversation often centered on new construction in the home, the need to buy a better car or computer? If this is the primary focus of parental discussion, then children are more likely to learn to value materialism over more meaningful values.

Help your children learn to distinguish between *wants* and *needs.* When planning to buy them gifts for birthdays or Chanukah, help them write wish lists that require that they prioritize what they want —making clear that they will not get everything that they ask for.

If your child has frequent tantrums when not given what he or she asks for, help him or her (after a calming-down period) to identify the underlying emotion feeding the tantrum. What are the underlying issues? If the child is bored and wants a new toy to combat the boredom, what are other ways of helping tolerate this frustration? If the issue is that friends have this toy, discuss the underlying feelings of social insecurity, etc.

Remember that it is fine to say "No," and fine for your child to be upset. Children learn very valuable, lifelong lessons by being required to deal with the frustration of not getting everything they need or want.

Giving children a weekly allowance can be a helpful tool for teaching a responsible approach toward money. Until approximately age 8, children may have difficulty understanding the concept of savings.

Early elementary school-age children can be taught, however, how to prioritize purchases. In the spirit of helping children distinguish *wants* from *needs* they can be encouraged to choose what they want most from their wish list. From third grade on, most children have a good understanding of the relationship between how much things cost and parents' ability to afford them. As children get older they can be given enough money on an incremental basis to gradually increase their responsibility for their purchases.

Balanced Parenting [New York: Shaar Press, 2014], pp. 57–75.

Excerpted with permission of the authors.

WHY CHINESE MOTHERS ARE SUPERIOR

BY AMY CHUA

A lot of people wonder how Chinese parents raise such stereotypically successful kids. They wonder what these parents do to produce so many math whizzes and music prodigies, what it's like inside the family, and whether they could do it too. Well, I can tell them, because I've done it. Here are some things my daughters, Sophia and Louisa, were never allowed to do:

- attend a sleepover

- have a playdate

- be in a school play

- complain about not being in a school play

- watch TV or play computer games

- choose their own extracurricular activities

- get any grade less than an A

- not be the No. 1 student in every subject except gym and drama

- play any instrument other than the piano or violin

- not play the piano or violin

I'm using the term "Chinese mother" loosely. I know some Korean, Indian, Jamaican, Irish and Ghanaian parents who qualify too. Conversely, I know some mothers of Chinese heritage, almost always born in the West, who are not Chinese mothers, by choice or otherwise. I'm also using the term "Western parents" loosely. Western parents come in all varieties.

All the same, even when Western parents think they're being strict, they usually don't come close to being Chinese mothers. For example, my Western friends who consider themselves strict make their children practice their instruments 30 minutes every day. An hour at most. For a Chinese mother, the first hour is the easy part. It's hours two and three that get tough.

Despite our squeamishness about cultural stereotypes, there are tons of studies out there showing marked and quantifiable differences between Chinese and Westerners when it comes to parenting.

In one study of 50 Western American mothers and 48 Chinese immigrant mothers, almost 70% of the Western mothers said either that "stressing academic success is not good for children" or that "parents need to foster the idea that learning is fun." By contrast, roughly 0% of the Chinese mothers felt the same way. Instead, the vast majority of the Chinese mothers said that they believe their children can be "the best" students, that "academic achievement reflects successful parenting," and that if children did not excel at school then there was "a problem" and parents "were not doing their job." Other studies indicate that compared to Western parents, Chinese parents spend approximately 10 times as long every day drilling academic activities with their children. By contrast, Western kids are more likely to participate in sports teams.

What Chinese parents understand is that nothing is fun until you're good at it. To get good at anything you have to work, and children on their own never want to work, which is why it is crucial to override their preferences. This often requires fortitude on the part of the parents because the child will resist; things are always hardest at the beginning, which is where Western parents tend to give up. But if done properly, the Chinese strategy produces a virtuous circle. Tenacious practice, practice, practice is crucial for excellence; rote repetition is underrated in America. Once a child starts to excel at something—whether it's math, piano, pitching or ballet—he or she gets praise, admiration and satisfaction. This builds confidence and makes the once not-fun activity fun. This in turn makes it easier for the parent to get the child to work even more.

Chinese parents can get away with things that Western parents can't. Once when I was young—maybe more than once—when I was extremely disrespectful to my mother, my father angrily called me "garbage" in our native Hokkien dialect. It worked really well. I felt terrible and deeply ashamed of what I had done. But it didn't damage my self-esteem or anything like that. I knew exactly how highly he thought of me. I didn't actually think I was worthless or feel like a piece of garbage.

As an adult, I once did the same thing to Sophia, calling her garbage in English when she acted extremely disrespectfully toward me. When I mentioned that I had done this at a dinner party, I was immediately ostracized. One guest named Marcy got so upset she broke down in tears and had to leave early. My friend Susan, the host, tried to rehabilitate me with the remaining guests.

The fact is that Chinese parents can do things that would seem unimaginable—even legally actionable—to Westerners. Chinese mothers can say to their daughters, "Hey fatty—lose some weight." By contrast, Western parents have to tiptoe around the issue, talking in terms of "health" and never ever mentioning the f-word, and their kids still end up in therapy for eating disorders and negative self-image. (I also once heard a Western father toast his adult daughter by calling her "beautiful and incredibly competent." She later told me that made her feel like garbage.)

Chinese parents can order their kids to get straight As. Western parents can only ask their kids to try their best. Chinese parents can say, "You're lazy. All your classmates are getting ahead of you." By contrast, Western parents have to struggle with their own conflicted feelings about achievement, and try to persuade themselves that they're not disappointed about how their kids turned out.

I've thought long and hard about how Chinese parents can get away with what they do. I think there are three big differences between the Chinese and Western parental mind-sets.

First, I've noticed that Western parents are extremely anxious about their children's self-esteem. They worry about how their children will feel if they fail at something, and they constantly try to reassure their children about how good they are notwithstanding a mediocre performance on a test or at a recital. In other words, Western parents are concerned about their children's psyches. Chinese parents aren't. They assume strength, not fragility, and as a result they behave very differently.

For example, if a child comes home with an A-minus on a test, a Western parent will most likely praise the child. The Chinese mother will gasp in horror and ask what went wrong. If the child comes home with a B on the test, some Western parents will still praise the child. Other Western parents will sit their child down and express disapproval, but they will be careful not to make their child feel inadequate or insecure, and they will not call their child "stupid," "worthless," or "a disgrace." Privately, the Western parents may worry that their child does not test well or have aptitude in the subject or that there is something wrong with the curriculum and possibly the whole school. If the child's grades do not improve, they may eventually schedule a meeting with the school principal to challenge the way the subject is being taught or to call into question the teacher's credentials.

If a Chinese child gets a B—which would never happen—there would first be a screaming, hair-tearing explosion. The devastated Chinese mother would then get dozens, maybe hundreds of practice tests and work through them with her child for as long as it takes to get the grade up to an A.

Chinese parents demand perfect grades because they believe that their child can get them. If their child doesn't get them, the Chinese parent assumes it's because the child didn't work hard enough. That's why the solution to substandard performance is always to excoriate, punish and shame the child. The Chinese parent believes that their child will be strong enough to take the shaming and to improve from it. (And when Chinese kids do excel, there is plenty of ego-inflating parental praise lavished in the privacy of the home.)

Second, Chinese parents believe that their kids owe them everything. The reason for this is a little unclear, but it's probably a combination of Confucian filial piety and the fact that the parents have sacrificed and done so much for their children. (And it's true that Chinese mothers get in the trenches, putting in long grueling hours personally tutoring, training, interrogating and spying on their kids.) Anyway, the understanding is that Chinese children must spend their lives repaying their parents by obeying them and making them proud.

By contrast, I don't think most Westerners have the same view of children being permanently indebted to their parents. My husband, Jed, actually has the opposite view. "Children don't choose their parents," he once said to me. "They don't even choose to be born. It's parents who foist life on their kids, so it's the parents' responsibility to provide for them. Kids don't owe their parents anything. Their duty will be to their own kids." This strikes me as a terrible deal for the Western parent.

Third, Chinese parents believe that they know what is best for their children and therefore override all of their children's own desires and preferences. That's why Chinese daughters can't have boyfriends in high school and why Chinese kids can't go to sleepaway camp. It's also why no Chinese kid would ever dare say to their mother, "I got a part in the school play! I'm Villager Number Six. I'll have to stay after school for rehearsal every day from 3:00 to 7:00, and I'll also need a ride on weekends." God help any Chinese kid who tried that one.

Don't get me wrong: It's not that Chinese parents don't care about their children. Just the opposite. They would give up anything for their children. It's just an entirely different parenting model.

Here's a story in favor of coercion, Chinese-style. Lulu was about 7, still playing two instruments, and working on a piano piece called "The Little White Donkey" by the French composer Jacques Ibert. The piece is really cute—you can just imagine a little donkey ambling along a country road with its master—but it's also incredibly difficult for young players because the two hands have to keep schizophrenically different rhythms.

Lulu couldn't do it. We worked on it nonstop for a week, drilling each of her hands separately, over and over. But whenever we tried putting the hands together, one always morphed into the other, and everything fell apart. Finally, the day before her lesson,

Lulu announced in exasperation that she was giving up and stomped off.

"Get back to the piano now," I ordered.

"You can't make me."

"Oh yes, I can."

Back at the piano, Lulu made me pay. She punched, thrashed and kicked. She grabbed the music score and tore it to shreds. I taped the score back together and encased it in a plastic shield so that it could never be destroyed again. Then I hauled Lulu's dollhouse to the car and told her I'd donate it to the Salvation Army piece by piece if she didn't have "The Little White Donkey" perfect by the next day. When Lulu said, "I thought you were going to the Salvation Army, why are you still here?" I threatened her with no lunch, no dinner, no Christmas or Hanukkah presents, no birthday parties for two, three, four years. When she still kept playing it wrong, I told her she was purposely working herself into a frenzy because she was secretly afraid she couldn't do it. I told her to stop being lazy, cowardly, self-indulgent and pathetic.

Jed took me aside. He told me to stop insulting Lulu—which I wasn't even doing, I was just motivating her—and that he didn't think threatening Lulu was helpful. Also, he said, maybe Lulu really just couldn't do the technique—perhaps she didn't have the coordination yet—had I considered that possibility?

"You just don't believe in her," I accused.

"That's ridiculous," Jed said scornfully. "Of course I do."

"Sophia could play the piece when she was this age."

"But Lulu and Sophia are different people," Jed pointed out.

"Oh no, not this," I said, rolling my eyes. "Everyone is special in their special own way," I mimicked sarcastically. "Even losers are special in their own special way. Well don't worry, you don't have to lift a finger. I'm willing to put in as long as it takes, and I'm happy to be the one hated. And you can be the one they adore because you make them pancakes and take them to Yankees games."

I rolled up my sleeves and went back to Lulu. I used every weapon and tactic I could think of. We worked right through dinner into the night, and I wouldn't let Lulu get up, not for water, not even to go to the bathroom. The house became a war zone, and I lost my voice yelling, but still there seemed to be only negative progress, and even I began to have doubts.

Then, out of the blue, Lulu did it. Her hands suddenly came together—her right and left hands each doing their own imperturbable thing—just like that.

Lulu realized it the same time I did. I held my breath. She tried it tentatively again. Then she played it more confidently and faster, and still the rhythm held. A moment later, she was beaming.

"Mommy, look—it's easy!" After that, she wanted to play the piece over and over and wouldn't leave the piano. That night, she came to sleep in my bed, and we snuggled and hugged, cracking each other up. When she performed "The Little White Donkey" at a recital a few weeks later, parents came up to me and said, "What a perfect piece for Lulu—it's so spunky and so *her*."

Even Jed gave me credit for that one. Western parents worry a lot about their children's self-esteem. But as a parent, one of the worst things you can do for your child's self-esteem is to let them give up. On the flip side, there's nothing better for building confidence than learning you can do something you thought you couldn't.

There are all these new books out there portraying Asian mothers as scheming, callous, overdriven people indifferent to their kids' true interests. For their part, many Chinese secretly believe that they care more about their children and are willing to sacrifice much more for them than Westerners, who seem perfectly content to let their children turn out badly.

I think it's a misunderstanding on both sides. All decent parents want to do what's best for their children. The Chinese just have a totally different idea of how to do that.

Western parents try to respect their children's individuality, encouraging them to pursue their true passions, supporting their choices, and providing positive reinforcement and a nurturing environment.

By contrast, the Chinese believe that the best way to protect their children is by preparing them for the future, letting them see what they're capable of, and arming them with skills, work habits and inner confidence that no one can ever take away.

Reprinted from the *Wall Street Journal*, January 8, 2011.

Excerpted with permission of the author from her memoir, *Battle Hymn of the Tiger Mother* (Penguin, 2011).

TIGER MOTHER, BURNING BRIGHT

BY JOHN BARNETT

Americans have always been anxious about how their kids are turning out. But at this moment in history —when that traditional source of anxiety has been joined by growing nervousness about the rise of China—any writer who hit upon the idea of connecting the two by arguing, essentially, that Chinese parentage is just better would have been guaranteed to strike a nerve. Just ask Amy Chua, whose recent Wall Street Journal piece, provocatively entitled "Why Chinese Mothers Are Superior," became an overnight internet smash.

Indeed, "strike a nerve" is not really an adequate metaphor to describe the impact of Chua's piece, which generated about one million page hits, 8,800 comments on the original page (at last count), a staggering 100,000-plus comments on Facebook, and countless responses around the web and in print. Besides the Penguin Press book that the original piece was drawn from, a movie deal is said to be in the works, and Chua's book tour is drawing crowds. Most recently, Chua started a website and appeared with her husband at the New York Public Library.

Personally, I felt almost compelled to respond to Chua, not only because I frequently write about Asia and have spent much of my adult life living in various Asian countries, but also because I earn a substantial portion of my income from private tutoring. Being a tutor in Asia for more than a decade has given me a highly unusual opportunity even for longtime

expatriates in this region: namely, the chance to observe the Asian parenting approach "in the field." I have spent thousands of hours in the homes of dozens of different families of Japanese, Korean, Thai, Vietnamese, and other Asian backgrounds. As for the Chinese parenting approach specifically, I have taught Chinese kids from mainland China, Hong Kong, Taiwan, Singapore, the U.S., and elsewhere.

For readers who missed Chua's article—there must be at least four or five—here are the main points. She basically advocates the following:

- extremely restricted autonomy for children, with harsh social restrictions (no playdates, no sleepovers, no boyfriends)

- limited or absent recreation (no TV, no computer games)

- emphasis on industry, not talent, as the key to success, and backing this up with borderline-abusive expectations for the child (like practicing piano for three hours a day)

- deep personal involvement of the parent in schoolwork (including tight control over extracurricular activities)

- a focus on outcomes considered desirable by society—not on expressing a child's individuality or protecting his or her "self-esteem" (hence, verbal abuse is acceptable if it gets results)

I know from personal experience, however, that the Chua approach is not fully accurate as a representation of "Asian parenting," if such a thing even exists. Many of my high school-aged students have had active social lives. Also, Chua's drastic anti-TV and videogame stance appears to be quite rare. Parental involvement with school is usually high, but most parents I've known are prepared to give their children more freedom to, say, pick extracurricular activities than Chua apparently was. And I have rarely witnessed verbal abuse, although this might not mean much, since Asians tend to conceal family discord from outsiders. In addition, of course, there are very considerable cultural differences in family behavior between different Asian groups, and as big as those differences are, the differences between individual families, even within the same national culture, can be greater still.

Still, "Chua-ism," or at least something like it, is very recognizable amongst the families I have dealt with. Compared to typical Americans, Asian parents really are stricter and intervene more deeply in their children's lives. They really do have higher expectations and stress hard work rather than talent. And their focus on educational outcomes (like getting into a top-25 university) verges on obsession. So if we grant that Chua-style parenting exists, the key question becomes, does it have any merit? Can Americans learn anything from Amy Chua, or is this controversy merely the latest in the long series of "yellow peril" panic attacks that have popped up in American culture since Asian immigration began in the 19th century?

The good points of Chua-ism...
Probably the most compelling point Chua makes is her defense of the value of rote repetition. As she says, "[w]hat Chinese parents understand is that nothing is fun until you're good at it. To get good at anything you have to work, and children on their own never want to work, which is why it is crucial to override their preferences." This observation is more than just a truism; it displays real wisdom, and few will doubt that many American children would benefit if their parents understood this principle better.

However, this insight is not uniquely Chinese. Personally, I first encountered it in the words of the great jazz trumpeter Wynton Marsalis: "Everyone wants to be the hero, but no one wants to slay the dragon"—the "dragon" being practice. In fact, practice is the key to mastering any instrument, irrespective of specifics; for evidence, read Keith Richards' autobiography, where he recalls spending endless hours obsessively teaching himself blues riffs. My own experience with piano also confirms Chua's view: my piano-playing career survived a tense confrontation with my mother in elementary school when I really, really wanted to quit. She insisted, I got a lot better, and predictably, playing piano has been one of my great pleasures in adult life. Chua's view on practice is also reminiscent of the "10,000 hour rule" popularized by Malcolm Gladwell in his book *Outliers*, which argued that, contrary to popular perceptions of the primacy of talent, the actual key to success in any endeavor is around 10,000 hours of practice at that endeavor, which produces a level of skill that is effectively unattainable to the vast majority of the population.

Chua makes another good point when she asserts that for youngsters, having "self-esteem" is not enough: they have to produce results. Without question, one of the most inane and socially destructive memes in Western culture over the last quarter century has been the uncritical promotion of self-esteem as an end in itself. The result, as others have noted, is a generation of college graduates who are practically unemployable due to a wildly exaggerated perception of their own abilities coupled with an inability to accept criticism. The self-esteem cult has profoundly damaged the lives of countless people shocked—shocked!—to learn that they are not really that "special" after all, notwithstanding years of assurances from well-meaning teachers, coaches, and parents. And the damage has not been limited to individuals; the cult has also drained away Americans' motivation to excel, at a moment when the competitive pressure on the U.S. internationally has never been greater.

Arguably, as well, our contemporary culture is characterized by an abnormal fascination with honest criticism, precisely because it has become verboten due to the strictures of self-esteem advocates. This phenomenon has probably contributed to the success of TV shows like *The Apprentice* or *American Idol* —for anyone raised within the self-esteem culture, seeing Simon Cowell coldly inform a tone-deaf contestant that "you cannot sing, and you should stop trying" can be breathtaking. The victims of self-esteem pampering can easily lose touch with reality, like the hapless *Idol* contestants. But more than that, through no fault of their own, these victims have been denied the benefit of "mastery experiences" — achieving goals that once seemed impossible via hard work and persistence. As Chua observes, "one of the worst things you can do for your child's self-esteem is to let them give up. On the flip side, there's nothing better for building confidence than learning you can do something you thought you couldn't."

Another wise Chua policy is to curtail the panoply of entertainment options available for children, or at least sharply limit the time they spend entertaining themselves instead of working. In modern-day America, opposing TV or computer games for kids is like being an atheist in colonial Massachusetts—apt to get you burned at the stake. But consider: the TV and computer game (or, if you like, "interactive entertainment") industries are staffed by people whose professional lives are dedicated to one thing—convincing viewers to keep watching, and players to keep playing, at any cost. Anyone who doubts that they have been successful should review the historical trends for per capita TV viewing hours in America, or the recent success of massively multiplayer online role-playing games (MMORPGs), which can be so frighteningly addictive as to replace real life even for adults.

Chua's restrictions on her daughters' social lives probably strike most Americans as not merely excessive, but inhuman. What, no slumber parties? Nevertheless, it may be simply an empirical fact that groups of teens together can be dangerous, both to society and to themselves, and the risk increases with the size of the group. Indeed, there has been recent research suggesting why this is the case: a Temple University study found that awareness that peers are engaged in some activity seems to suppress perceptions of the risk of that activity in the brain of a young person. In all likelihood, there is a straightforward evolutionary explanation for this: in a group of starving young hominids trying to bring down a woolly mammoth, it's probably beneficial for the young Cro-Magnon to stand his ground and hurl that spear, even if doing so risks his own skin. The contemporary manifestation of this trait may be the woeful toll of drunk-driving deaths and unplanned pregnancies among teens. To be sure, in modern America, it is probably impossible to put the teenage-dating genie back in the bottle, but that doesn't mean that Chua is wrong when she suggests that the downside of adolescent romance far outweighs the upside (especially since, statistically, few high school relationships result in lasting marriages).

...and the bad points

Whether it was because of or in spite of her draconian methods, Amy Chua's daughters apparently turned out all right—her older daughter, Sophia, became so proficient at piano that she performed at Carnegie Hall. Sophia even wrote a letter to the *New York Post* defending her mother after the controversy erupted. And Ms. Chua, by her own account, has moderated her approach in recent years. For example, her younger daughter, Lulu, is apparently now allowed to have an iPod and even go to sleepovers.

Nonetheless, parenting is one human endeavor where a one-size-fits-all approach is least likely to succeed. Regarding grades, Chua asserts:

> [I]f a child comes home with an A-minus on a test, a Western parent will most likely praise the child. The Chinese mother will gasp in horror and ask what went wrong... If a Chinese child gets a B—which would never happen—there would first be a screaming, hair-tearing explosion. The devastated Chinese mother would then get dozens, maybe hundreds of practice tests and work through them with her child for as long as it takes to get the grade up to an A.

Well, my work experience allows me to tell you with absolute certainty that this account of "Chinese mothers" could not possibly be true in more than a minority of cases. First of all, even after allowing for grade inflation, it is mathematically impossible for every Chinese pupil to be bringing home As all the time, or even most of the time. Second, in every ethnic group, without exception, there are many kids who simply are not capable of straight-A academic performance—and trying to force them into that mold will only cause enormous pain for both the parents and the child. What about kids with learning disabilities, for example? Responding to Chua's article, many Asian adults left comments describing how their relationships with their parents had been destroyed by impossibly high expectations.

Moreover, intensifying the pressure for high grades can have undesirable consequences, such as increasing the temptation to cheat. Academic dishonesty in its various forms, including cheating and plagiarizing, is now a huge and underpublicized social problem in this country. It is not enough just to reward excellence—we need to create an environment where it is understood that excellence is worthless if earned by breaking the rules. (It hardly needs to be said that the importance of this principle is not limited to academic undertakings.)

Another, even more extreme consequence of focusing children on school to the exclusion of almost everything else can be seen in the notorious "hikikomori" phenomenon of Japan, in which adolescents unable to cope with the extreme demands of the Japanese education system respond by dropping completely out of society and disappearing into their rooms, sometimes for years, emerging only to eat or use the bathroom. This phenomenon has been mostly limited to Japan, probably because the country combines an extremely high level of educational stress with an extremely indulgent family environment. However, peculiarly Japanese though it may be, the "hikikomori" syndrome does suggest that ratcheting up academic pressure on teenagers may be very harmful for a subset of vulnerable individuals.

As for curtailing TV or computer games (especially the latter), whatever the value of this step, it will be much easier to advocate it than to actually do it. Moreover, the idea that losing time to video games is a problem that happens only to Western kids is about as wrong as you can get. In actuality, for Asian youngsters, who tend to be introverted, the seductive power of computer technology has been an even greater problem than it has been in the U.S. —Google "internet addiction Korea" for some truly hair-raising stories of extreme cases (such as the infant who died of starvation while her parents were at an internet cafe feeding their virtual child). Destructively excessive internet use has become a tremendous social problem everywhere in East Asia, and mainland China is no exception. When I relocated to the PRC several years ago, internet cafes could be found on almost every block; the overwhelming majority of users were under 30, and their favorite internet activities were chat, internet dating sites, and games. Looking around my terminal in these cafes, I was typically the sole person doing anything so prosaic as sending an e-mail. For better or for worse, the internet addiction cat is long out of the bag in Asia, and to suggest that Asian families are somehow immune to this problem is just factually incorrect.

Another Chua error is her dogmatic insistence that certain extracurricular activities are "just better" than others. Speaking as someone who has often, and successfully, advised Asian kids on U.S. university admission, I can tell you that privileging certain extracurriculars over others is wrongheaded. In particular, Chua's antipathy for drama reaches such absurd heights that one wonders if there is some unspoken personal reason for it. In my opinion, if an Ivy League admissions officer had to choose between two evenly matched Asian applicants, one with extraordinary achievement in piano and another with extraordinary achievement in acting, I think he or she would take the actor. After all, Asian students who excel in piano are a dime a dozen, but brilliant Asian actors are rare. Every student is a unique individual with a unique set of interests—even in Asia. University admissions committees in the U.S. expect to see this uniqueness and will respond positively to it.

In fact, if anything, Asian students, influenced by powerful social pressure to conform, underperform as university applicants precisely because they fail to differentiate themselves from similar applicants. When it comes to extracurriculars, the most important factor is excellence in that activity, whatever it is. The second-most important factor is depth of commitment—excelling in one or two activities is better than participating shallowly in six or seven just to "pad the resume." And the third-most important factor is to participate in something that is unique or unusual, or shows real leadership capacity.

Finally, there is no question that academic achievement is relatively high in East Asian populations, both within East Asia and in Asian immigrant communities. But tension in inter-generational relationships is also high. And every year, during the national university entrance examinations—an event all-important to a child's future in most Asian nations—there is a wave of suicides.

What are we doing right?

Fundamentally, the United States is an inward-looking culture. We are so focused on our own problems that we tend to underestimate the difficulties other societies face. This tendency is greatly exacerbated by media bias and multiculturalism; the former causes the seriousness of American shortcomings to become greatly exaggerated in the minds of the American public (a "muckraking journalist" has a strong professional incentive to make the "muck" sound filthier than it actually is), and the latter causes the very serious issues faced by other countries, which could put our own woes in much-needed perspective, to be minimized or even ignored. Arguably, a writer like myself, who has spent years abroad, has a special responsibility to correct these imbalances.

So is the U.S. under dire threat from a horde of hyper-competitive Asians created by Amy Chua's superior parenting model? Well, no, and here's why. America's greatest and most underappreciated strength as an international player is its incredible capacity to create and innovate. To a far greater extent than any other country in the world, the U.S. is receptive to new ideas and provides a cultural environment, in-

cluding (crucially) in its education system, that facilitates this. Somewhere in America, the next Thomas Edison or Bill Gates or Mark Zuckerberg is in school. And maybe he (or she) hasn't thought of his greatest idea yet. But when he does think of it, American society is not going to crush him instantaneously for threatening established interests, behaving contrarily to his parents' expectations, or daring to stand out from the crowd.

In most of the world, all three of these things would tend to happen—and East Asia is no exception to this general rule. In fact, even though the extreme importance of creativity, innovation, and entrepreneurship is widely recognized in Asia nowadays, it has still been excruciatingly difficult for these countries to accommodate it—because doing so requires violating cultural habits of unquestioning conformity and deference to "superiors" that have been deeply ingrained for millennia. To some extent, the history of modern Asia is simply a series of attempts to adjust, with varying success, to the never-ending torrent of new technologies and ideas pouring in from the West.

Asia's creativity problem

The cultures of East Asia have many virtues to admire. When the proper economic and political context is in place, they reliably produce orderly, safe, affluent societies with excellent infrastructure, high levels of education, and a diligent, skilled labor force. What they do not produce, however, is a high level of technological or artistic innovation. In fact, East Asia is as creatively impoverished as it is economically wealthy.

I am stepping deeply into politically incorrect territory by saying this, but speaking as the teacher of hundreds of Asian kids, these youngsters consistently display a noticeable deficiency in creative thinking. Brainstorming, for example, is excruciatingly difficult for them. At every educational level, from elementary school to graduate school, generating genuinely original thoughts seems to be virtually an insuperable challenge for these students (which is not to say that it is necessarily easy for other ethnic groups).

"Tiger Mother"-like parenting practices, with their emphasis on absolute obedience to authority, mastering existing knowledge, and mimicking the thoughts of others, almost certainly contribute to this problem. Chua is rightly proud of her daughter's skill on piano, but playing classical piano pieces, admirable though it may be, ultimately consists of duplicating the musical ideas of the composer. There are thousands of classical musicians of East Asian descent, but how many East Asian classical composers are there?

Anti-creative parenting is reinforced by the education systems used in Asia, which focus almost entirely on rote learning, repetition, and memorization. For students accustomed to this environment, coming up with new ideas yourself can actually seem bizarre and unnatural—like running a footrace backwards. In South Korea, I heard a story that illustrates this: if you show a class of Korean students a picture of a dog and ask them to "draw a dog," almost every student will effortlessly produce a perfect copy. But if you instead just ask them to "draw a dog," without the picture, they will flounder helplessly—even if they do eventually come up with something, it will probably be inept, and the stack of results will be filled with copies of the work of the few students in the class who can draw from memory.

I do not hold my students, or even their national cultures per se, ultimately responsible for this situation. In fact, it is likely that two specific features of classical Chinese culture are responsible: namely, the character-based written language, and the institution of the imperial examination system.

China's character-based script, which was also used in modified form by Japan and (until the relatively recent past) Korea and Vietnam, requires prodigious memory skills to achieve even basic literacy. This system unified the country because the same characters were used by all Chinese regardless of local dialects, but it also condemned a substantial fraction of the population to illiteracy.

Those who succeeded in learning the characters, however, could aspire to attempt the imperial examinations. For about 1,300 years, high-ranking offi- cials in China were selected from top performers on these exams, which required applicants to memorize vast amounts of text by classical authors. Success in the examinations—probably the first standardized tests in the history of the world—provided social mobility in China by allowing talented individuals to rise to a high position, regardless of their origin. However, because the tests emphasized rote memo- ry over innovative thinking, and because those who were successful at them often became the wealthy progenitors of large families, the examinations may have unintentionally, in effect, bred the Chinese pop- ulation for rote memory proficiency—a result only amplified by the memory-intensive nature of written Chinese. And because the precursor states of mod- ern-day Korea and Vietnam adopted an essentially similar system, this effect was not limited to China.

To be sure, I am not saying that it is impossible for East Asians to be creative; I am personally aware of a great many counterexamples. I'm saying only that outstanding creativity is rarer, statistically, than it is in the West—especially in the U.S.

Also, it is obvious that the rote-learning-and-mim- icry strategy can be highly successful —if there is an innovative culture available to mimic. In fact, entire countries in East Asia have based their economic strategy on producing Western innovations with su- perior quality and low prices. However, at the same time, Japan's economic woes since the 1990s show that surpassing the West is vastly more difficult than catching up to the West. And the limitations of this strategy suggest that Chua-ism may simply be inap- propriate for American culture: there is every reason to believe that practices which developed in East Asia may work less well here, and even if they did work, is it really a good idea for Americans to change a cul- ture that has given us such a high level of innova- tive prowess?

Finally, there is a political dimension to this discus- sion. Rote learning, with its implication of mindless obedience, simply does not sit well with American culture. This rejection brings a substantial benefit: Americans revolutionize our culture on a regular basis, but we have never had a Cultural Revolution—and that is a good thing.

Chua-ism in China

Interestingly, the Chua phenomenon met with a skeptical or even hostile reception within China itself. Chinese are certainly proud of their students' high performance on examinations, but they are also deeply worried about the country's underperformance at the highest levels of intellectual achievement. For example, Lu Jun, director of an English school in Beijing, told China Daily: "It is exciting to see so many Chinese kids excelling in math tests, but so far China has no Nobel laureates. By contrast, more than 70% [of] the global Nobel laureates are Americans whose population is less than 5% of the world." Lu added, "A key reason is that the teaching methods of Chinese schools and parents are test-oriented, which fails to inspire kids to use their knowledge in real life."

Many Chinese internet users were scornful towards the "Tiger Mother." One person commented, "Is she brainwashed? She violated her child's human rights! They have a right to happy childhood memories." Another observer also found it hard to reconcile Western human rights notions with Chua's strictness: "To some extent, her behavior can be called child abuse... In her book, Chua says that if her child can't finish their homework, they won't be not allowed to sleep... However, science has demonstrated that if people cannot get enough sleep, brain activity will be reduced. As a university professor, how can [Chua] be so lacking in common sense!" And a Shanghainese friend of the author even dismissed the entire notion that Chinese parents provide their kids with a superior environment, attributing the success of Chua's daughters to "great genes... that's all."

Conclusion

It would be a mistake to take Amy Chua too seriously; she is no heavyweight in the child-development field, and in all fairness, she never really claimed to be one. Her book was intended as a personal account, not a parenting manual, and it reflects the softening of her initially hard-line approach over time. The sensationalized coverage of the book, intended to pump up sales, has had the effect of exaggerating her actual claims.

Having said that, although Chua makes some good points, her approach is definitely no panacea, and it may have limited or no applicability in many family situations. There are also many good parenting ideas from Asia that Chua never mentions, such as the importance of providing a clean, well-lit, and quiet place in the home for studying. However, the "Tiger Mother" phenomenon has undoubtedly produced one useful result: it reminded Americans that the world is not standing still. We live in a competitive international environment, and we need to benchmark ourselves against what others are doing and be open to new approaches—even if those ideas come from foreigners, and even if they are in areas as culturally sensitive as parenting.

Reprinted from John Barnett. "Tiger Mother, Burning Bright." *The American Thinker,* May 23, 2011.

the art of parenting

Lesson 3

On Good Authority

The question is one that children have asked their parents since time immemorial: "But why?" Today, as subjectivity seems to have conquered objectivity, as the unchallenged system of rights and wrongs on which our grandparents were reared is subjected to evaluation and rejection, as "Yes, sir!" is replaced by "But why?", this question assumes even greater urgency. Will our children listen to us? Should they?

JLI
JEWISH LEARNING INSTITUTE

Introduction

Text 1

Rabbi Yosef Yitschak Schneersohn, *Sefer Hama'amarim* 5710, p. 244 📖

וועֶן מעֶן הָאט מיך מחַנֵך געֶווָעזֶען זָאגעֶן מוֹדֶה אֲנִי, הָאט מעֶן מיר געֶהייסעֶן צו-
לייגעֶן איין די צוויטעֶ, און איינבּוֹיגעֶן די קָאפּ און אַזוֹי זָאגעֶן מוֹדֶה אֲנִי.

וועֶן איך בּין געֶווָארעֶן אַ בּיסעֶל עֶלטעֶר, אָבּעֶר אַלץ נָאך אין די
קינדעֶר-יָאהרעֶן, הָאבּ איך געֶפּרעֶגט כּבוֹד קדוּשת אאמו"ר
הרה"ק: פַארווָאס וועֶן מעֶן זָאגט מוֹדֶה אֲנִי, דאַרף מעֶן צו-לייגעֶן
איין די אַנדעֶרעֶ, און מאַרכין זיין אֶת הָרֹאש. הָאט עֶר מיר
געֶעֶנטפעֶרט: בֶּאֱמֶת דאַרף מעֶן טָאן ניט פרעֶגעֶנדיק פַארווָאס . . .

הָאט הוֹד כּבוֹד קדוּשת אאמו"ר הרה"ק אַרייִנגעֶרוּפעֶן ר' יוֹסֵף מָרְדְכַי דעֶם
מְשָׁרֵת, אַ איִד אַ בֶּן שמוֹנִים און הָאט אים געֶפּרעֶגט: ווי אַזוֹי זָאגסטו אין
דעֶר פְּרֵי מוֹדֶה אֲנִי. עֶנטפעֶרט ר' יוֹסֵף מָרְדְכַי: איך לייג צו איין האַנד צו די
אַנדעֶרעֶ און בּוֹיג איין דעֶם קָאפּ. פרעֶגט אים ווייטעֶר הוֹד כּבוֹד קדוּשת
אאמו"ר הרה"ק: פַארווָאס טוּסטו אַזוֹי. עֶנטפעֶרט ר' יוֹסֵף מָרְדְכַי: איך ווייס
ניט. וועֶן איך בּין געֶווָען אַ קליין קינד הָאט מעֶן מיך געֶלעֶרעֶנט אַזוֹי.

זעֶהסט. — זָאגט צו מיר הוֹד כּבוֹד קדוּשת אאמו"ר הרה"ק — עֶר טוּט
ווייל זיין טאַטעֶ הָאט אים אַזוֹי געֶלעֶרעֶנט. און אַזוֹי פריעֶר בּיז משֶׁה
רבֵּינוּ און אַברָהָם אָבינוּ, ווָאס אַברָהָם אָבינוּ עָלָיו השָׁלוֹם איז געֶווען
דעֶר עֶרשטעֶר איד. מעֶן דאַרף טָאן ניט פרעֶגעֶנדיק פַארווָאס . . .

אָט דָאס הייסט חינוך אַמיתּי.

When I was taught to recite *Modeh Ani*, I was told to put my hands together, bow my head, and say *Modeh Ani*. When I was a little older, but still a young child, I asked my father [Rabbi Shalom DovBer, the fifth Chabad-Lubavitch rebbe]: "Why when we say *Modeh Ani*, do we put our hands together and bow our head?" He answered me: "We need to do as we are told without asking why." . . .

Rabbi Yosef Yitschak Schneersohn
(Rayats, Frierdiker Rebbe, Previous Rebbe)
1880–1950

Chasidic rebbe, prolific writer, and Jewish activist. Rabbi Yosef Yitschak, the 6th leader of the Chabad movement, actively promoted Jewish religious practice in Soviet Russia and was arrested for these activities. After his release from prison and exile, he settled in Warsaw, Poland, from where he fled Nazi occupation, and arrived in New York in 1940. Settling in Brooklyn, Rabbi Schneersohn worked to revitalize American Jewish life. His son-in law, Rabbi Menachem Mendel Schneerson, succeeded him as the leader of the Chabad movement.

My father called over Reb Yosef Mordechai, his eighty-year-old aide, and asked him: "How do you say *Modeh Ani* in the morning?" He replied, "I put my hands together and bow my head." My father asked him further, "Why do you do it that way?" Reb Yosef Mordechai answered, "I don't know. When I was a small child, that's what I was taught to do."

"See!" my father told me, "He does it because that's what his father taught him. And before him was Moses and Abraham, the first Jew. We need to do without asking why." . . .

This is the embodiment of true education.

QUESTIONS FOR DISCUSSION

1. What are the advantages of this parenting style (if any)?
2. What are the disadvantages of this parenting style (if any)?
3. Can you think of times when you were asked a similar question? How did you respond?

A Shift in Parenting Techniques

Loosening the Reins

QUESTION FOR DISCUSSION

In which way(s) does your parenting style differ from your parents' parenting style?

Text 2

Lori Gottlieb, "How to Land Your Kid in Therapy," *The Atlantic*, June 7, 2011

never said to my son, "Here's your grilled-cheese sandwich." I'd say, "Do you want the grilled cheese or the fish sticks?" On a Saturday, I'd say, "Do you want to go to the park or the beach?" Sometimes, if my preschooler was having a meltdown over the fact that we had to go to the grocery store, instead of swooping him up and wrestling him into the car, I'd give him a choice: "Do you want to go to Trader Joe's or Ralphs?" (Once we got to the market, it was "Do you want the vanilla yogurt or the peach?") . . .

Lori Gottlieb

American journalist and author. Occasional commentator for National Public Radio and a contributor to the *Atlantic Monthly*. Best known as the author of the self-help book, *Marry Him: The Case for Settling for Mr. Good Enough*.

When I was my son's age, I didn't routinely get to choose my menu, or where to go on weekends—and the friends I asked say they didn't, either. There was some negotiation, but not a lot, and we were content with that. We didn't expect so much choice, so it didn't bother us not to have it.

QUESTION FOR DISCUSSION

What is the common thread that underlies the various shifts in parenting style?

Amy McCready, "Because I Said So? Not Anymore,"
Huffington Post, August 10, 2011

Amy McCready

Parenting expert. After being introduced to Adlerian Psychology and Positive Discipline, McCready became a certified Positive Discipline Instructor and founded Positive Parenting Solutions, Inc.

Ever tried any of these on your kids? "Wait until your father gets home." "Don't make me come in there." Or the famous, "You'll do it because I said so." How'd it work? If you're among the millions of parents whose kids don't exactly snap to attention, take heart. While these words may have peppered your own childhood—and worked—there are some very real reasons they don't fly nowadays with your kids, no matter how many veins stick out in your forehead as you utter them. In fact, while demanding compliance may have gotten you and your siblings to listen up, nowadays, it will only push your own kids further away.

You can thank some very positive societal shifts for your kids' refusal to jump into action when you bark orders. Just look around, and you'll see that cooperation, rather than dominance, is the new norm. . . .

This new order is why we see more pushback, power struggles and negotiation than we ever have in past generations. You can blame it on everything from CSPAN to social media, but kids intuitively sense that everything's up for debate in the world around them. This leads them to respond to your best, "You'll do it because I said so!" with, "You're not the boss of me!"

The iPros and iCons

LEARNING EXERCISE 2

The modern-day lessening of parental authority is positive because

_____

_____

_____

_____

The modern-day lessening of parental authority is negative because

_____

_____

_____

_____

Text 4a

Joel Stein, "The New Greatest Generation," *Time*, May 20, 2013

Here's the cold hard data: The incidence of narcissistic personality disorder is nearly three times as high for people in their 20s as for the generation that's now 65 or older, according to the National Institutes of Health; 58% more college students scored higher on a narcissism scale in 2009 than in 1982. Millennials got so many participation trophies growing up that a recent study showed that 40% believe they should be promoted every two years, regardless of performance. They are fame-obsessed: three times as many middle school girls want to grow up to be a personal assistant to a famous person as want to be a Senator, according to a 2007 survey; four times as many would pick the assistant job over CEO of a major corporation. . . .

Millennials consist, depending on whom you ask, of people born from 1980 to 2000. . . . In the U.S., millennials are the children of baby boomers, who are also known as the Me Generation, who then produced the Me Me Me Generation.

Joel Stein

American journalist. His columns appear in the *Los Angeles Times* and *Time* magazine.

Text 4b

Joel Stein, ibid.

What millennials are most famous for besides narcissism is its effect: entitlement. If you want to sell seminars to middle managers, make them about how to deal with young employees who e-mail the CEO directly and beg off projects they find boring.

Text 4c

Joel Stein, ibid.

They're so convinced of their own greatness that the National Study of Youth and Religion found the guiding morality of 60% of millennials in any situation is that they'll just be able to feel what's right.

Text 4d

Tim Elmore, "Employers: Ready or Not, Here Comes Generation iY," *Huffington Post*, June 11, 2013

They appear to be cocky . . . they believe they offer something valuable. Raised by "peer-ants," (parents are like peers), they've always had a say. Seventy-six percent of [Millennials] believe "my boss could learn a lot from me." Sixty-five percent say "I should be mentoring older coworkers when it comes to tech and getting things done." This doesn't mean they don't think they have a lot to learn from a boss. It's a sense that learning is a two-way street, regardless of seniority.

Tim Elmore

Author and president of Growing Leaders, a nonprofit organization that helps develop leadership qualities in young people. Author of more than 25 books including the best-selling, *Habitudes: Images that Form Leadership Habits and Attitudes.*

I Do!

Text 5

Exodus 24:3–7

וַיָּבֹא מֹשֶׁה וַיְסַפֵּר לָעָם אֵת כָּל דִּבְרֵי ה'. . . וַיֹּאמְרוּ,
"כֹּל אֲשֶׁר דִּבֶּר ה' נַעֲשֶׂה וְנִשְׁמָע".

Moses came [from atop Mount Sinai] and told the nation all of God's words. . . . The people responded, "All [the commands] that God spoke we will do and we will understand."

A Tale of Two Authorities

Illegitimate Sovereignty

Text 6a

Numbers 15:16 📖

הַקָּהָל, חֻקָּה אַחַת לָכֶם וְלַגֵּר הַגָּר, חֻקַּת עוֹלָם לְדֹרֹתֵיכֶם כָּכֶם כַּגֵּר יִהְיֶה לִפְנֵי ה'. תּוֹרָה אַחַת וּמִשְׁפָּט אֶחָד יִהְיֶה לָכֶם וְלַגֵּר הַגָּר אִתְּכֶם.

One law applies to the entire assembly, both you and the foreigner. This shall be an eternal rule for your future generations: you and the foreigner are equal before God. There shall be one Torah and one law for you and the foreigner who resides with you.

Text 6b

Paul Johnson, *A History of the Jews* [New York: Harper & Row, 1987], p. 585

Paul Johnson

English journalist, historian, speechwriter, and author. First came to prominence in the 1950s as a journalist writing for, and later editing, the *New Statesman* magazine. He has written over 40 books and contributed to numerous magazines and newspapers. In 2006, Johnson was honored with the Presidential Medal of Freedom by U.S. President George W. Bush.

Certainly, the world without the Jews would have been a radically different place. Humanity might have eventually stumbled upon all the Jewish insights. But we cannot be sure. All the great conceptual discoveries of the human intellect seem obvious and inescapable once they had been revealed, but it requires a special genius to formulate them for the first time. The Jews had this gift. To them we owe the idea of equality before the law, both divine and human; of the sanctity of life and the dignity of human person.

The Authority Advantage

Text 7

Zohar III:108a

כְּהַאי תּוֹרָא דְּיָהֲבִין עֲלֵיהּ עוֹל בְּקַדְמִיתָא, בְּגִין לְאַפְקָא מִנֵּיהּ טַב לְעָלְמָא, וְאִי לֹא קַבִּיל עֲלֵיהּ הַהוּא עוֹל, לֹא עָבִיד מִדִּי, הָכִי נַמִי אִצְטְרִיךְ לֵיהּ לְבַר נַשׁ לְקַבְּלָא עֲלֵיהּ עוֹל בְּקַדְמִיתָא, וּלְבָתַר דְּיִפְלַח בֵּיהּ בְּכָל מַה דְּאִצְטְרִיךְ, וְאִי לֹא קַבִּיל עֲלֵיהּ הַאי בְּקַדְמִיתָא, לֹא יֵיכוּל לְמִפְלַח. הֲדָא הוּא דִּכְתִיב, (תהלים ק ב) עִבְדוּ אֶת ה' בְּיִרְאָה.

We place a yoke upon an ox while it is still young so that it should bring benefit to the world. If, however, the ox does not accept the yoke, it will not be productive. So, too, a human must accept the yoke from the beginning and then he can serve God as is required. If, however, he does not accept the yoke from the beginning, he is unable to serve. This is the meaning of the verse "Serve God with awe" (Psalms 100:2).

Zohar

The seminal work of Kabbalah, Jewish mysticism. The Zohar is a mystical commentary on the Torah, written in Aramaic and Hebrew. According to Arizal, the Zohar contains the teachings of Rabbi Shimon bar Yocha'i who lived in the Land of Israel during the 2nd century. The Zohar has become one of the indispensable texts of traditional Judaism, alongside and nearly equal in stature to the Mishnah and Talmud.

Text 8

The Rebbe, Rabbi Menachem M. Schneerson,
Correspondence, January 21, 1982.

Rabbi Menachem Mendel Schneerson
1902–1994

The towering Jewish leader of the 20th century, known as "the Lubavitcher Rebbe," or simply as "the Rebbe." Born in southern Ukraine, the Rebbe escaped Nazi-occupied Europe, arriving in the U.S. in June 1941. The Rebbe inspired and guided the revival of traditional Judaism after the European devastation, impacting virtually every Jewish community the world over. The Rebbe often emphasized that the performance of just one additional good deed could usher in the era of Mashiach. The Rebbe's scholarly talks and writings have been printed in more than 200 volumes.

As an educator, you know that children need motivation, but that is only one aspect of the problem. The most important aspect, in my opinion, in this day and age, is the lack of *Kabolas Ol* [acceptance of the yoke], not only of *Ol Malchus Shomayim* [the yoke of the sovereignty of Heaven], but also general insubmission to authority, including the authority of parents at home and of teachers in school, and the authority of law and order in the street. There remains only the fear of punishment as a deterrent, but that fear has been reduced to a minimum because there has in recent years been what amounts to a breakdown of law enforcement, for reasons which need not be discussed here.

On the other hand, American children have been brought up on the spirit of independence and freedom, and on the glorification of personal prowess and smartness. It has cultivated a sense of cockiness and self-assurance to the extent that one who is bent on mischief or anti-social activity feels that one can outsmart a cop on the beat, and even a judge on the bench; and, in any event, there is little to fear in the way of punishment.

As with every health problem, physical, mental or spiritual, the cure lies not in treating the symptoms, but in attacking the cause, although the former may sometimes be necessary for relief in acute cases.

Since, as mentioned, the root of the problem is the lack of *Kabolas Ol*, I thought long and hard about finding a way of inducing an American child to get used to the idea of subordination to a higher authority, despite all the influence to the contrary—in the school, in the street, and even at home, where parents—not wishing to be bothered by their children—have all too often abdicated their authority, and left it to others to deal with truancy, juvenile delinquency, etc.

I came to the conclusion that there was no other way than trying to effect a basic change in the nature, through a system of discipline and obedience to rules which she/he can be induced to get accustomed to. Moreover, for this method to be effective, it would be necessary that it should be freely and readily accepted without coercion. . . .

Thus, a "pilot" Tzivos Hashem was instituted. It immediately proved a great success in getting the children to do good things in keeping with the motto *V'Ohavto L'Reacho Komocho* (Thou shalt love thy neighbor as thyself), coupled with love and obedience to the "Commander-in-Chief" of Tzivos Hashem, namely *Hashem Elokei Tzivo'os* (the G-d of Hosts).

Application Time

Text 9

Rabbi Samson Raphael Hirsch, *Yesodot Hachinuch* 2:53–54

מַדּוּעַ כֹּה קָשֶׁה לְהוֹרִים לְהַרְגִּיל אֶת בְּנֵיהֶם לַמִּדָּה הַיְסוֹדִית שֶׁל מִשְׁמַעַת חוֹפְשִׁית בִּלְתִּי כְּפוּיָה? יִתָּכֵן שֶׁאֶת הַסִּבָּה הָאֲמִיתִּית לְתוֹפָעָה זוּ יֵשׁ לִרְאוֹת בְּעוּבְדָה שֶׁהַמִּשְׁמַעַת הִיא אוּלַי הַמִּדָּה הַיְחִידָה שֶׁאֵין הַיְלָדִים מוֹצְאִים אוֹתָהּ אֵצֶל הַהוֹרִים. אָנוּ מוֹפִיעִים לִפְנֵי יְלָדֵינוּ רַק כִּמְפַקְּדִים וּמְצַוִּים, וּמִנַּיִן יִלְמְדוּ אֶת מִדַּת הַמִּשְׁמַעַת?

בְּרַם, אֵצֶל הוֹרִים יְהוּדִיִּים מוֹעִיל בְּהַרְבֵּה אוֹרַח-הַחַיִּים הַיְהוּדִים, שֶׁהוּא כּוּלוֹ רָצוּף מִשְׁמַעַת מִתּוֹךְ שִׂמְחָה וְרָצוֹן חוֹפְשִׁי, וְהַמִּצְוֹת הֵן יְסוֹד-הַיְסוֹדוֹת שֶׁל כָּל הַמִּדּוֹת הַטּוֹבוֹת. בְּעֵינֵי הַיֶּלֶד נִמְשֶׁלֶת הַתּוֹרָה לַהוֹרֵי הוֹרָיו, וְאוֹתָהּ שִׂמְחָה-שֶׁל-מִצְוָה שֶׁבָּהּ הַהוֹרִים סָרִים לְמִשְׁמַעַת הַתּוֹרָה וּמְדַקְדְּקִים בְּכָל אִיסּוּרֶיהָ וְהֶיתֵּרֶיהָ בְּחַיֵּי יוֹם-יוֹם, מְהַוָּוה דֻגְמָא מְאַלֶּפֶת וּמַלְהִיבָה לְהַרְגִּילָם בְּמִדַּת הַמִּשְׁמַעַת וּבְכָל שְׁאָר הַמִּדּוֹת הַטּוֹבוֹת.

Why is it so difficult for parents to instill within their children the foundational value of accepting authority of their own volition? Perhaps the true reason is that acceptance of authority may be the only value that children don't see exemplified by their parents, for we tend to relate to our children as commanders and instructors. From whence then shall they learn the importance of subordination?

Jewish parents, however, have the advantage of leading a Jewish way of life, which is infused and suffused with subservience. We freely choose to submit to G-d's commandments and accept them as the foundation of our value system; doing so brings us great joy. In the eyes of a child, the Torah constitutes the parents of his/her parents. The joy that the parents take in subordinating themselves to Torah and its instructions is a wonderful model for the child to emulate.

Rabbi Samson Raphael Hirsch
1808–1888

Born in Hamburg, Germany; rabbi and educator; intellectual founder of the *Torah Im Derech Eretz* school of Orthodox Judaism, which advocates combining Torah with secular education. Beginning in 1830, Hirsch served as chief rabbi in several prominent German cities. During this period he wrote his *Nineteen Letters on Judaism*, under the pseudonym of Ben Uziel. His work helped preserve traditional Judaism during the era of the German Enlightenment. He is buried in Frankfurt am Main.

Text 10

Rabbi Samson Raphael Hirsch, *Yesodot Hachinuch* 2:54 📖

מְלַמֶּדֶת אוֹתָנוּ תוֹרַת-הַחִנּוּךְ לְהוֹפִיעַ בִּפְנֵי הַיְלָדִים כְּאוֹסְרִים וּמַתִּירִים רַק
מִתּוֹךְ מַשְׁמַעַת. הָאוֹפֶן בּוֹ אָנוּ אוֹסְרִים עַל הַיֶּלֶד אוֹ מַתִּירִים לוֹ, וְהַשִּׂמְחָה
בָּהּ אָנוּ מַעֲנִיקִים לוֹ אֶת הַחֵירוּת לַעֲשׂוֹת כִּרְצוֹנוֹ, מוֹכִיחִים בַּעֲלִיל כִּי הָאִסּוּר
אוֹ הַהֶיתֵּר אֵינָם נוֹבְעִים מִתּוֹךְ מַצָּב רוּחַ אַרְעַי מִתּוֹךְ שְׁאִיפָה לִשְׁלוֹט אוֹ
מִתּוֹךְ עַקְשָׁנוּת גְּרֵידָא, אֶלָּא מִתּוֹךְ שִׁיקוּל-דַּעַת בְּכוֹבֶד-רֹאשׁ, וְכִי אֵין אָנוּ
אוֹסְרִים אוֹ מַתִּירִים אֶלָּא רַק מַה שֶׁאָנוּ חַיָּבִים לֶאֱסוֹר אוֹ לְהַתִּיר.

Instructions that we issue to our children must not be a product of whim, but should noticeably flow from our own sense of duty and understanding of right and wrong. When we are thoughtful in the manner in which we allow or disallow a child to do something, and when we are visibly joyful when we give the child the autonomy to do as he or she wishes [when appropriate], we demonstrate that whatever we permit or prohibit is not a product of a transient mood, the result of our desire to control the child, or due to our stubbornness. Rather, the child sees that our instruction is a result of careful and objective consideration and thought.

EXERCISES FOR THE WEEK

a) **Write down a recent example of an occasion on which you exerted unhealthy authority over your child(ren).**

In the coming week, if you have the urge to react in an authoritative manner, first ask yourself whether it will benefit your child in the long run.

b) **Write down a recent example of an occasion on which you exerted healthy authority over your child(ren), in a way that taught them to act responsibly**

In the coming week, praise something your child does (or has done in the past) that demonstrates his or her sense of responsibility to another person or to God.

Key Points

1. The modern-day weakening of parental authority results in societal advantages (e.g., greater sensitivity to the needs of children and the discarding of many institutionalized injustices) and disadvantages (e.g., moral subjectivity and greater frequency of narcissistic tendencies).

2. There are two types of authority, one positive and one negative, and both are on the wane. Parents need to completely eliminate the negative authority from their parenting arsenal, while embracing and reinforcing the positive type.

3. Illegitimate authority is power that is exerted for the benefit of a powerful party. The Torah exhorts the powerful—including parents—never to take utilize their natural authority to oppress those with less power.

4. The duties and responsibilities that we all have toward God and society constitute the legitimate authority in our lives. Judaism places a premium on the importance of this authority, making our duties and responsibilities the center of our lives.

5. It is important for children to learn from a young age to respect this healthy authority and to have a responsibility-first attitude.

6. We enhance our children's sense of and appreciation for responsibility/duty/authority by role modeling such behavior and also by not always explaining the reasons behind rules, instead emphasizing the importance of following rules simply because we must.

7. We minimize the amount of unhealthy authority we exert over our children by taking our egos out of the equation and not making an issue of ourselves and our authority.

Appendix A

Text 1

The Rebbe, Rabbi Menachem M. Schneerson, *Likutei Sichot* 19:91–92

דֶער רַבִּי דֶער שְׁווֶער הָאֶט דֶערצֵיילְט, אַז ווֶען דִי קִינְדֶער – דִי קִינְדֶער
פוּן רַבִּי'ן – זַיינֶען גֶעווֶען קְלֵיין, הָאֶט מֶען פַאר זֵיי גֶענוּמֶען אַ מְלַמֵד. דֶער
מְלַמֵד הָאֶט גֶעהאַלְטֶן אַז קִינְדֶער דאַרְף מֶען נִיט דֶערצֵיילְן עִנְיָנִים בְּיַהֲדוּת
פוּן הַבְהָלָה – מוֹפְתִים ווָאֶס זַיינֶען נִיט עַל פִּי שֵׂכֶל, עִנְיָנֵי פְּלָאִים ווָאֶס לֵייגְן
זִיך נִיט אַין אַין שֵׂכֶל. דאַס אִיז פאַר עֶרוואַקְסֶענֶע ווָאֶס בּאַנֶעמֶען כְּדְבָּעֵי דִי
עִנְיָנִים שֶׁעַל פִּי שֵׂכֶל, דאַן קֶענֶען זֵיי צוּנֶעמֶען עִנְיָנִים פוּן מוֹפְתִים. אָבֶּער
בֵּיי קִינְדֶער אִיז דאָס נאָר מַבְהִיל אֶת הָרַעְיוֹן, מִיט זֵיי – הָאֶט גֶעהאַלְטֶן
דֶער מְלַמֵד – דאַרְף מֶען רֵיידְן נאָר עִנְיָנֵי יַהֲדוּת שֶׁעַל פִּי שֵׂכֶל.

ווֶען דֶער רַבִּי (מוֹהריי"ב) נ"ע הָאֶט זִיך דֶערוואוּסְט ווֶעגְן דֶעם
מְלַמֵד'ס שִׁיטָה, הָאֶט מֶען אִים בּאַלְד אָפְּגֶעזאָגְט.

מֶען דאַרְף אָנְהוֹיבְּן דַוְקָא מִיט אֱמוּנָה וְקַבָּלַת עוֹל אוּן נִיט מִיט
שֵׂכֶל; אוֹיך דִי עִנְיָנִים הַמוּבָנִים בְּשֵׂכֶל דאַרְף מֶען טאָן מִיט קַבָּלַת
עוֹל. אוּן אַזוֹי אִיז אוֹיך אִין עִנְיַן הַחִינוּך: מֶען דאַרְף דֶערצֵיילְן
קִינְדֶער עִנְיָנִים פוּן מוֹפְתִים, ווָאֶס זַיינֶען הֶעכֶער פוּן שֵׂכֶל,

דאָס פְלאַנְצְט אַיין אִין זֵיי אֱמוּנָה.

My father-in-law, the Rebbe [Rabbi Yosef Yitschak Schneersohn of Lubavitch] related that when his daughters were yet young, a tutor was retained to instruct them in Judaic studies. This tutor was of the opinion that young children should not be taught the supernatural aspects of Judaism: miracles that defy logic or other inexplicable ideas. Such matters, this tutor felt, are best left for adults who have developed minds and philosophies. Such people have the necessary intellectual sophistication to process the concept of miracles. Such stories, however, can only serve to unnecessarily excite the imagination of children.

When Rabbi Shalom DovBer of Lubavitch [the girls' grandfather] became aware of the tutor's educational theory, he arranged for his immediate termination.

Our starting point must be faith and *kabalat ol* [acceptance of the yoke], not intellect. Even matters that are logical must be embraced with *kabalat ol*. The same is true of education. We must educate children about the miraculous, matters that transcend the intellect. This instills faith in them.

ADDITIONAL READINGS

TANYA IN PLAIN ENGLISH
CHAPTER 41
BY RABBI TZVI FREEMAN

Nevertheless, you must always remember
where all divine service begins,

and its backbone,

and its root.

And that is the following:

That although a sense of awe of G-d
inspires you to stay away from evil,

and a sense of love of G-d inspires you to do good,

nevertheless, it is not enough to
awaken love alone to do good.

Even to do good, you must awaken at
least the innate sense of awe hidden
within every Jewish heart,

that sense that was explained earlier

that does not allow you to rebel
against the King of kings,

against He Who transcends all, may He be blessed.

You must bring out this sense of
awe openly in your heart

or at least in your mind,

meaning that you must contemplate—

at the very least, contemplate just in thought—

the greatness of the Infinite, may He be blessed,

and His dominion,

for He reigns over all worlds,

higher worlds and lower worlds.

And He fills every world from within

and encompasses all worlds from beyond.

As is written,

"Do I not fill the heavens and the earth?"

And He puts aside this whole idea of
what is higher and what is lower

and instead singles out His people
Israel as His domain

—in general, but in particular,

He singles out you,

for every person must say, "The world
was created for my sake."

And you, you too accept upon yourself
the yoke of His dominion,

so that He becomes king over you.

and so that you will serve Him,

and do His will,

in all the ways that servants do their master's will.

Now conceive of this:

The One who brings all into existence

is standing over you, relying on you,

and all the earth is full of His glory,

and He is staring at you,

determining the state of your
inner self and your heart,

to know whether you are serving Him properly.

If so, obviously you have to serve
Him with awe and fear,

just as someone who is standing before the king.

Reprinted with permission of the author and Chabad.org.

THE TASTE OF WATER

BY RABBI YANKI TAUBER

Draw water with joy from the wellsprings of salvation

Isaiah 12:3

The Pouring of the Water was performed on all seven days [of Sukkot] . . .

The one who was doing the pouring was told, "Raise your hands" (so that all could see him pouring the water on the altar). This was because there was once a Sadducee who spilled the water on his feet, and the entire people pelted him with their etrogim...

Talmud, Sukkah 42b and 48b

When the Holy Temple stood in Jerusalem, the "Pouring of the Water" *(nisuch hamayim)* was an important feature of the festival of Sukkot.

Throughout the year, the daily offerings in the Temple were accompanied by the pouring of wine on the altar. On Sukkot, water was poured in addition to the wine. The drawing of water for this purpose was preceded by all-night celebrations in the Temple courtyard, with music-playing Levites, torch-juggling sages and huge oil-burning lamps that illuminated the entire city. The singing and dancing went on until daybreak, when a procession would make its way to the Shiloach spring which flowed in a valley below the Temple.

A golden pitcher, holding three lugim, *was filled from the Shiloach spring. When they arrived at the Water Gate, the* shofar *was sounded . . . [The priest] ascended the ramp [of the altar] and turned to his left . . . where there were two bowls of silver . . . with small holes [in their bottom], one wider and the other narrower so that both should empty at the same time—the western one was for the water and the eastern one for wine. . .*

"For all the days of the water-drawing," recalled Rabbi Joshua ben Chananiah, "our eyes saw no sleep," for the nights of Sukkot were devoted to the singing, dancing and merrymaking in preparation to "draw water with joy." And the Talmud declares: "One who did not see the joy of the water-drawing celebrations, has not seen joy in his life."

The Sadducees

There was, however, a segment of the Jewish community that was not party to the joy of the water-drawing celebrations.

The Sadducees were a breakaway Jewish sect who denied the oral tradition received by Moses at Sinai and handed down through the generations, arguing that they had the right to interpret the Torah according to their own understanding. Unlike the pouring of the wine, which is explicitly commanded by the Torah, the pouring of the water on Sukkot is derived by interpretation. In the verses (Numbers 29:19, 29 and 33) where the Torah speaks of the libations to accompany the Sukkot offerings, there are three extra letters; according to the Sinaitic tradition, these letters are combined to form the word *mayim* (water). The Sadducees, who rejected the "Oral Torah," maintained that only wine was to be poured on the altar on Sukkot, as on every day of the year.

During the Second Temple era, there were times when the Sadducees amassed political power, and even gained the high priesthood—the highest spiritual office in Israel. Thus it came to pass that one Sukkot, the honor of pouring the water on the altar was given to a Sadducee priest; but instead of pouring the water into its prescribed bowl on the southwest corner of the altar, this priest spilled it on his feet to demonstrate his opposition to the practice. The assembled crowd expressed its outrage by pelting him with the *etrogim* which, this being Sukkot, they held in their hands.

Water and Wine

There are two basic components to man's endeavor to serve his Creator.

First, there is what the Talmud calls *kabbalat ol malchut shamayim*, "the acceptance of the yoke of the sovereignty of Heaven." *Kabbalat ol* is the basis and foundation of Torah: without a recognition of G-d as our Master and a commitment to obey His will, the very concept of a mitzvah (divine commandment) has no meaning.

But G-d gave us more than a body and a nervous system, which is all we would have required if our purpose in life were only the carrying out of commands with robotic obedience. He created us with a searching mind and a feeling heart because He desired that these, too, should form an integral part of our relationship with Him.

Thus the Torah states: "See, I have taught you statutes and laws . . . for this is your wisdom and understanding before the nations"; "You shall know today, and take into your heart, that the L-rd is G-d"; "Know the G-d of your fathers and serve Him with a whole heart and desirous soul"; "You shall love G-d . . . with all your heart"; "Serve G-d with joy." G-d wants us to know, understand, appreciate, love, desire and enjoy our mission in life.

In the language of Kabbalah and Chassidism, these two elements in our service of G-d are referred to as "water" and "wine." Water—tasteless, scentless and colorless, yet a most basic requisite of life—is the intellectually and emotionally vacuous, yet fundamentally crucial, "acceptance of the yoke of Heaven." Wine—pleasing to the eye, nose and palate, intoxicating to the brain and exhilarating to the heart—is the sensually gratifying aspect of our divine service: our understanding of the inner significance of the mitzvot, and the fulfillment and joy we experience in our relationship with G-d.

In light of this, "the joy of the water-drawing" seems a contradiction in terms. If water represents the "flavorless," emotionally devoid aspect of our service of G-d, why did the pouring of water upon the altar on Sukkot yield a joy not only greater than that produced by the pouring of wine, but a joy such as was not equaled by any other joy in the world?

The Full Moon of Tishrei

A clue to unraveling the paradox of the "tasty water" of Sukkot might be found in what *halachah* (Torah law) has to say about the taste or non-taste of water.

The law is that "it is forbidden to derive pleasure from this world without a *berachah*"—a blessing of praise and thanks to G-d. Thus, even the smallest amount of food or drink requires a *berachah*, since, even if the amount consumed is of little nutritional value, the person derives pleasure from its taste. Water, however, has no taste, so it does not require a *berachah* unless "one drinks water out of thirst," in which case, explains the Talmud, a person derives pleasure from this otherwise tasteless liquid.

To a thirsty man, a cup of water is tastier than the most delectable wine. In the spiritual sense, this means that when a soul experiences a "thirst" for G-d—when it recognizes how vital its connection to G-d is for its very existence—the prosaic "water" of commitment is a feast for its senses. To the soul who thirsts for G-d, a self-negating act of *kabbalat ol* is more exhilarating than the most profound page of Talmud, the most sublime Kabbalistic secret, the most ecstatic flight of prayer or the most intense spiritual experience. To such a soul, the "water" it draws from its deepest self to pour onto its altar of service to G-d is a greater source of joy than the flesh and wine offered upon its altar or the incense wafting through its Temple.

And Sukkot is the time when we are most open to experiencing pleasure and joy in the ordinarily prosaic act of "accepting the yoke of the sovereignty of Heaven."

Rosh Hashanah, which occurs fifteen days before Sukkot, on the first of Tishrei, is our fountainhead of *kabbalat ol* for the entire year: this is the day on which we crown G-d as our King, and reiterate our acceptance of His sovereignty. But on Rosh Hashanah, the joy of the thirsting soul in its elemental "water" is subdued by the awe that pervades the occasion, as the entirety of creation trembles in anticipation of the annual renewal of the divine kingship. Sukkot is the celebration of this joy, the revelation of what was implicit fifteen days earlier on Rosh Hashanah.

The connection between Rosh Hashanah and Sukkot derives from their respective positions in the month of Tishrei. The Jewish calendar is a lunar calendar, in which each month begins on the night of the new moon, progresses as the moon grows in the night sky, and reaches its apex on the fifteenth of the month, the night of the full moon. This is why so many of the festivals and special days of the Jewish year fall on the fifteenth of the month, this being the day on which the particular month's special quality is most expressed and manifest. In the month of Tishrei, Rosh Hashanah coincides with the birth of the new moon on the first of the month, while Sukkot coincides with the full moon on the fifteenth. Thus, Sukkot is the revelation and manifestation of what was hidden and concealed on Rosh Hashanah.

(Thus does Chassidic teaching interpret the verse, "Blow the *shofar* on the new moon, in concealment to the day of our festival." "Blow the *shofar*," proclaiming our acceptance of the sovereignty of Heaven, "on the new moon," Rosh Hashanah; this, however, remains "in concealment to [i.e., until] the day of our festival," Sukkot, when it erupts in a seven-day feast of joy.)

Throughout the year, only wine was poured on the altar, for ordinarily, only the "savory" and "aromatic" elements of our service of G-d are a source of joy to us. But on Sukkot, when the full import of our *kabbalat ol* is revealed to us, the joy we experience in the "water" of life is the greatest joy in the world, surpassing even the joy of its "wine."

Anatomical Statement
The Sadducees, however, opposed the Pouring of the Water on Sukkot.

The Sadducees refused to accept the divinely ordained interpretation of Torah transmitted to Moses at Sinai and handed down through the generations.

While recognizing the divine origin of Torah, they regarded it as a series of laws open to personal interpretation—an interpretation dictated solely by the interpreter's understanding and feelings.

In other words, for the Sadducee, there is no true submission to the divine authority. To the Jew who accepts both the Written and Oral Torahs, the basis and end of everything he does is to serve the divine will. The "wine" of his divine service—the intellectual and emotional fulfillment that he experiences in the process—is also part and parcel of this end: this, too, is something that G-d desires from him. The Sadducee, on the other hand, sees the "wine" as the end and objective of his observance of the mitzvot: everything he does is subject to his personal understanding and appreciation.

The Sadducee might accept the need for "water" in one's life, but only as an accessory to the wine. He might acknowledge the need for unquestioning obedience to Torah on the part of the masses, for not every man is capable of interpreting these laws himself. He might acknowledge the need for such obedience on the part of even the wisest of men, for no man can expect to understand everything. But the Sadducee will always see such "mindless" and "unfeeling" obedience as a necessity rather than the ideal—the ideal being a fulfillment of Torah based on the observer's understanding and appreciation.

So for the Sadducee, there is no joy in submission to the divine will, no taste to the water of commitment. The Sadducee does not *thirst* for this water; if he obeys G-d's laws, it is only as a means to an end—to enable him to savor their intellectual flavor and emotional aroma.

This is why the Sadducee priest poured the water on his *feet*. He was not condemning the phenomenon of "water" in serving G-d; he was regulating it to the feet—to the "foot soldiers" of the nation, or to the lower extremities of the human form. Water might be necessary in certain individuals and in certain circumstances, but it is hardly the fluid to grace the altar in the year's most joyous celebration of man's relationship with G-d.

A Hail of Fruit

The people responded by pelting him with their *etrogim*.

The Midrash tells us that the "Four Kinds" taken on Sukkot—the *etrog* (citron), *lulav* (palm frond), *hadas* (myrtle branch) and *aravah* (willow branch)—represent four types of individuals. The *etrog*, which has both a taste and a fragrant smell, represents the perfect individual who is both knowledgeable in Torah and proficient in the observance of mitzvot. The *lulav* is the branch of the date palm, whose fruit has a taste but no smell, representing those accomplished in Torah though less so in regard to the mitzvot. The *hadas*—tasteless but aromatic—represents the type who, though lacking in Torah knowledge, has many mitzvot to his credit. Finally, the tasteless, scentless *aravah* represents the individual who lacks both Torah and mitzvot.

On a deeper level, the "Four Kinds" represent four personas within every individual, each with its own domain in his psyche and its appropriate place in his life. In this sense, "Torah" is the intellectual apprecia-tion of the divine wisdom, and "mitzvot" are the love and awe of G-d experienced in the observance of the commandments. Thus, the *lulav* is the "intellectual" in man who does not allow feeling to cloud the purity of knowledge and comprehension; the *hadas* is the emotional self, who sets experience as the highest ideal, even at the expense of the intellect; the *etrog* is the force that strives for a synthesis of mind and heart; and the *aravah* is the capacity for acceptance and commitment, for setting aside intellect and feeling to commit oneself absolutely to a higher ideal.

When the Sadducee priest spilled the water on his feet, the "entire people pelted him with their *etrogim*." We reject what you represent, the people were saying, not only with the self-negating *aravah* in us, not only with our intellectual or emotional personas, but also with the synthesis of wisdom and feeling that defines what is highest and most perfect in man. For also— and especially—the *etrog* within us recognizes the water of life as our ultimate source of joy.

Reprinted from Chabad.org with permission of the Meaningful Life Center.

RULES WITHOUT RELATIONSHIP LEAD TO REBELLION

BY MARK L. BRENNER, MFT, PhD

If all we do as parents is impart too many rules, re-main rigid, and tell our children what they can't do, rebellion isn't a matter of if, it's just a matter of when. You never win cooperation on the strength of your arguments; you win on the strength of your relation-ship, which is why rules without relationship lead to rebellion. At the same time, being overly permissive feeds feelings of entitlement and lack of self-control. Obviously all parents agree that children need limits. What they don't agree on are the methods and the timing for setting them: iPad time is over, no more snacks, have the car back by 10 p.m., bedtime is 8:30, dinner in five minutes. Most parents live with their children from moment to moment, exacting obe-dience or excusing disobedience on impulse rather than on principle. Unenforced consequences cause increased anxiety in a child, as a result of not know-ing when or where the hammer of discipline will fall. The child will come to think, "I know I broke the lim-it," and become anxious when the consequence will arrive. At the same time, a parent who is not skilled in enforcing limits also gives away his or her author-ity to the child. The child thinks, "I'm smarter and tougher than you." It's confirmation that he has de-feated an adult. Although he celebrates his victory, he is also fearful of his new power. Who will keep me safe? Who will protect me?

When you enforce limits consistently, you teach about the laws of nature, the laws of man and, of course, the laws above us all. When you exercise consequences consistently, children acquire the life skill of self-control. Self-control also leads to self-respect. The operative word is consistency. Some parents beg, some threaten, some hit, some yell, and some finally give in. Setting limits without enforcement is not discipline, it is confusion. That's why parents must think twice before setting a limit or rule. They must ask themselves, "Is this limit necessary? Does it fit the situation? And most importantly, can I enforce it?" There is no sense in telling your teenager or small child, "The next time you do that again we're leaving," if in fact you are unable to leave! The real secret of enforcing a consequence is not severity, but predictability and a calm style. It makes no difference if your child is seven or 17. When you do set a limit, your tone must sound relaxed and optimistic, as though your child will abide no matter how unlikely. "Harold, I know I can count on you to let your sister use your iPad."

One often-missed opportunity when a child does comply with maintaining the limit is to immediately express authentic appreciation. "Sarah, I really appreciate the way you did not fight back when I asked you to log off the Internet." Say it relaxed and low-key. "Thank you, Brian, for turning off your laptop when you said you would!" Talking this way brings about high levels of cooperation. It is the same principle when they complete a consequence successfully. "Adam, you could have fought me when I asked you to go to your room, but you didn't. You waited there and controlled yourself. I really appreciated that. Thank you. I know you felt good about yourself, too!"

Be Specific When You Set Limits
Other ways to make limit setting more effective is to be specific rather than general in what you will allow or not allow. For example, if a parent says, "David, you can only stay on the Internet a little while longer," David will see this as an invitation to test the limit. Does "little" mean 10 minutes or 30 minutes? Better to say, "David, you can use the Internet for three more minutes." Although he will probably still push the limit, David will not be confused about what the

limit was when you enforce the consequence. You will become unpopular, but not unfair. Children and teenagers respond better to limit-setting when parents give concrete information rather than abstract information. Eight-year-old Nathan will respond better to, "It's time to leave in five minutes," than, "Soon it will be time to leave." With older children, when it is time to enforce a consequence, often it is best to make the consequences harsher so your child comes to believe you mean business. Of course you must remain calm and elegant as you enforce the consequence. For example, a teenager who does not bring the car back on time without calling first should be met with a quiet consequence of: "Asher, I know you know you're a half-hour late. No car for one week. The time will pass quickly and you'll be back in the driver's seat again." An 11-year-old who throws a tantrum in a store does not get to go to her favorite place for two weeks.

Avoid the Word Punishment
I want to underscore the psychological importance of not using the word "punishment" when we refer to a consequence. As a practical matter, obviously a consequence is punishment. However, the word serves as trigger. Swapping out those words will help shift the focus away from the parent as the enforcer back to the child or teenager who blew past the limit. It's subtle but it's true. There is a world of difference when a parent says, "Your consequence is staying home for the afternoon," versus, "Your punishment is staying home all afternoon." That simple change in language allows the child to focus much more on what they did to cause that outcome. Your child will still be upset about the consequence, but you'll become less of a target for retaliation.

Nagging and Whining
It is worth repeating from *Relationship Exercise 1* that you should not set a time limit on how long you allow your child to whine or nag. In other words, there are no consequences just for whining. Naturally, it's disturbing to listen to non-stop whining and carrying-on. It's easy to react angrily and quickly. "Justin, act like a big boy. Quit crying already!" "I'm going to ignore you if you keep nagging me!" It's also easy to see how this can become an ideal window to

model empathy as your child learns how to develop self-control. Yes, it will take many more months for your child to acquire self-control, but that's nothing compared to a new realization, Wow, I can control myself. Each child has a different tolerance during this exercise.

The key is not to appear angry, detached or uncaring during these episodes. Your child will continue to test you, to see if you will break your calm ways. "Justin, I know you don't like me now for not giving you what you want. It hurts me too when see how upset you are, but I respect you too much to give in to you. I know you will control yourself. You can stay upset for as long as you like and I will understand. I know you will control yourself."

Obviously if you're in public, it is best to leave and find a private place to allow your child to continue to carry on. If you can prove to your child you will not give in and at the same time not detach, you will have passed a crucial milestone. Allowing a child to cry, whine, or complain for as long as they like without losing your cool and respect will, over time, create that tipping point for change. By reacting in these counter-intuitive ways, you are reinforcing emotional trust. Again, the secret is to ignore the obnoxious behaviors without ignoring the child! "Justin, you can take as long as you want to remain upset. I know this is not easy for you to accept. I also know you understand why I am not going along with what you want." You must maintain a high level of respect and empathy during these stress points. Try not to become embarrassed by other adult reactions.

Change the Behavior, Not the Child!
There is a huge difference between accepting a child's feelings and accepting his behavior. Bad feelings are always tolerated, bad behavior is not. Allowing a child to express genuine negative feelings in the moment to any family member must always be accepted. A teenager or middle school child who may say, "I wish I had a different father" during a moment of intense conflict must be met with a heartfelt reaction, "I can understand now why you feel that way. There's no question you wish I wasn't your father right now." Validating those feelings reduces tension.

A critical element when enforcing consequences is to remain respectful (*Relationship Exercise 2*). Parents get so caught up in making sure they enforce the consequence, they ignore their style of communication and, as a result, diminish the child's self-worth. I cannot over-emphasize the importance of remaining elegant and respectful as you enforce a consequence. **In order to enforce limits effectively, we need to do two things: be consistent and be respectful.** When your child inevitably does step over the limit, move right in with the consequence. No warning, no negotiations, no reiteration of the rule. Just your calm manner. "Deana, now you only get one scoop of ice cream instead of two." Your children will come to believe you mean what you say and you say what you mean, all without sounding mean. Do not threaten with statements like, "If you do that again I'm going to add another hour of punishment" or, "I'm not kidding this time."

Never match your child's intensity, especially if your child is already high strung and wound tight. Give no emotional energy to unwanted behavior. If your child amps up, you amp down! Do not energize negativity with extra words. "Ben, when you scream at your sister, it drains my energy and generosity. Because of this, I'm no longer willing to drive you to get those sneakers we talked about. I know you understand. I also know you can control yourself completely." This may sound like too much of a formal way to speak, but it is not. "Ben, I am going to another room now. When you are ready to acknowledge what happened, you will find me there." Then, walk out of the room calmly, separating yourself from his tantrum. Refuse to get drawn into matching your child's negative energy with smirks, sarcasm, loudness or other disrespectful behaviors. Remember, the goal is to change behavior, not the child. Another way to understand this approach is, *tough love is not tough parenting!*

Stop Saying the Word "No"
I wrote an entire book on this word (*When No Gets You Nowhere!*, Rocklin, CA: Prima Publishers). It's easy to say "No," especially when we're running late. The word "No" rarely works anyway. Children hear it over 200 times a day from teachers, parents, grandparents, almost everyone. The word automatically

shuts down the thinking process and encourages conflict. Instead, give the facts about why you won't or can't do something. "Danny, I wish I could take you. Unfortunately I must leave now for my office for a business appointment." Keep the reason simple. No more than 5 seconds. Stay elegant and respectful as you repeat with heartfelt regret why you are unable to do what your child wants. Do not be drawn into debate. Do not say the word NO! It's not how fast you can get a child to stop, but how fast you can get him to think. Here are 4 more reasons:

- *Allows the child the time to think and reason.*

- *Shows respect for the child's ability to figure things out.*

- *Does not make the parent the messenger of the word "No."*

- *Takes the focus away from the perception and feeling that the parent is just doling out arbitrary Nos.*

Excerpted with permission of the author from his upcoming book *The Best Parenting Book Ever: How to Have a Struggle-Free Relationship with Your Children.*

the art of parenting

Lesson 4

Competence and Confidence

How important is self-esteem and what is the most productive way to build our children's self-esteem? How do we help our children recognize and develop their unique talents and abilities?

Regarding the Self

Climbing the Pyramid of Needs

Text 1

Matthew McKay, PhD, and Patrick Fanning, *Self-Esteem*
[Oakland, CA: New Harbinger Publications, 2000], p. 2

Matthew McKay, PhD

Professor at the Wright Institute in Berkeley, CA. McKay has authored and coauthored numerous books, including *The Relaxation and Stress Reduction Workbook, Self-Esteem, Thoughts and Feelings, When Anger Hurts,* and *Act on Life Not on Anger.* McKay received his PhD in clinical psychology from the California School of Professional Psychology.

Patrick Fanning

Professional writer in the mental health field. Fanning has authored and coauthored eight self-help books, including *Self-Esteem, Thoughts and Feelings, Couple Skills,* and *Mind and Emotions.*

Self-esteem is essential for psychological survival, it is an emotional *sine qua non.* . . .

Judging and rejecting yourself causes enormous pain. And in the same way that you would favor and protect a physical wound, you find yourself avoiding anything that might aggravate the pain of self-rejection in any way. You take fewer social, academic, or career risks. You make it more difficult for yourself to meet people, interview for a job, or push hard for something where you might not succeed. You limit your ability to open yourself with others . . . be the center of attention, hear criticism, ask for help, or solve problems.

To avoid more judgments and self-rejection, you erect barriers of defense. Perhaps you blame and get angry, or bury yourself in perfectionistic work. Or you brag. Or you make excuses. Sometimes you turn to alcohol or drugs.

Text 2

Rabbi Tsadok Hakohen Rabinowitz, *Tsidkot Hatsadik* 154 📖

כְּשֵׁם שֶׁצָּרִיךְ אָדָם לְהַאֲמִין בְּהַשֵּׁם בְּהַשֵּׁם יִתְבָּרַךְ, כַּךְ צָרִיךְ אַחַר כַּךְ לְהַאֲמִין
בְּעַצְמוֹ. רָצָה לוֹמַר, שֶׁיֵּשׁ לְהַשֵּׁם יִתְבָּרֵךְ עֵסֶק עִמּוֹ וְשֶׁאֵינֶנּוּ פּוֹעֵל
בָּטֵל . . . רַק צָרִיךְ לְהַאֲמִין כִּי נַפְשׁוֹ מִמְּקוֹר הַחַיִּים יִתְבָּרֵךְ שְׁמוֹ
וְהַשֵּׁם יִתְבָּרֵךְ מִתְעַנֵּג וּמִשְׁתַּעֲשֵׁעַ בָּה כְּשֶׁעוֹשָׂה רְצוֹנוֹ.

Just as we must believe in God, we must also believe in ourselves. We must believe that God cares about us, that we are not worthless laborers . . . that we possess divine souls, and that God takes pleasure and joy when we fulfill His desire.

Rabbi Tsadok Hakohen Rabinowitz
1823–1900

Chasidic master and thinker. Rabbi Tsadok was born into a Lithuanian rabbinic family and later joined the Chasidic movement. He was a follower of the Chasidic leaders Rabbi Mordechai Yosef Leiner of Izbica and Rabbi Leibel Eiger. He succeeded Rabbi Eiger after his passing and became a rebbe in Lublin, Poland. He authored many works on Jewish law, Chasidism, Kabbalah, and ethics, as well as scholarly essays on astronomy, geometry, and algebra.

LEARNING EXERCISE 1

Rate your child(ren)'s overall self-esteem.
3 = healthy and robust; 2 = average; 1 = weak and needs reinforcement

Bullying

LEARNING EXERCISE 2

Which of the following is bully behavior?

(a) A six-year-old consistently grabs toys from his five-year-old sibling.	☐ Yes ☐ No ☐ Maybe
(b) A twelve-year-old is part of a clique that regularly humiliates the less popular kids in class.	☐ Yes ☐ No ☐ Maybe
(c) A nine-year-old, when upset, physically lashes out at her siblings.	☐ Yes ☐ No ☐ Maybe

Text 3

"Bullying Definition," www.stopbullying.gov

Bullying is unwanted, aggressive behavior among school-aged children that involves a real or perceived power imbalance. The behavior is repeated, or has the potential to be repeated, over time. Both kids who are bullied and who bully others may have serious, lasting problems.

In order to be considered bullying, the behavior must be aggressive and include:

* *An Imbalance of Power*: Kids who bully use their power—such as physical strength, access to embarrassing information, or popularity—to control or harm others. . . .

* *Repetition*: Bullying behaviors happen more than once or have the potential to happen more than once.

Text 4a

"Effects of Bullying," www.stopbullying.gov

Kids who are bullied can experience negative physical, school, and mental health issues.

Kids who are bullied are more likely to experience:

* Depression and anxiety, increased feelings of sadness and loneliness, changes in sleep and eating patterns, and loss of interest in activities they used to enjoy. These issues may persist into adulthood.

* Health complaints

* Decreased academic achievement—GPA and standardized test scores—and school participation. They are more likely to miss, skip, or drop out of school.

Text 4b

Ibid.

Kids who bully others can also engage in violent and other risky behaviors into adulthood. Kids who bully are more likely to:

- Abuse alcohol and other drugs in adolescence and as adults

- Get into fights, vandalize property, and drop out of school

- Engage in early sexual activity

- Have criminal convictions and traffic citations as adults

- Be abusive toward their romantic partners, spouses, or children as adults

QUESTIONS FOR DISCUSSION

1. What causes a child to bully others?

2. What makes a particular child more attractive as a target for bullies?

Text 5

Michael J. Formica, "Ego, Insecurity, and the Destructive Narcissist," *Psychology Today*, November 6, 2009

The bully's ego is artifice. His arrogance is a hollow confidence. . . . This ego for him is a fragile thing, driven by fear and narcissism, not by power, nor by the power he wishes so desperately to possess. . . . He feeds on our fear, but his hunger is driven solely by his own.

The key for the bullied is to recognize that the bully's bullying is not about us—it's about him, and his weakness. It's about his sense of being threatened, and his horror at being found out as an imposter or a poser. He is afraid—quite afraid—and all the time.

Michael J. Formica

Counselor, executive coach, and self-development expert. Formica attended Columbia University's Teachers College and earned three advanced degrees in psychology. He writes and lectures extensively on spirituality and psychology, and he has developed a broad clinical focus that centers on compulsive dependency, addiction, anxiety, depression, and a number of personality disorders.

Text 6

Pesach and Chana Burston, "Superiority," *Chicken Soup to Warm the Neshama*

Pesach and Chana Burston
Co-directors of Chabad of
Orange County, NY.

As a small child, Reb Zalman Aharon (the "Raza"), the older brother of Rebbe Sholom DovBer of Lubavitch (the "Rashab"), often complained that he was noticeably shorter than his younger brother.

One day, the Raza sneaked up behind his brother and pushed him lightly into a small ditch. As the Rashab stood up in surprise, the Raza seized the moment and pointed out that now he was taller.

Rabbi Shmuel of Lubavitch, the father of the two boys, observed the entire episode. The Rebbe asked for a chair, ordered the Raza to stand on it, and asked him, "Tell me, who's taller now?"

The Raza answered excitedly that yet again he was taller.

"Aha!" said Rabbi Shmuel. "There you are! To be bigger than your friend, there is no need to pull him down. Simply elevate yourself!"

Building Healthy Self-Esteem

Competence and Intrinsic Worth

LEARNING EXERCISE 3

Describe the advantages or disadvantages (or both) of the self-concepts of the following four children.

	Feels competent	Feels incompetent
Feels intrinsically worthy	Child A:	Child B:
Feels intrinsically unworthy	Child C:	Child D:

Text 7

Rabbi Abraham Twerski, MD, *Let Us Make Man*
[Brooklyn: CIS Publication, 1989], p. 11 🔲

Rabbi Abraham J. Twerski, MD
1930–

Psychiatrist and noted author. Rabbi Twerski is a scion of the Chernobyl Chasidic dynasty and a well-known expert in the field of substance abuse. He has authored more than 50 books on self-help and Judaism, and has served as a pioneer in heightening awareness of the dangers of addiction, spousal abuse, and low self-esteem. He served as medical director of the Gateway Rehabilitation Center in Pittsburgh and as associate professor of psychiatry at the University of Pittsburgh School of Medicine.

As I studied the negative self-image problem, I found that the most profound feelings of low self-esteem paradoxically occur most often in those who are in reality most gifted and competent. It appears that the person who develops a negative self-image sees himself as if he were looking through a trick lens which distorts the perception in such a manner that the person sees himself as the opposite of what he actually is.

Action Matters

QUESTIONS FOR DISCUSSION

1. What parenting techniques help our children feel more competent?

2. What parenting techniques help our children feel intrinsically valuable?

3. What are things parents can do that might negatively harm a child's self-esteem?

Text 8

The Rebbe, Rabbi Menachem M. Schneerson, *Correspondence*,
5 Teves 5745 [December 29, 1984] 📖

You surely know that nowadays such problems with children are very common.... Usually, the final decision as to how to deal with children who have such problems lies with the administration of the school, after discussing the situation with the parents and being advised of the way the child is handled at home. . . . It is also well to bear in mind that a significant number of such problems are usually straightened out in the course of time. . . .

What surprises me is that there is a factor in the situation which is rarely, if ever, used. This is to give a problem child a role of leadership with a group of younger children, through some school activity and the like. This usually goes a long way to encourage the child's self-confidence, as well as making the child more sociable, etc. I trust that this method could be used also in your situation—of course with the approval, and under the supervision, of the school administration.

Rabbi Menachem Mendel Schneerson
1902–1994

The towering Jewish leader of the 20th century, known as "the Lubavitcher Rebbe," or simply as "the Rebbe." Born in southern Ukraine, the Rebbe escaped Nazi-occupied Europe, arriving in the U.S. in June 1941. The Rebbe inspired and guided the revival of traditional Judaism after the European devastation, impacting virtually every Jewish community the world over. The Rebbe often emphasized that the performance of just one additional good deed could usher in the era of Mashiach. The Rebbe's scholarly talks and writings have been printed in more than 200 volumes.

Text 9

The Rebbe, Rabbi Menachem M. Schneerson, *Likutei Sichot* 16:625

כְּדַאי וְנָכוֹן בִּמְאֹד מְאֹד, אֲשֶׁר מְנַהֲלֵי וּמוֹרֵי כָּל בָּתֵּי הַסֵּפֶר . . . יְעוֹרְרוּ וִיזָרְזוּ אֶת הַתַּלְמִידִים וְהַתַּלְמִידוֹת – כּוֹלֵל וּבִפְרָט קְטַנִּים וּקְטַנּוֹת שֶׁלֹּא הִגִּיעוּ עֲדַיִן לְגִיל בַּר-מִצְוָה אוֹ בַּת-מִצְוָה (שֶׁהֵם זְקוּקִים לְהַסְבָּרָה יְתֵרָה) – לְהוֹסִיף בְּ . . . מַעֲשֵׂה הַצְּדָקָה – שֶׁהַתַּלְמִידִים וְהַתַּלְמִידוֹת דְּכָל בֵּית סֵפֶר וְכוּ' (אוֹ דְכָל כִּתָּה) יְיַסְּדוּ קֶרֶן גְּמַ"ח . . . וְשֶׁכָּל אֶחָד וְאַחַת יִתְרְמוּ מִזְמַן לִזְמַן מִמָּמוֹנָם לְקֶרֶן זוֹ . . .

בִּכְדֵי לְהַשְׁרִישׁ בְּלֵב הַיְלָדִים וְהַיְלָדוֹת שֶׁיִּהְיוּ לֹא רַק "נְדִיבִים בְּמָמוֹנָם" אֶלָּא גַם "נְדִיבִים בְּגוּפָם" – נָכוֹן בִּמְאֹד, שֶׁקֶּרֶן הַגְּמַ"ח יִתְנַהֵל עַל יְדֵי הַיְלָדִים וְהַיְלָדוֹת עַצְמָם. שֶׁתַּלְמִידֵי בֵּית הַסֵּפֶר (אוֹ הַכִּתָּה) וְכוּ' יִבְחֲרוּ מִתּוֹכָם מְנַהֵל הַקֶּרֶן, גִּזְבָּר, וְכוּ',

אֲשֶׁר זֶה גַם יַגְבִּיר רֶגֶשׁ הָאַחֲרָיוּת [וּבְמֵילָא, יוֹסִיף גַם חַיּוּת וְהִתְלַהֲבוּת] וְהַקֶּשֶׁר לְהַגְּמַ"ח דְּכָל תַּלְמִידֵי בֵּית הַסֵּפֶר וְכוּ' – הוֹאִיל וְגַם עֲשִׂיַּית הַחֶסֶד בְּפוֹעַל הִיא עַל יְדֵי שְׁלוּחֵיהֶם וּבָאֵי כּוֹחָם.

וּמַה טּוֹב שֶׁהַנְהָלַת קֶרֶן הַגְּמַ"ח וַחֲלוּקַת הַתַּפְקִידִים (מְנַהֵל, גִּזְבָּר, מְנַהֵל חֶשְׁבּוֹנוֹת וְכוּ') תִּתְחַלֵּף לְעִתִּים לֹא רְחוֹקוֹת (עַל יְדֵי בְּחִירַת הַתַּלְמִידִים וְהַתַּלְמִידוֹת) – בִּכְדֵי לְאַפְשֵׁר לְכָל תַּלְמִידֵי בֵּית הַסֵּפֶר וְכוּ' אוֹ לְרֻבָּם עַל כָּל פָּנִים, לִהְיוֹת לֹא רַק נְדִיבִים בְּמָמוֹנָם אֶלָּא גַם נְדִיבִים בְּגוּפָם.

I t is very appropriate and worthwhile for school principals and teachers . . . to recommend and encourage the students, boys and girls, including and especially those who have not yet reached the age of bar or bat mitzvah, to increase . . . their charitable activities. Namely, the students of each school (or each class) should establish a free-loan fund . . . and from time to time each student should contribute of his or her own money to this fund. . . .

In order to instill in the students' hearts the importance of personal charitable involvement and volunteer work—in addition to monetary generosity—it is most proper that these free-loan funds be directed by the boys and girls themselves, with the students of the school (or the class) choosing from among themselves a director, a treasurer, etc.

The fact that this fund is being administered by the students' representatives will cause them to have a stronger feeling of responsibility and personal commitment to the cause (which will, in turn, increase their energy and enthusiasm as well).

It would be best to alternate from time to time (by way of student vote) the directorship of the free-loan fund as well as its various management positions (director, treasurer, bookkeeper, etc.), in order to enable all the students, or at the least a majority, to be (not just donors of money but also) donors of their time and energy.

Parenting Individuals

Text 10a

Proverbs 22:6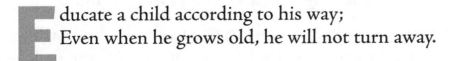

חֲנֹךְ לַנַּעַר עַל פִּי דַרְכּוֹ,

גַּם כִּי יַזְקִין לֹא יָסוּר מִמֶּנָּה.

Educate a child according to his way;
Even when he grows old, he will not turn away.

Text 10b

Paraphrase of commentary by Rabbi Eliyahu of Vilna, ad loc.

כִּי הָאָדָם אִי אֶפְשָׁר לוֹ לִשְׁבּוֹר דַּרְכּוֹ, כְּלוֹמַר מַזָּלוֹ שֶׁנּוֹלַד בּוֹ, כְּמוֹ שֶׁאָמְרוּ (שַׁבָּת
קנו,א), "הַאי מַאן דִּבְצֶדֶק, יְהִי גְּבַר צַדְקָן" וכו'. אֶלָּא שֶׁנִּתְּנָה הַבְּחִירָה בְּיַד הָאָדָם
שֶׁיּוּכַל לֶאֱחוֹז בְּמַזָּלוֹ וּלְהַעֲמִידוֹ כְּפִי שֶׁיִּרְצֶה, אוֹ צַדִּיק, אוֹ רָשָׁע, אוֹ בֵּינוֹנִי.
וּכְמוֹ שֶׁכָּתוּב בְּשַׁבָּת שָׁם: "הַאי מַאן דִּבְמַאֲדִים יְהְיֶה גְּבַר אַשִׁיד דָּמָא (שׁוֹפֵךְ
דָּמִים). אָמַר רַב אַשִׁי: אִי אוּמָּנָא (מַקִּיז דָּם), אִי גַּנְבָּא (לִסְטִים), אִי טַבָּחָא,
אִי מוֹהֲלָא". וְזָכַר אֵלּוּ הַשְּׁלוֹשָׁה לְפִי שֶׁמַּזָּלוֹ מוֹרֶה שֶׁיִּהְיֶה שׁוֹפֵךְ דָּמִים, אַךְ
בִּבְחִירָתוֹ יוּכַל לִבְחוֹר בְּאֵלּוּ הַשְּׁלוֹשָׁה, אִי מוֹהֲלָא — וְהוּא צַדִּיק שֶׁעוֹשֶׂה מִצְווֹת,
אִי טַבָּחָא — הוּא בֵּינוֹנִי, אִי לִסְטִים — וְהוּא רָשָׁע שׁוֹפֵךְ דָּמִים כְּמַשְׁמָעוֹ.

וְזֶה שֶׁנֶּאֱמַר "חֲנֹךְ לַנַּעַר עַל פִּי דַרְכּוֹ" — לְפִי דֶרֶךְ מַזָּלוֹ וְטִבְעוֹ תְחַנְּכֵהוּ
וְתַדְרִיכֵהוּ לַעֲשׂוֹת מִצְווֹת, וְאָז גַּם כַּאֲשֶׁר "יַזְקִין לֹא יָסוּר מִמֶּנָּה". אֲבָל
כְּשֶׁאַתָּה מַכְרִיחוֹ נֶגֶד טִבְעוֹ, עַתָּה יִשְׁמַע לְךָ, מִיִּרְאָתוֹ אוֹתְךָ, אֲבָל אַחַר כָּךְ,
בְּעֵת יוּסַר עֻלְךָ מֵעַל צַוָּארוֹ, יָסוּר מִזֶּה, כִּי אִי אֶפְשָׁר לוֹ לִשְׁבּוֹר מַזָּלוֹ.

Rabbi Eliyahu of Vilna
(Vilna Ga'on, Gra)
1720–1797

Talmudist, halachist, and Kabbalist. The Vilna Ga'on was one of the greatest scholars of his day. In addition to Talmud, he excelled in all aspects of Torah study, including Kabbalah, and was proficient in secular subjects as well. He left a tremendous legacy, both from his vast writings on the Tanach, Talmud, and Shulchan Aruch, and from the many students that he inspired to Torah and scholarship.

We cannot escape our innate personality, but we can choose how to channel it. We can utilize our inborn nature for positive, negative, or neutral causes.

Thus, the Talmud (Shabbat 156a) says that a person born with a violent nature who is inclined to spill blood can turn out to be a *mohel* (circumcisor), a *shochet* (ritual slaughterer), or a murderer. This illustrates how the same nature can be utilized for a holy objective (circumcision), a neutral purpose (slaughtering animals), or an evil end (murder).

Hence, the verse instructs us to educate a child "according to his way," in a manner that is consistent with the child's nature; for then, "even when he grows old, he will not turn away." If, however, we attempt to compel a child to act in a manner that is inconsistent with his or her nature, the child may listen to us now, in deference to our authority, but afterwards, when the child matures and sheds the yoke of our authority, he or she will "turn away" from the education we provided, for it tried to accomplish the impossible—the alteration of a person's innate nature.

Text 11

Rabbi Adin Even-Israel Steinsaltz, Interview with the JLI Curriculum Development Team, August 7, 2014 ▌

Parenting is like tending a garden. To properly care for it, you first have to know what you have in it. Do you have potatoes? Do you have roses? Do you have thorns? Then you have to take care and nurture each organism according to its unique needs.

Rabbi Adin Even-Israel Steinsaltz
1937–

Talmudist, author, and philosopher. Rabbi Even-Israel Steinsaltz is considered one of the foremost Jewish thinkers of the 20th century. Praised by *Time* magazine as a "once-in-a-millennium scholar," he has been awarded the Israel Prize for his contributions to Jewish study. He lives in Jerusalem and is the founder of the Israel Institute for Talmudic Publications, a society dedicated to the translation and elucidation of the Talmud.

LEARNING EXERCISE 4

Analyze the twenty-four character traits listed below* and try to identify (some of) your child's signature strengths. Do this exercise for each of your children.

Wisdom and Knowledge		
Creativity	Thinking of new and interesting ways to perceive and do things	1. Very much like my child 2. Like my child 3. Neutral 4. Unlike my child 5. Very much unlike my child
Curiosity	Exploring and discovering; finding certain topics to be fascinating	1. Very much like my child 2. Like my child 3. Neutral 4. Unlike my child 5. Very much unlike my child
Open-Mindedness	Contemplating matters from multiple angles; forming conclusions after weighing the evidence	1. Very much like my child 2. Like my child 3. Neutral 4. Unlike my child 5. Very much unlike my child
Love of Learning	A thirst for new knowledge and a desire to master new skills, whether formally or independently	1. Very much like my child 2. Like my child 3. Neutral 4. Unlike my child 5. Very much unlike my child

*Reprinted from Christopher Peterson, PhD and Martin E.P. Seligman, PhD, *Character Strengths and Virtues: A Handbook and Classification* (Washington, DC: American Psychological Association; New York: Oxford University Press, 2004).

Perspective	Having a knack for offering wise counsel	1. Very much like my child 2. Like my child 3. Neutral 4. Unlike my child 5. Very much unlike my child
Courage		
Bravery	Not backing down from challenge, despite threat or pain; doing the right thing even when it's unpopular	1. Very much like my child 2. Like my child 3. Neutral 4. Unlike my child 5. Very much unlike my child
Persistence	Continuing a course of action despite setbacks and obstacles	1. Very much like my child 2. Like my child 3. Neutral 4. Unlike my child 5. Very much unlike my child
Integrity	Acting in a way that is genuine and sincere; taking responsibility for actions	1. Very much like my child 2. Like my child 3. Neutral 4. Unlike my child 5. Very much unlike my child
Vitality	Approaching life with energy and excitement	1. Very much like my child 2. Like my child 3. Neutral 4. Unlike my child 5. Very much unlike my child

Humanity		
Love	Having close, loving relationships	1. Very much like my child 2. Like my child 3. Neutral 4. Unlike my child 5. Very much unlike my child
Kindness	Helping and caring for others	1. Very much like my child 2. Like my child 3. Neutral 4. Unlike my child 5. Very much unlike my child
Social Intelligence	Knowing what makes other people tick, understanding how they feel, and how to behave in different social situations	1. Very much like my child 2. Like my child 3. Neutral 4. Unlike my child 5. Very much unlike my child
Justice		
Citizenship	Working well with others; being loyal to the group	1. Very much like my child 2. Like my child 3. Neutral 4. Unlike my child 5. Very much unlike my child
Fairness	Treating people equally and giving them a fair chance	1. Very much like my child 2. Like my child 3. Neutral 4. Unlike my child 5. Very much unlike my child

Leadership	Helping a group organize activities and coalesce	1. Very much like my child 2. Like my child 3. Neutral 4. Unlike my child 5. Very much unlike my child
Temperance		
Forgiveness and Mercy	Giving people a second chance when they have done wrong; accepting people's shortcomings	1. Very much like my child 2. Like my child 3. Neutral 4. Unlike my child 5. Very much unlike my child
Humility	Letting accomplishments speak for themselves; not bragging	1. Very much like my child 2. Like my child 3. Neutral 4. Unlike my child 5. Very much unlike my child
Prudence	Choosing carefully, ensuring that there are no regrets later on	1. Very much like my child 2. Like my child 3. Neutral 4. Unlike my child 5. Very much unlike my child
Self-Regulation	Being in control of emotions; self-discipline	1. Very much like my child 2. Like my child 3. Neutral 4. Unlike my child 5. Very much unlike my child

Transcendence		
Appreciation of Beauty and Excellence	Noticing and appreciating all the wonderful things in life, from nature to art to everyday experiences	1. Very much like my child 2. Like my child 3. Neutral 4. Unlike my child 5. Very much unlike my child
Gratitude	Being thankful and expressing gratefulness for the good things in life	1. Very much like my child 2. Like my child 3. Neutral 4. Unlike my child 5. Very much unlike my child
Hope	Believing in and working toward a brighter future and expecting things to work out for the best	1. Very much like my child 2. Like my child 3. Neutral 4. Unlike my child 5. Very much unlike my child
Humor	Enjoying smiles and laughter	1. Very much like my child 2. Like my child 3. Neutral 4. Unlike my child 5. Very much unlike my child
Spirituality	Spiritually sensitive; enjoys prayer and other religious experiences; seeks meaning and searches for answers to metaphysical questions	1. Very much like my child 2. Like my child 3. Neutral 4. Unlike my child 5. Very much unlike my child

Intrinsic Worth

Text 12a

Genesis 22:2

וַיֹּאמֶר: קַח נָא אֶת בִּנְךָ אֶת יְחִידְךָ אֲשֶׁר אָהַבְתָּ, אֶת יִצְחָק, וְלֶךְ לְךָ אֶל אֶרֶץ הַמֹּרִיָּה.

God said [to Abraham], "Please, take your son, your only one, whom you love, Isaac, and go to the land of Moriah...."

Text 12b

Talmud, Sanhedrin 79b

"אֶת בִּנְךָ" — שְׁנֵי בָּנִים יֵשׁ לִי.

"אֶת יְחִידְךָ" — זֶה יָחִיד לְאִמּוֹ וְזֶה יָחִיד לְאִמּוֹ.

"אֲשֶׁר אָהַבְתָּ" — תַּרְוַיְיהוּ רְחִימְנָא לְהוּ.

"אֶת יִצְחָק".

"Take your son . . ." God instructed.

"I have two sons!" Abraham responded.

"Your only one."

"Isaac is *his* mother's only child, and Ishmael is *his* mother's only child!"

"[The one] whom you love."

"I love them both!"

"Take Isaac."

Babylonian Talmud

A literary work of monumental proportions that draws upon the legal, spiritual, intellectual, ethical, and historical traditions of Judaism. The 37 tractates of the Babylonian Talmud contain the teachings of the Jewish sages from the period after the destruction of the 2nd Temple through the 5th century CE. It has served as the primary vehicle for the transmission of the Oral Law and the education of Jews over the centuries; it is the entry point for all subsequent legal, ethical, and theological Jewish scholarship.

Text 13

The Rebbe, Rabbi Menachem M. Schneerson,
Correspondence, Chanukah 5721 [1960] ▌

I received your letter, in which you ask my advice with regard to certain educational problems, especially how to influence the children to get rid of undesirable habits, etc.

Needless to say, these problems cannot be adequately discussed in a letter. . . .

Nevertheless I would like to make one general point which can be universally applied in educational problems, a point which is emphasized in the teachings of Chassidus. I refer to the effort to make the children aware that they possess a soul which is a part of G-d, and that they are always in the presence of G-d (as explained in Chapters 2 and 41 of the Tanya). When this is done persistently, and on a level which is suitable to the age group and background of the children, the children come to realize that they possess a great and holy quality which is directly linked with G-d, the Creator and Master of the world, and that it would therefore be quite unbecoming and unworthy of them to do anything which is not good. At the same time they come to realize that they have the potential to overcome temptation or difficulty, and if they would only make a little effort on their part they would receive considerable assistance from On high to live up to the Torah and Mitzvoth, which constitute the will and wisdom of G-d.

EXERCISE FOR THE WEEK

Spend some time reviewing your child(ren)'s strengths, as identified earlier in Learning Exercise 4, and brainstorm different activities and responsibilities that will call upon and highlight these strengths.

Key Points

1. We need to see to it that our children are emotionally stable and happy, and self-esteem is a big part of that.

2. Self-esteem is essential for psychological survival. Low self-esteem negatively impacts a person in many ways, including inhibiting his or her spiritual growth.

3. A particularly detrimental consequence of low self-esteem is that it puts a child at higher risk for engaging in bully behavior or for being a target of bully behavior. Building our children's self-esteem helps prevent their becoming bullies or being bullied.

4. Self-esteem is comprised of two primary elements: a feeling of personal competence and a feeling of intrinsic worth. We want our children to love and value themselves for *what they can do* and for *who they are*.

5. The most effective way to build children's self-esteem is to treat them as worthy and competent beings. We do so by entrusting them with positions of responsibility.

6. Our children feel competent when they see success in their endeavors. It is important to tailor our parenting to the uniqueness of each child, and to guide each child to activities that call upon his or her signature strengths.

7. We nurture our children's feeling of intrinsic worth by loving them unconditionally and not differentiating in our love between one child and the next. This intrinsic worth is grounded in the understanding that every child is defined by the infinite value of his or her divine soul.

ADDITIONAL READINGS

HOW TO LAND YOUR KID IN THERAPY

BY LORI GOTTLIEB

If there's one thing I learned in graduate school, it's that the poet Philip Larkin was right. ("They $#&% you up, your mum and dad, / They may not mean to, but they do.") At the time, I was a new mom with an infant son, and I'd decided to go back to school for a degree in clinical psychology. With baby on the brain and term papers to write, I couldn't ignore the barrage of research showing how easy it is to screw up your kids. Of course, everyone knows that growing up with "Mommy Dearest" produces a very different child from one raised by, say, a loving PTA president who has milk and homemade cookies waiting after school. But in that space between Joan Crawford and June Cleaver, where most of us fall, it seemed like a lot could go wrong in the kid-raising department.

As a parent, I wanted to do things right. But what did "right" mean? One look in Barnes & Noble's parenting section and I was dizzy: child-centered, collaborative, or RIE? Brazelton, Spock, or Sears?

The good news, at least according to Donald Winnicott, the influential English pediatrician and child psychiatrist, was that you didn't have to be a perfect mother to raise a well-adjusted kid. You just had to be, to use the term Winnicott coined, a "good-enough mother." I was also relieved to learn that we'd moved beyond the concept of the "schizophrenogenic mother," who's solely responsible for making her kid crazy. (The modern literature acknowledges that genetics—not to mention fathers—play a role in determining mental health.) Still, in everything we studied—from John Bowlby's "attachment theory" to Harry Harlow's monkeys, who clung desperately to cloth dummies when separated from their mothers—the research was clear: fail to "mirror" your children, or miss their "cues," or lavish too little affection on them, and a few decades later, if they had

the funds and a referral, they would likely end up in one of our psychotherapy offices, on the couch next to a box of tissues, recounting the time Mom did this and Dad didn't do that, for 50 minutes weekly, sometimes for years.

Our main job as psychotherapists, in fact, was to "re-parent" our patients, to provide a "corrective emotional experience" in which they would unconsciously transfer their early feelings of injury onto us, so we could offer a different response, a more attuned and empathic one than they got in childhood.

At least, that was the theory. Then I started seeing patients.

My first several patients were what you might call textbook. As they shared their histories, I had no trouble making connections between their grievances and their upbringings. But soon I met a patient I'll call Lizzie. Imagine a bright, attractive 20-something woman with strong friendships, a close family, and a deep sense of emptiness. She had come in, she told me, because she was "just not happy." And what was so upsetting, she continued, was that she felt she had nothing to be unhappy about. She reported that she had "awesome" parents, two fabulous siblings, supportive friends, an excellent education, a cool job, good health, and a nice apartment. She had no family history of depression or anxiety. So why did she have trouble sleeping at night? Why was she so indecisive, afraid of making a mistake, unable to trust her instincts and stick to her choices? Why did she feel "less amazing" than her parents had always told her she was? Why did she feel "like there's this hole inside" her? Why did she describe herself as feeling "adrift"?

I was stumped. Where was the distracted father? The critical mother? Where were the abandoning, devaluing, or chaotic caregivers in her life?

As I tried to make sense of this, something surprising began happening: I started getting more patients like her. Sitting on my couch were other adults in their 20s or early 30s who reported that they, too, suffered from depression and anxiety, had difficulty choosing or committing to a satisfying career path, struggled with relationships, and just generally felt a sense of emptiness or lack of purpose—yet they had little to quibble with about Mom or Dad.

Instead, these patients talked about how much they "adored" their parents. Many called their parents their "best friends in the whole world," and they'd say things like "My parents are always there for me." Sometimes these same parents would even be funding their psychotherapy (not to mention their rent and car insurance), which left my patients feeling both guilty and utterly confused. After all, their biggest complaint was that they had nothing to complain about!

At first, I'll admit, I was skeptical of their reports. Childhoods generally aren't perfect—and if theirs had been, why would these people feel so lost and unsure of themselves? It went against everything I'd learned in my training.

But after working with these patients over time, I came to believe that no florid denial or distortion was going on. They truly did seem to have caring and loving parents, parents who gave them the freedom to "find themselves" and the encouragement to do anything they wanted in life. Parents who had driven carpools, and helped with homework each night, and intervened when there was a bully at school or a birthday invitation not received, and had gotten them tutors when they struggled in math, and music lessons when they expressed an interest in guitar (but let them quit when they lost that interest), and talked through their feelings when they broke the rules, instead of punishing them ("logical consequences" always stood in for punishment). In short, these were parents who had always been "attuned," as we thera-pists like to say, and had made sure to guide my patients through any and all trials and tribulations of childhood. As an overwhelmed parent myself, I'd sit in session and secretly wonder how these fabulous parents had done it all.

Until, one day, another question occurred to me: Was it possible these parents had done too much?

Here I was, seeing the flesh-and-blood results of the kind of parenting that my peers and I were trying to practice with our own kids, precisely so that they wouldn't end up on a therapist's couch one day. We were running ourselves ragged in a herculean effort to do right by our kids—yet what seemed like grown-up versions of them were sitting in our offices, saying they felt empty, confused, and anxious. Back in graduate school, the clinical focus had always been on how the lack of parental attunement affects the child. It never occurred to any of us to ask, what if the parents are too attuned? What happens to those kids?

Child-rearing has long been a touchy subject in America, perhaps because the stakes are so high and the theories so inconclusive. In her book *Raising America: Experts, Parents, and a Century of Advice About Children*, Ann Hulbert recounts how there's always been a tension among the various recommended parenting styles—the bonders versus the disciplinarians, the child-centered versus the parent-centered—with the pendulum swinging back and forth between them over the decades. Yet the underlying goal of good parenting, even during the heyday of don't-hug-your-kid-too-much advice in the 1920s ("When you are tempted to pet your child, remember that mother love is a dangerous instrument," the behavioral psychologist John Watson wrote in his famous guide to child-rearing), has long been the same: to raise children who will grow into productive, happy adults. My parents certainly wanted me to be happy, and my grandparents wanted my parents to be happy too. What seems to have changed in recent years, though, is the way we think about and define happiness, both for our children and for ourselves.

Nowadays, it's not enough to be happy—if you can be even happier. The American Dream and the pursuit of happiness have morphed from a quest for general contentment to the idea that you must be happy at all times and in every way. "I am happy," writes Gretchen Rubin in *The Happiness Project*, a book that topped the *New York Times* best-seller list and that has spawned something of a national movement in happiness-seeking, "but I'm not as happy as I should be."

How happy should she be? Rubin isn't sure. She sounds exactly like some of my patients. She has two wonderful parents; a "tall, dark, and handsome" (and wealthy) husband she loves; two healthy, "delightful" children; a strong network of friends; a beautiful neo-Georgian mansion on the Upper East Side; a law degree from Yale; and a successful career as a freelance writer. Still, Rubin writes, she feels "dissatisfied, that something [is] missing." So to counteract her "bouts of melancholy, insecurity, listlessness, and free-floating guilt," she goes on a "happiness journey," making lists and action items, buying three new magazines every Monday for a month, and obsessively organizing her closets.

At one point during her journey, Rubin admits that she still struggles, despite the charts and resolutions and yearlong effort put into being happy. "In some ways," she writes, "I'd made myself less happy." Then she adds, citing one of her so-called Secrets of Adulthood, "Happiness doesn't always make you feel happy."

Modern social science backs her up on this. "Happiness as a byproduct of living your life is a great thing," Barry Schwartz, a professor of social theory at Swarthmore College, told me. "But happiness as a goal is a recipe for disaster." It's precisely this goal, though, that many modern parents focus on obsessively—only to see it backfire. Observing this phenomenon, my colleagues and I began to wonder: Could it be that by protecting our kids from unhappiness as children, we're depriving them of happiness as adults?

Paul Bohn, a psychiatrist at UCLA who came to speak at my clinic, says the answer may be yes. Based on what he sees in his practice, Bohn believes many parents will do anything to avoid having their kids experience even mild discomfort, anxiety, or disappointment—"anything less than pleasant," as he puts it—with the result that when, as adults, they experience the normal frustrations of life, they think something must be terribly wrong.

Consider a toddler who's running in the park and trips on a rock, Bohn says. Some parents swoop in immediately, pick up the toddler, and comfort her in that moment of shock, before she even starts crying. But, Bohn explains, this actually prevents her from feeling secure—not just on the playground, but in life. If you don't let her experience that momentary confusion, give her the space to figure out what just happened (Oh, I tripped), and then briefly let her grapple with the frustration of having fallen and perhaps even try to pick herself up, she has no idea what discomfort feels like, and will have no framework for how to recover when she feels discomfort later in life. These toddlers become the college kids who text their parents with an SOS if the slightest thing goes wrong, instead of attempting to figure out how to deal with it themselves. If, on the other hand, the child trips on the rock, and the parents let her try to reorient for a second before going over to comfort her, the child learns: That was scary for a second, but I'm okay now. If something unpleasant happens, I can get through it. In many cases, Bohn says, the child recovers fine on her own—but parents never learn this, because they're too busy protecting their kid when she doesn't need protection.

Which made me think, of course, of my own sprints across the sand the second my toddler would fall. And of the time when he was 4 and a friend of mine died of cancer and I considered … not telling him! After all, he didn't even know she'd been sick (once, commenting on her head scarves, he'd asked me if she was an Orthodox Jew, and like a wuss, I said no, she just really likes scarves). I knew he might notice that we didn't see her anymore, but all of the parenting listservs I consulted said that hearing about a parent's death would be too scary for a child, and that, without lying (because God forbid that we enlightened, attuned parents ever lie to our children), I should sugarcoat it in all these ways that I knew would never withstand my preschooler's onslaught of cross-examining whys.

In the end, I told my son the truth. He asked a lot of questions, but he did not faint from the shock. If anything, according to Bohn, my trusting him to handle the news probably made him more trusting of me, and ultimately more emotionally secure. By telling him, I was communicating that I believed he could tolerate sadness and anxiety, and that I was here to help him through it. Not telling him would have sent a very different message: that I didn't feel he could handle discomfort. And that's a message many of us send our kids in subtle ways every day.

Dan Kindlon, a child psychologist and lecturer at Harvard, warns against what he calls our "discomfort with discomfort" in his book *Too Much of a Good Thing: Raising Children of Character in an Indulgent Age*. If kids can't experience painful feelings, Kindlon told me when I called him not long ago, they won't develop "psychological immunity."

"It's like the way our body's immune system develops," he explained. "You have to be exposed to pathogens, or your body won't know how to respond to an attack. Kids also need exposure to discomfort, failure, and struggle. I know parents who call up the school to complain if their kid doesn't get to be in the school play or make the cut for the baseball team. I know of one kid who said that he didn't like another kid in the carpool, so instead of having their child learn to tolerate the other kid, they offered to drive him to school themselves. By the time they're teenagers, they have no experience with hardship. Civilization is about adapting to less-than-perfect situations, yet parents often have this instantaneous reaction to unpleasantness, which is 'I can fix this.'"

Wendy Mogel is a clinical psychologist in Angeles who, after the publication of her book *The Blessing of a Skinned Knee* a decade ago, became an adviser to schools all over the country. When I talked to her this spring, she said that over the past few years, college deans have reported receiving growing numbers of incoming freshmen they've dubbed "teacups" because they're so fragile that they break down anytime

things don't go their way. "Well-intentioned parents have been metabolizing their anxiety for them their entire childhoods," Mogel said of these kids, "so they don't know how to deal with it when they grow up."

Which might be how people like my patient Lizzie end up in therapy. "You can have the best parenting in the world and you'll still go through periods where you're not happy," Jeff Blume, a family psychologist with a busy practice in Los Angeles, told me when I spoke to him recently. "A kid needs to feel normal anxiety to be resilient. If we want our kids to grow up and be more independent, then we should prepare our kids to leave us every day."

But that's a big if. Blume believes that many of us today don't really want our kids to leave, because we rely on them in various ways to fill the emotional holes in our own lives. Kindlon and Mogel both told me the same thing. Yes, we devote inordinate amounts of time, energy, and resources to our children, but for whose benefit?

"We're confusing our own needs with our kids' needs and calling it good parenting," Blume said, letting out a sigh. I asked him why he sighed. (This is what happens when two therapists have a conversation.) "It's sad to watch," he explained. "I can't tell you how often I have to say to parents that they're putting too much emphasis on their kids' feelings because of their own issues. If a therapist is telling you to pay less attention to your kid's feelings, you know something has gotten way of out of whack."

Last October, in an article for the *New York Times Magazine*, Renée Bacher, a mother in Louisiana, described the emptiness she felt as she sent her daughter off to college in the Northeast. Bacher tried getting support from other mother friends, who, it turned out, were too busy picking up a refrigerator for a child's college dorm room or rushing home to turn off a high-schooler's laptop. And while Bacher initially justified her mother-hen actions as being in her daughter's best interest—coming up with excuses to vet her daughter's roommate or staying too long in her daughter's dorm room under the guise of helping her move in—eventually she concluded: "As with all Helicopter Parenting, this was about me."

Bacher isn't unusual. Wendy Mogel says that colleges have had so much trouble getting parents off campus after freshman orientation that school administrators have had to come up with strategies to boot them. At the University of Chicago, she said, they've now added a second bagpipe processional at the end of opening ceremonies—the first is to lead the students to another event, the second to usher the parents away from their kids. The University of Vermont has hired "parent bouncers," whose job is to keep hovering parents at bay. She said that many schools are appointing an unofficial "dean of parents" just to wrangle the grown-ups. Despite the spate of articles in recent years exploring why so many people in their 20s seem reluctant to grow up, the problem may be less that kids are refusing to separate and individuate than that their parents are resisting doing so.

"There's a difference between being loved and being constantly monitored," Dan Kindlon told me. And yet, he admitted, even he struggles. "I'm about to become an empty-nester," he said, "and sometimes I feel like I'd burn my kids' college applications just to have somebody to hang around with. We have less community nowadays—we're more isolated as adults, more people are divorced—and we genuinely like spending time with our kids. We hope they'll think of us as their best friends, which is different from parents who wanted their kids to appreciate them, but didn't need them to be their pals. But many of us text with our kids several times a day, and would miss it if it didn't happen. So instead of being peeved that they ask for help with the minutiae of their days, we encourage it."

Long work hours don't help. "If you've got 20 minutes a day to spend with your kid," Kindlon asked, "would you rather make your kid mad at you by arguing over cleaning up his room, or play a game of Boggle together? We don't set limits, because we want our kids to like us at every moment, even though it's better for them if sometimes they can't stand us."

Kindlon also observed that because we tend to have fewer kids than past generations of parents did, each becomes more precious. So we demand more from them—more companionship, more achievement, more happiness. Which is where the line between selflessness (making our kids happy) and selfishness (making ourselves happy) becomes especially thin.

"We want our kids to be happy living the life we envision for them—the banker who's happy, the surgeon who's happy," Barry Schwartz, the Swarthmore social scientist, told me, even though those professions "might not actually make them happy." At least for parents of a certain demographic (and if you're reading this article, you're likely among them), "we're not so happy if our kids work at Walmart but show up each day with a smile on their faces," Schwartz says. "They're happy, but we're not. Even though we say what we want most for our kids is their happiness, and we'll do everything we can to help them achieve that, it's unclear where parental happiness ends and our children's happiness begins."

His comment reminded me of a conversation I'd just had with a camp director when I inquired about the program. She was going down the list of activities for my child's age group, and when she got to basketball, T-ball, and soccer, she quickly added, "But of course, it's all noncompetitive. We don't encourage competition." I had to laugh: all of these kids being shunted away from "competition" as if it were kryptonite. Not to get too shrink-y, but could this be a way for parents to work out their ambivalence about their own competitive natures?

It may be this question—and our unconscious struggle with it—that accounts for the scathing reaction to Amy Chua's memoir, *Battle Hymn of the Tiger Mother*, earlier this year. Chua's efforts "not to raise a soft, entitled child" were widely attacked on blogs and mommy listservs as abusive, yet that didn't stop the book from spending several months on the *New York Times* best-seller list. Sure, some parents might have read it out of pure voyeurism, but more likely, Chua's book resonated so powerfully because she isn't so different from her critics. She may have been obsessed with her kids' success at the expense of their happiness—but many of today's parents who are obsessed with their kids' happiness share Chua's drive, just wrapped in a prettier package. Ours is a have-your-cake-and-eat-it-too approach, a desire for high achievement without the sacrifice and struggle that this kind of achievement often requires. When the Tiger Mom looked unsparingly at her parental contradictions, perhaps she made the rest of us squirm because we were forced to examine our own.

Chua, says Wendy Mogel, "was admitting in such a candid way what loads of people think but just don't own up to." In her practice, Mogel meets many parents who let kids off the hook for even basic, simple chores so they can spend more time on homework. Are these parents being too lenient (letting the chores slide), or too hard-core (teaching that good grades are more important than being a responsible family member)? Mogel and Dan Kindlon agree that whatever form it takes—whether the fixation is happiness or success—parental overinvestment is contributing to a burgeoning generational narcissism that's hurting our kids.

A few months ago, I called up Jean Twenge, a co-author of *The Narcissism Epidemic* and professor of psychology at San Diego State University, who has written extensively about narcissism and self-esteem. She told me she wasn't surprised that some of my patients reported having very happy childhoods but felt dissatisfied and lost as adults. When ego-boosting parents exclaim "Great job!" not just the first time a young child puts on his shoes but every single morning he does this, the child learns to feel that everything he does is special. Likewise, if the kid participates in activities where he gets stickers for "good tries," he never gets negative feedback on his performance. (All failures are reframed as "good tries.") According to Twenge, indicators of self-esteem have risen consistently since the 1980s among middle-school, high-school, and college students. But, she says, what starts off as healthy self-esteem can quickly morph into an inflated view of oneself—a self-absorption and sense of entitlement that looks a lot like narcissism. In fact, rates of narcissism among college students have increased right along with self-esteem.

Meanwhile, rates of anxiety and depression have also risen in tandem with self-esteem. Why is this? "Narcissists are happy when they're younger, because they're the center of the universe," Twenge explains. "Their parents act like their servants, shuttling them to any activity they choose and catering to their every desire. Parents are constantly telling their children how special and talented they are. This gives them an inflated view of their specialness compared to other human beings. Instead of feeling good about themselves, they feel better than everyone else."

In early adulthood, this becomes a big problem. "People who feel like they're unusually special end up alienating those around them," Twenge says. "They don't know how to work on teams as well or deal with limits. They get into the workplace and expect to be stimulated all the time, because their worlds were so structured with activities. They don't like being told by a boss that their work might need improvement, and they feel insecure if they don't get a constant stream of praise. They grew up in a culture where everyone gets a trophy just for participating, which is ludicrous and makes no sense when you apply it to actual sports games or work performance. Who would watch an NBA game with no winners or losers? Should everyone get paid the same amount, or get promoted, when some people have superior performance? They grew up in a bubble, so they get out into the real world and they start to feel lost and helpless. Kids who always have problems solved for them believe that they don't know how to solve problems. And they're right—they don't."

Last month, I spoke to a youth soccer coach in Washington, D.C. A former competitive college athlete and now a successful financier, he told me that when he first learned of the youth league's rules—including no score-keeping—he found them "ridiculous."

How are the kids going to learn? he thought. He valued his experience as an athlete, through which he had been forced to deal with defeat. "I used to think, If we don't keep score, we're going to have a bunch of wusses out there. D.C. can be very PC, and I thought this was going too far."

Eventually, though, he came around to the new system, because he realized that some kids would be "devastated" if they got creamed by a large margin. "We don't want them to feel bad," he said. "We don't want kids to feel any pressure." (When I told Wendy Mogel about this, she literally screamed through the phone line, "Please let them be devastated at age 6 and not have their first devastation be in college! Please, please, please let them be devastated many times on the soccer field!") I told the coach this sounded goofy, given that these kids attend elite, competitive schools like Georgetown Day School or Sidwell Friends, where President Obama's daughters go. They're being raised by parents who are serious about getting their kids into Harvard and Yale. Aren't these kids exposed to a lot of pressure? And besides, how is not keeping score protecting anyone, since, as he conceded, the kids keep score on their own anyway? When the score is close, the coach explained, it's less of an issue. But blowouts are a problem.

He told me about a game against a very talented team. "We lost 10–5, and the other team dominated it. Our kids were very upset. They said, 'We got killed!' and I said, 'What are you talking about? You guys beat the spread! The team we beat last week lost 14–1!' The kids thought about this for a second and then were like, 'You're right, we were great! We rule!' They felt so much better, because I turned it around for them into something positive. When you get killed and there's no positive spin, the kids think they're failures. It damages their self-esteem."

At the end of the season, the league finds a way to "honor each child" with a trophy. "They're kind of euphemistic," the coach said of the awards, "but they're effective." The Spirit Award went to "the troublemaker who always talks and doesn't pay attention, so we spun it into his being very 'spirited,'" he said. The Most Improved Player Award went to "the kid who has not an ounce of athleticism in his body, but he tries hard." The Coaches' Award went to "the kids who were picking daisies, and the only thing we could think to say about them is that they showed up on time. What would that be, the Most Prompt Award? That seemed lame. So we called it the Coaches' Award." There's also a Most Valuable Player Award, but the kid who deserved it three seasons in a row got it only after the first season, "because we wanted other kids to have a chance to get it." The coach acknowledged that everyone knew who the real MVP was. But, he said, "this is a more collaborative approach versus the way I grew up as a competitive athlete, which was a selfish, Me Generation orientation."

I asked Wendy Mogel if this gentler approach really creates kids who are less self-involved, less "Me Generation." No, she said. Just the opposite: parents who protect their kids from accurate feedback teach them that they deserve special treatment. "A principal at an elementary school told me that a parent asked a teacher not to use red pens for corrections," she said, "because the parent felt it was upsetting to kids when they see so much red on the page. This is the kind of self-absorption we're seeing, in the name of our children's self-esteem."

Paradoxically, all of this worry about creating low self-esteem might actually perpetuate it. No wonder my patient Lizzie told me she felt "less amazing" than her parents had always said she was. Given how "amazing" her parents made her out to be, how could she possibly live up to that? Instead of acknowledging their daughter's flaws, her parents, hoping to make her feel secure, denied them. "I'm bad at math," Lizzie said she once told them, when she noticed that the math homework was consistently more challenging for her than for many of her classmates. "You're not bad at math," her parents responded. "You just have a different learning style. We'll get you a tutor to help translate the information into a format you naturally understand."

With much struggle, the tutor helped Lizzie get her grade up, but she still knew that other classmates were good at math and she wasn't. "I didn't have a different learning style," she told me. "I just suck at math! But in my family, you're never bad at anything. You're just better at some things than at others. If I ever say I'm bad at something, my parents say, 'Oh, honey, no you're not!'"

Today, Wendy Mogel says, "every child is either learning-disabled, gifted, or both—there's no curve left, no average." When she first started doing psychological testing, in the 1980s, she would dread having to tell parents that their child had a learning disability. But now, she says, parents would prefer to believe that their child has a learning disability that explains any less-than-stellar performance, rather than have their child be perceived as simply average. "They believe that 'average' is bad for self-esteem."

The irony is that measures of self-esteem are poor predictors of how content a person will be, especially if the self-esteem comes from constant accommodation and praise rather than earned accomplishment. According to Jean Twenge, research shows that much better predictors of life fulfillment and success are perseverance, resiliency, and reality-testing—qualities that people need so they can navigate the day-to-day.

Earlier this year, I met with a preschool teacher who told me that in her observation, many kids aren't learning these skills anymore. She declined to be named, for fear of alienating parents who expect teachers to agree with their child-rearing philosophy, so I'll call her Jane.

Let's say, Jane explained, that a mother is over by the sign-in sheet, and her son has raced off to play. Suddenly the mother sees her kid fighting over a toy with a classmate. Her child has the dump truck, and the other kid grabs it. Her child yells, "No! That's mine!" The two argue while the other kid continues to play with the truck, until finally the other kid says, "This one is yours!" and tosses her child a crappy one. Realizing the other kid won't budge, her child says, "Okay," and plays with the crappy toy.

"Her kid is fine," Jane said. "But the mother will come running over and say, 'But that's not fair! Little Johnnie had the big truck, and you can't just grab it away. It was his turn.' Well, the kids were fine with it. Little Johnnie was resilient! We do teach the kids not to grab, but it's going to happen sometimes, and kids need to learn how to work things out themselves. The kid can cope with adversity, but the parent is reeling,

and I end up spending my time calming down the parent while her kid is off happily playing."

Jane told me that because parents are so sensitive to how every interaction is processed, sometimes she feels like she's walking on eggshells while trying to do her job. If, for instance, a couple of kids are doing something they're not supposed to—name-calling, climbing on a table, throwing sand—her instinct would be to say "Hey, knock it off, you two!" But, she says, she'd be fired for saying that, because you have to go talk with the kids, find out what they were feeling, explain what else they could do with that feeling other than call somebody a "poopy face" or put sand in somebody's hair, and then help them mutually come up with a solution.

"We try to be so correct in our language and our discipline that we forget the true message we're trying to send—which is, don't name-call and don't throw the sand!" she said. "But by the time we're done 'talking it through,' the kids don't want to play anymore, a rote apology is made, and they'll do it again five minutes later, because they kind of got a pass. 'Knock it off' works every time, because they already know why it's wrong, and the message is concise and clear. But to keep my job, I have to go and explore their feelings."

Another teacher I spoke with, a 58-year-old mother of grown children who has been teaching kindergarten for 17 years, told me she feels that parents are increasingly getting in the way of their children's development. "I see the way their parents treat them," she said, "and there's a big adjustment when they get into my class. It's good for them to realize that they aren't the center of the world, that sometimes other people's feelings matter more than theirs at a particular moment—but it only helps if they're getting the same limit-setting at home. If not, they become impulsive, because they're not thinking about anybody else."

This same teacher—who asked not to be identified, for fear of losing her job—says she sees many parents who think they're setting limits, when actually, they're just being wishy-washy. "A kid will say, 'Can we get ice cream on the way home?' And the parent will say, 'No, it's not our day. Ice-cream day is Friday.' Then the child will push and negotiate, and the parent, who probably thinks negotiating is 'honoring her child's opinion,' will say, 'Fine, we'll get ice cream today, but don't ask me tomorrow, because the answer is no!'" The teacher laughed. "Every year, parents come to me and say, 'Why won't my child listen to me? Why won't she take no for an answer?' And I say, 'Your child won't take no for an answer, because the answer is never no!'"

Barry Schwartz, at Swarthmore, believes that well-meaning parents give their kids so much choice on a daily basis that the children become not just entitled, but paralyzed. "The ideology of our time is that choice is good and more choice is better," he said. "But we've found that's not true."

In one study Schwartz and his team conducted, kids were randomly divided into two groups and then asked to draw a picture. Kids in one group were asked to choose a marker to use from among three; kids in the other group were asked to choose from among 24 markers. Afterward, when the pictures were evaluated by an elementary-school art teacher who did not know which group had produced which pictures, the drawings rated the "worst" were by and large created by kids in the 24-marker group. Then, in a second part of the experiment, the researchers had the kids pick one marker from their set to keep as a gift. Once the kids had chosen, the researchers tried to persuade them to give back their marker in exchange for other gifts. The kids who had chosen from 24 markers did this far more easily than those who had chosen from only three markers. According to Schwartz, this suggests that the kids who had fewer markers to select from not only focused better on their drawings, but also committed more strongly to their original gift choice.

What does this have to do with parenting? Kids feel safer and less anxious with fewer choices, Schwartz says; fewer options help them to commit to some things and let go of others, a skill they'll need later in life.

"Research shows that people get more satisfaction from working hard at one thing, and that those who

always need to have choices and keep their options open get left behind," Schwartz told me. "I'm not saying don't let your kid try out various interests or activities. I'm saying give them choices, but within reason. Most parents tell kids, 'You can do anything you want, you can quit any time, you can try this other thing if you're not 100 percent satisfied with the other.' It's no wonder they live their lives that way as adults, too." He sees this in students who graduate from Swarthmore. "They can't bear the thought that saying yes to one interest or opportunity means saying no to everything else, so they spend years hoping that the perfect answer will emerge. What they don't understand is that they're looking for the perfect answer when they should be looking for the good-enough answer."

The message we send kids with all the choices we give them is that they are entitled to a perfect life—that, as Dan Kindlon, the psychologist from Harvard, puts it, "if they ever feel a twinge of non-euphoria, there should be another option." Mogel puts it even more bluntly: what parents are creating with all this choice are anxious and entitled kids whom she describes as "handicapped royalty."

As a parent, I'm all too familiar with this. I never said to my son, "Here's your grilled-cheese sandwich." I'd say, "Do you want the grilled cheese or the fish sticks?" On a Saturday, I'd say, "Do you want to go to the park or the beach?" Sometimes, if my preschooler was having a meltdown over the fact that we had to go to the grocery store, instead of swooping him up and wrestling him into the car, I'd give him a choice: "Do you want to go to Trader Joe's or Ralphs?" (Once we got to the market, it was "Do you want the vanilla yogurt or the peach?") But after I'd set up this paradigm, we couldn't do anything unless he had a choice. One day when I said to him, "Please put your shoes on, we're going to Trader Joe's," he replied matter-of-factly: "What are my other choices?" I told him there were no other choices—we needed something from Trader Joe's. "But it's not fair if I don't get to decide too!" he pleaded ingenuously. He'd come to expect unlimited choice.

When I was my son's age, I didn't routinely get to choose my menu, or where to go on weekends—and the friends I asked say they didn't, either. There was some negotiation, but not a lot, and we were content with that. We didn't expect so much choice, so it didn't bother us not to have it until we were older, when we were ready to handle the responsibility it requires. But today, Twenge says, "we treat our kids like adults when they're children, and we infantilize them when they're 18 years old."

Like most of my peers, I'd always thought that providing choices to young children gave them a valuable sense of agency, and allowed them to feel more in control. But Barry Schwartz's research shows that too much choice makes people more likely to feel depressed and out of control.

It makes sense. I remember how overwhelmed and anxious I felt that day I visited the parenting aisle at Barnes & Noble and was confronted by all those choices. How much easier things would be if there weren't hundreds of parenting books and listservs and experts that purport to have the answers, when the truth is, there is no single foolproof recipe for raising a child.

And yet, underlying all this parental angst is the hopeful belief that if we just make the right choices, that if we just do things a certain way, our kids will turn out to be not just happy adults, but adults that make us happy. This is a misguided notion, because while nurture certainly matters, it doesn't completely trump nature, and different kinds of nurture work for different kinds of kids (which explains why siblings can have very different experiences of their child-

hoods under the same roof). We can expose our kids to art, but we can't teach them creativity. We can try to protect them from nasty classmates and bad grades and all kinds of rejection and their own limitations, but eventually they will bump up against these things anyway. In fact, by trying so hard to provide the perfectly happy childhood, we're just making it harder for our kids to actually grow up. Maybe we parents are the ones who have some growing up to do—and some letting go.

As Wendy Mogel likes to say, "Our children are not our masterpieces."

Indeed. Recently, I noticed that one of my patients had, after a couple of sessions of therapy, started to seem uncomfortable. When I probed a bit, he admitted that he felt ambivalent about being in treatment. I asked why.

"My parents would feel like failures if they knew I was here," he explained. "At the same time, maybe they'd be glad I'm here, because they just want me to be happy. So I'm not sure if they'd be relieved that I've come here to be happier, or disappointed that I'm not already happy."

He paused and then asked, "Do you know what I mean?"

I nodded like a therapist, and then I answered like a parent who can imagine her son grappling with that very same question one day. "Yes," I said to my patient. "I know exactly what you mean."

Reprinted from *The Atlantic*, June 7, 2011, with permission of *The Atlantic* and the author.

ORIGINS OF LOW SELF-ESTEEM

BY RABBI ABRAHAM J. TWERSKI, MD

The prevalence of the negative self-image problem is so great that the question is obvious: What causes so many people to have such distortions of self-perception and such unwarranted feelings of inadequacy?

One might think that the negative self-image problem would occur only in people who suffered severe deprivation in their childhood or who were subject to a great deal of emotional trauma. This does not appear to be true. I have seen instances of very profound negative self-image problems in people who had good homes and loving parents, and in whose histories there is no evidence of emotional trauma.

It should also be noted that negative self-image distortions can often be detected in very young children. Some five- and six-year olds exhibit unwarranted feelings of negativity, and even at this tender age, may manifest some of the character traits we have described.

Is it possible that some negative self-image feelings are hereditary? Is it possible that there are intrauterine factors that can affect one's self-perception? At this point in time we do not have any definitive answers to these questions. What is more important is to realize that whatever the source of these feelings, they are amenable to correction.

However, there is one predisposition to the development of a negative self-image which is universal. Of all living things, the human being has the longest period of dependency on others. Young animal cubs are ambulatory shortly after birth, and become self-sufficient within a relatively short period of time. Their period of dependence on their parents is thus quite brief. The human infant, however, is totally dependent on its parents for a very long period of time, not only for food, but also for shelter and all personal care. Human infants cannot ambulate for months, and even as they grow they cannot obtain and prepare their own food, or provide their own clothing and shelter for years. They usually do not become financially independent for decades.

Dependence on others lowers one's self-esteem. There appears to be an instinctive resentment of dependence, as is evidenced by tiny children who insist on doing things by themselves and refuse adult assistance. Dependence is perceived as equivalent to powerlessness and helplessness, and seems to be resented as demeaning even at an age when a child has not yet developed any cultural value of independence or a concept of pride. The drive for the emergence of a self seems to be innate, and to the extent that we are dependent or are under the domination of others, to that extent we feel the "self" stifled. It thus appears that we may all begin life with at least a predisposition to low self-esteem.

During the early years of life many things are apt to happen that can depress self-esteem, even with parents who are caring and devoted. Parents must discipline children and teach them not to do wrong. However, in telling children that something they have done was wrong there is a risk that the children will feel that they are bad people, and it requires great ingenuity to achieve the necessary discipline without conveying to the child a feeling of badness. I recall my father reprimanding me when I did something wrong by saying, "Es past nisht" (that does not befit you). The message was, "You are too good for behavior like that." Parental techniques such as this can help avoid some of the ego-depressing effects of discipline.

A child may observe a sibling getting more parental attention than himself, and this may impact on his self-esteem. Whether this extra attention is really favoritism or whether the sibling requires extra care because of some problem may make little difference to the child who feels relatively neglected. Some remarks or critical attitudes by parents, grandparents, teachers and other significant adults may also contribute to a self-esteem problem.

When parents require children to perform certain functions before the children have the capacity to do so, the children are apt to consider themselves defective. They reason that the parents must be right in their demands on them, and that their failure to perform is indicative of something being wrong with them. On the other hand, doing too much for children and not giving them the opportunity to develop their skills may also result in their feeling inadequate. There is a narrow latitude in just how much to demand of a child at any given time in his development. It is little wonder that even the most dedicated parents may stray beyond these narrow limits, and unwittingly contribute to lowering the child's self-esteem.

There is good reason to assume that children have a need to perceive the world around them as rational and predictable. As adults we have come to recognize that there is neither much rationality nor predictability to even natural phenomena, let alone human behavior which is subject to caprice. But that is not how children view the world. To children a capricious world would be too anxiety-provoking, and they have to assume that there is order in the world. Hence, when something irrational or unexpected happens, children are not likely to conclude that the world is crazy, but rather that they do not understand what is going on because there is something wrong with them. Instead of recognizing the world to be as chaotic as it really is, children are more likely *to blame themselves* for failing to comprehend it. When this happens, the child loses confidence in his ability to understand things and considers himself deficient.

Another consequence of juvenile thinking is the development of unwarranted guilt feelings. Children's thinking often operates on a simple principle of cause and effect. Every effect must have an apparent cause. When things go wrong and they do not readily understand why, they are likely to blame themselves as somehow being the cause. Many children harbor guilt feelings which seem completely groundless to adult logic, but children can easily hold themselves responsible for many things, even though there is in fact not even the remotest reason for their feeling this way.

These two characteristics of juvenile thought, the tendency to consider oneself deficient when the world appears incomprehensible, and the tendency to assume blame for things when one cannot see an evident cause, profoundly depress a child's self-confidence and self-esteem.

* * *

Self-esteem is comprised of two principal ingredients: feelings of competence and feelings of worthiness. Contemporary culture tends to identify worthiness with competence. In a civilization which is so productivity oriented, great emphasis is placed on a person's capacity to perform or produce. People who are not productive are frequently looked upon as liabilities. Indeed, many of the problems facing the elderly population may reflect an unspoken resentment that they are parasitic to society, and that their upkeep drains too much from the younger, productive population. The only redeeming feature that is heard about the elderly is that they deserve our respect and consideration because of their many years of work, but the emphasis still remains on productivity as the ultimate value. In other words, we are indebted to them for what they *did* and for what they *were,* rather than respect them for what they *are.* If we will only be truthful with ourselves, we will recognize that our culture devalues people once they cease to be productive.

The idea that human value is linked to productivity has far-reaching consequences. Only several decades ago, abortion was a crime roughly equivalent to murder. It then went through a rather remarkable change, first being decriminalized, and then becoming essentially a virtuous act, supported by public funds. How did abortion metamorphose so rapidly from a crime to a virtue?

The answer is painfully simple. When infant mortality was high, when epidemics were rampant, when young mothers died of childbed fever, and when tuberculosis killed young people in the prime of their lives, every additional human being had value. People were needed for their productivity. Doing away with a fetus was detrimental to the welfare of the community, hence terminating a pregnancy was evil. Now that medical science has eradicated the mass killers of young people, and now that population control has become the banner of social planners, humans are no longer an unquestioned desirable *commodity*. There is the key word. Our society often looks upon human life as a commodity. It does not always see an intrinsic value in human life, but only value in terms of productivity, and today that source of productivity is no longer in short supply.

When worthiness is totally contingent on competence, self-esteem is dealt a mortal blow. Once a person sees himself as incompetent, there is no concept of an intrinsic worthiness to fall back on.

* * *

Many of the factors responsible for depletion of self-esteem existed before the advent of our super-industrialized society. Today there are even more depressants of self-esteem. The computer era has converted us into numbered cards rather than people with names. Factors such as the mobility of families, resulting in the lack of strong family ties and community roots, have had their impact. Little wonder that the prevalence of the negative self-image problem is now so great.

Reprinted from *Let Us Make Man* [New York: CIS Publishers, 1991], pp. 53–59, with permission of the author.

the art of

parenting

Lesson 5

Feedback and Consequences

We know that it is necessary, but usually it does not leave us feeling great about ourselves. Instead, we are left with a sinking feeling in our stomach and wondering whether we did it all wrong. We are discussing discipline, of course. What is the correct way to discipline? For that matter, what is the correct way to praise or reward?

JLI

JEWISH LEARNING INSTITUTE

Introduction

Text 1

Po Bronson, "How Not to Talk to Your Kids," *New York Magazine*, August 3, 2007

Po Bronson

American journalist and author. Bronson coauthored *NurtureShock*, an influential book about children, which was on the *New York Times* bestseller list for six months and was translated into 16 languages. He is also the author of *What Should I Do with My Life?* and *Bombardiers*.

Since the 1969 publication of *The Psychology of Self-Esteem,* in which Nathaniel Branden opined that self-esteem was the single most important facet of a person, the belief that one must do whatever he can to achieve positive self-esteem has become a movement with broad societal effects. Anything potentially damaging to kids' self-esteem was axed. Competitions were frowned upon. Soccer coaches stopped counting goals and handed out trophies to everyone. Teachers threw out their red pencils. Criticism was replaced with ubiquitous, even undeserved, praise.

QUESTION FOR DISCUSSION

Do you agree that ample praise and reward foster healthy self-esteem while frequent criticism inhibits it?

Praise

How to Phrase the Praise

LEARNING EXERCISE 1A

Write down two positive things that your child recently did and how you responded to them.

1. _____

   _____

   _____

   _____

   _____

2. _____

   _____

   _____

   _____

   _____

LEARNING EXERCISE 1B

Analyze the following compliments and determine whether they are likely to have a positive or negative effect on a child's self-esteem.

Compliment	Impact on Child's Self-esteem
"You're so smart! I'm very proud."	Positive / Negative / Neutral
"You're an absolute angel! The best!"	Positive / Negative / Neutral
"You did a great job. Look at how perfect the work is!"	Positive / Negative / Neutral
"You worked really hard. That is wonderful!"	Positive / Negative / Neutral

Text 2

Po Bronson, ibid.

For a few decades, it's been noted that a large percentage of all gifted students (those who score in the top 10 percent on aptitude tests) severely underestimate their own abilities. . . . When parents praise their children's intelligence, they believe they are providing the solution to this problem. According to a survey conducted by Columbia University, 85 percent of American parents think it's important to tell their kids that they're smart. . . .

But a growing body of research—and a new study from the trenches of the New York public-school system—strongly suggests it might be the other way around. Giving kids the label of "smart" does not prevent them from underperforming. It might actually be causing it.

For the past ten years, psychologist Carol Dweck and her team at Columbia (she's now at Stanford) studied the effect of praise on students in a dozen New York schools. Her seminal work—a series of experiments on 400 fifth-graders—paints the picture most clearly.

Dweck sent four female research assistants into New York fifth-grade classrooms. The researchers would take a single child out of the classroom for a nonverbal IQ test consisting of a series of puzzles—puzzles easy enough that all the children would do fairly well. . . . Some [of the children] were praised for their *intelligence*. They were told, "You must be smart at this." Other students were praised for their *effort*: "You must have worked really hard." . . .

Then the students were given a choice of test for the second round. One choice was a test that would be more difficult than the first, but the researchers told the kids that they'd learn a lot from attempting the puzzles. The other choice, Dweck's team explained, was an easy test, just like the first. Of those praised for their effort, 90 percent chose the *harder* set of puzzles. Of those praised for their intelligence, a majority chose the *easy* test. The "smart" kids took the cop-out.

QUESTION FOR DISCUSSION

Why would praising intelligence have a detrimental effect on children?

Rewarding Toil

Text 3

Mishnah, Ethics of the Fathers 2:16 📖

הוּא הָיָה אוֹמֵר: לֹא עָלֶיךָ הַמְּלָאכָה לִגְמוֹר, וְלֹא אַתָּה בֶן חוֹרִין לִבָּטֵל מִמֶּנָּה.

Rabbi Tarfon would say: It is not incumbent upon you to finish the task, but neither are you free to absolve yourself from it.

Pirkei Avot
(Ethics of Our Fathers)

A 6-chapter work on Jewish ethics that is studied widely by Jewish communities, especially during the summer. The first 5 chapters are from the Mishnah, tractate Avot. Avot differs from the rest of the Mishnah in that it does not focus on legal subjects; it is a collection of the sages' wisdom on topics related to character development, ethics, healthy living, piety, and the study of Torah.

Text 4

Job 5:7

כִּי אָדָם לְעָמָל יוּלָּד.

Man was created to toil.

Text 5

Talmud, Berachot 28b

בִּיצִיאָתוֹ מַהוּ אוֹמֵר?

מוֹדֶה אֲנִי לְפָנֶיךָ ה' אֱלֹקַי שֶׁשַּׂמְתָּ חֶלְקִי מִיוֹשְׁבֵי בֵּית
הַמִּדְרָשׁ וְלֹא שַׂמְתָּ חֶלְקִי מִיוֹשְׁבֵי קְרָנוֹת.

שֶׁאֲנִי מַשְׁכִּים וְהֵם מַשְׁכִּימִים; אֲנִי מַשְׁכִּים לְדִבְרֵי
תוֹרָה, וְהֵם מַשְׁכִּימִים לִדְבָרִים בְּטֵלִים.

אֲנִי עָמֵל וְהֵם עֲמֵלִים; אֲנִי עָמֵל וּמְקַבֵּל שָׂכָר, וְהֵם עֲמֵלִים וְאֵינָם מְקַבְּלִים שָׂכָר.

Upon exiting the *beit midrash* (Torah study hall), what does one say?

I thank You, my God, for You have established my lot among those who inhabit the *beit midrash*, and have not established my lot among those who do not study Torah.

For both I and they rise early. I rise early to study Torah; they rise early for matters of [relative] idleness.

Both I and they toil. I toil and receive reward; they toil and do not receive reward.

Babylonian Talmud

A literary work of monumental proportions that draws upon the legal, spiritual, intellectual, ethical, and historical traditions of Judaism. The 37 tractates of the Babylonian Talmud contain the teachings of the Jewish sages from the period after the destruction of the 2nd Temple through the 5th century CE. It has served as the primary vehicle for the transmission of the Oral Law and the education of Jews over the centuries; it is the entry point for all subsequent legal, ethical, and theological Jewish scholarship.

Praise with Purpose

Text 6

Rabbi Abraham J. Twerski, MD, and Dr. Ursula Verena Schwartz, *Positive Parenting* [Brooklyn, NY: Mesorah, 1996], p. 89

Rabbi Abraham J. Twerski, MD
1930–

Psychiatrist and noted author. Rabbi Twerski is a scion of the Chernobyl Chasidic dynasty and a well-known expert in the field of substance abuse. He has authored more than 50 books on self-help and Judaism, and has served as a pioneer in heightening awareness of the dangers of addiction, spousal abuse, and low self-esteem. He served as medical director of the Gateway Rehabilitation Center in Pittsburgh and as associate professor of psychiatry at the University of Pittsburgh School of Medicine.

Ursula Verena Schwartz, PhD

Psychologist. Schwartz practices in the Squirrel Hill section of Pittsburgh, Pennsylvania. Schwartz's areas of expertise include early and middle childhood disorders, adolescent depression and anxiety, and effective parenting. She received her PhD in educational psychology from Indiana University in Bloomington, Indiana. She then completed a predoctoral internship in clinical psychology at Children's Hospital of Pittsburgh.

When my grandchild was seven, he began taking violin lessons, and after his fourth lesson he wanted to audition for me. Needless to say, his performance was a bit less than that of a virtuoso, but I was able to recognize the melody, even with all the sharps and flats that were uncalled for. My first impulse was to compliment him, "that was beautiful!" But I caught myself in time, realizing that this would be a lie, because it was not beautiful. Instead, I said, "I know that tune. Play it again, and I'll sing it along with you." We did so twice, and we had a duet which pleased him to no end, as his facial expressions revealed. I had complimented him on his performance without lying to him.

Punishment and Reprimand

LEARNING EXERCISE 2

Your nine-year-old daughter has been acting rudely to her younger brother for the past hour. Now she slammed a door in his face and barked some nasty comments at him. What should your response be?

_____

_____

_____

_____

_____

_____

_____

_____

_____

_____

Text 7

Amos 3:2 📖

רַק אֶתְכֶם יָדַעְתִּי מִכֹּל מִשְׁפְּחוֹת הָאֲדָמָה, עַל כֵּן אֶפְקֹד עֲלֵיכֶם אֵת כָּל עֲוֹנֹתֵיכֶם.

Only you did I love above all the families of the earth; therefore, I visit upon you [the consequences of] all your iniquities.

Text 8

Rabbi Abraham J. Twerski, MD, and Dr. Ursula Verena Schwartz, ibid., p. 90–91 📖

Many of the interactions that can affect self-esteem are not dramatic or traumatic events, but rather things to which we ascribe little significance. For example, the child asks you something while you are absorbed reading an article, and with your eyes on the paper or at best halfway on the paper, you respond to the child's question, "Um, yeah, I guess it's okay." No big deal, is it?

But think about it a moment. The child's question, perhaps whether he may go over to a friend's house, may be trivial to you, but it is important to him. Suppose you wanted to ask your employer something that was of importance to you, and he gave your question scant attention, mumbling some kind of answer while he was absorbed doing something else. How would you feel? Would that give you the feeling that your employer is really concerned about you and your cares? That is how the child feels when you act similarly.

You are not required to put the paper or the magazine aside, but you might say, "Honey, I'm in the middle of reading this, and I want to hear what you have to say. I'll be through with this in just a few moments, and then I can listen to you." When you finish the article or come to a break, you can then listen to his question attentively, and perhaps even ask what he plans to do at the friend's house. The child should have reason to feel that his needs are considered important.

Do you know the names of all your child's teachers? These people are very important to him. They are his authorities. In addition to knowing their names, you should care about how the child feels about his teachers. Also, you should know the names of at least his closest friends. It is a sign of his significance to you when you show concern about the people with whom he associates.

Text 9

The Rebbe, Rabbi Menachem M. Schneerson, *Torat Menachem* 5750, 3:194

Rabbi Menachem Mendel Schneerson
1902–1994

The towering Jewish leader of the 20th century, known as "the Lubavitcher Rebbe," or simply as "the Rebbe." Born in southern Ukraine, the Rebbe escaped Nazi-occupied Europe, arriving in the U.S. in June 1941. The Rebbe inspired and guided the revival of traditional Judaism after the European devastation, impacting virtually every Jewish community the world over. The Rebbe often emphasized that the performance of just one additional good deed could usher in the era of Mashiach. The Rebbe's scholarly talks and writings have been printed in more than 200 volumes.

וְעוֹד וְעִיקָר – פְּעוּלַת הַחִינּוּךְ הִיא מִתּוֹךְ אַהֲבָה וְקֵירוּב, כְּפִי שֶׁרוֹאִים בְּמוּחָשׁ שֶׁחִינּוּךְ מִתּוֹךְ אַהֲבָה גְּלוּיְ **מַצְלִיחַ יוֹתֵר** מֵחִינּוּךְ מִתּוֹךְ יִרְאָה וּפַחַד. נוֹסָף לְכַךְ שֶׁבִּכְלָל יֵשׁ לְהִמָּנַע מֵהַפְחָדַת יֶלֶד כְּדֵי שֶׁיּוּכַל לִחְיוֹת חַיָּיו וּלְנַצֵּל כּוֹחוֹתָיו מִתּוֹךְ מְנוּחָה וְשַׁלְוָה, שִׂמְחָה וְטוּב לֵבָב, וְאָז יוּכַל לְנַצֵּל כּוֹחוֹתָיו בִּשְׁלֵימוּת.

Education needs to be implemented with love and affection. We see quite plainly that education that flows from revealed love is more effective and successful than education that is imposed through fear and trepidation.

In general, it is inadvisable to cause a child anxiety, for this inhibits his or her ability to live a life of tranquility, serenity, and joy—all necessary ingredients to maximize one's potential.

Text 10

Midrash, *Devarim Rabah* 1:4

Devarim Rabah

A homiletic commentary on the Book of Deuteronomy. It was first published in Constantinople in 1512, with four other Midrashic works on the other four books of the Pentateuch. The homilies are structured similarly; each episode begins with a question of religious law and is followed by an answer, which opens with the words, "Our sages taught." Most commentaries end with reassurances and promises of the redemption.

רְאוּיוֹת הָיוּ הַתּוֹכָחוֹת לוֹמַר מִפִּי בִּלְעָם וְהַבְּרָכוֹת מִפִּי מֹשֶׁה. אֶלָּא, אִילוּ הוֹכִיחָם בִּלְעָם הָיוּ יִשְׂרָאֵל אוֹמְרִים, "שׂוֹנֵא מוֹכִיחֵנוּ". וְאִילוּ בֵּרְכָם מֹשֶׁה הָיוּ אוּמּוֹת הָעוֹלָם אוֹמְרִים, "אוֹהֲבָן בֵּרְכָן". אָמַר הַקָּדוֹשׁ בָּרוּךְ הוּא, "יוֹכִיחָן מֹשֶׁה שֶׁאוֹהֲבָן וִיבָרְכָן בִּלְעָם שֶׁשּׂוֹנְאָן".

It would have been proper for the reprimands to emanate from the mouth of Balaam and the blessings from the mouth of Moses. However, had Balaam rebuked, the Jews would have [dismissed his words and] said, "Our enemy is rebuking us?" Had Moses blessed the Jews, the nations of the world would have [dismissed the blessings and] said, "He who loves them has blessed them." God, therefore, said, "Let Moses who loves them rebuke them and let Balaam who detests them bless them."

Text 11

Rabbi Abraham J. Twerski, MD, and Dr. Ursula Verena Schwartz, *Positive Parenting* [Brooklyn, NY: Mesorah, 1996], p. 91

While there are few rules that are without any exceptions, here is one that is absolute. Never, but never, humiliate a child. Discipline does not require his being shamed. A child should not be humiliated in the presence of his friends or even his own sisters or brothers. When reprimand or punishment is necessary, call the child aside, and in privacy carry out the required discipline. Although the child may resent the reprimand, he will appreciate your concern for his self-respect. On the other hand, if you reprimand him in the presence of others, the pain of being humiliated may be so intense that it obscures the message of the reprimand, and the discipline is of little value.

Text 12

Rabbi Yosef Yitschak Schneersohn, *Principles of Education and Guidance*, ch. 5 ▯

הַמְחַנֵּךְ וְהַמַדְרִיךְ צָרִיךְ לָדַעַת כִּי לֹא רַק פִּתְגָּמִים מַתְאִימִים לְעִנְיְנֵי הוֹרָאוֹתָיו
נוֹגְעִים בְּעִיקָרֵי תּוֹעֶלֶת הַחִינוּךְ וְהַהַדְרָכָה, אֶלָּא גַּם אוֹפֶן בִּיטוּי הַפִּתְגָּמִים, אִם
בְּנִימוּס וּמְתִינוּת אוֹ בְּהִתְרַגְּשׁוּת וְזִלְזוּל, נוֹגֵעַ בִּיסוֹדֵי תּוֹעֶלֶת הַחִינוּךְ וְהַהַדְרָכָה. . .

רַבִּים מֵהַמְחַנְכִים וְהַמַדְרִיכִים טוֹעִים בָּזֶה מַה שֶׁחוֹשְׁבִים אֲשֶׁר בְּהִתְרַגְּשׁוּת
בְּקוֹל רַעַם וָרַעַשׁ יַגִּיעוּ לְמַטָּרָתָם בְּחִינוּךְ וְהַדְרָכָה, וּמֵהֶם מִתְנַפְּלִים עַל
הַמְחוּנָּךְ וְהַמוּדְרָךְ בְּדִבְרֵי רוֹגֶז בִּדְבָרִים קָשִׁים כְּגִידִים וְיֶחֱרְפֵנוּ וִיגַדְּפֵנוּ,
וּבֶאֱמֶת הִנֵּה גַּם אִם לְשָׁעָה מִתְרַגֵּשׁ הַמְחוּנָּךְ וְהַמוּדְרָךְ מִלַּפִּידֵי אֵשׁ אִמְרֵי
פִּי הַמְחַנֵּךְ וְהַמַדְרִיךְ וְלִבָּבוֹ מִתְכַּוֵּץ מִצַּעַר וּלְפְעָמִים הִנֵּה גַּם יִבְכֶּה בְּמַר
נַפְשׁוֹ, הִנֵּה חִינוּךְ וְהַדְרָכָה זוֹ לֹא יָבִיאוּ שׁוּם תּוֹעֶלֶת וְכַחֲלוֹם יָעוּף.

Rabbi Yosef Yitschak Schneersohn
(Rayats, Frierdiker Rebbe, Previous Rebbe)
1880–1950

Chasidic rebbe, prolific writer, and Jewish activist. Rabbi Yosef Yitschak, the 6th leader of the Chabad movement, actively promoted Jewish religious practice in Soviet Russia and was arrested for these activities. After his release from prison and exile, he settled in Warsaw, Poland, from where he fled Nazi occupation, and arrived in New York in 1940. Settling in Brooklyn, Rabbi Schneersohn worked to revitalize American Jewish life. His son-in law, Rabbi Menachem Mendel Schneerson, succeeded him as the leader of the Chabad movement.

An educator or counselor must understand that not only is it important to appropriately phrase his or her words, but that the manner in which the words are expressed—with politeness and patience or with agitation and derision—profoundly impacts the effectiveness of the educational message. . . .

Many educators and counselors err in this area. They imagine that their emotional outbursts that are accompanied by much commotion and shouting help them achieve their educational goals. Some assault their students with harsh and angry words and berate and insult them.

In truth, however, even if the pupil is temporarily upset by the fiery words of the educator or counselor and his or her heart contracts from pain, even if the pupil cries bitter tears, this type of education yields no lasting benefit whatsoever. Any [temporary positive] effect will vanish like a fleeting dream.

Text 13

The Rebbe, Rabbi Menachem Mendel Schneerson,
Correspondence, Chanukah 5721 [1960]

I would like to add one more point, which is also emphasized in the teachings of Chassidus, namely, to be careful that in admonishing children, the teacher or parent should not evoke a sense of helplessness and despondency on the part of the child; in other words, the child should not get the impression that he is good-for-nothing and that all is lost, etc., and therefore he can continue to do as he wishes. On the contrary, the child should always be encouraged in the feeling that he is capable of overcoming his difficulties and that it is only a matter of will and determination.

Text 14a

Proverbs 9:8 🕮

אַל תּוֹכַח לֵץ פֶּן יִשְׂנָאֶךָּ, הוֹכַח לְחָכָם וְיֶאֱהָבֶךָּ.

Reprove not a scoffer lest he hate you; reprove a wise man and he will love you.

Text 14b

Rabbi Yeshayahu Halevi Horowitz, *Shenei Luchot Haberit, Parashat Devarim* 🕮

כְּשֶׁאַתָּה רוֹצֶה לְהוֹכִיחַ אֶת אֶחָד, אַל תֹּאמַר לוֹ, "כָּךְ וְכָךְ אַתָּה גָּרוּעַ", כִּי אָז יִשְׂנָאֶךָּ וְלֹא יִשְׁמַע לִדְבָרֶיךָ. וְזֶהוּ שֶׁאָמַר, "אַל תּוֹכַח לֵץ", שֶׁלֹא תוֹכִחַ אוֹתוֹ בְּדֶרֶךְ זִלְזוּל לוֹמַר לוֹ, "לֵץ אַתָּה". רַק, אַדְרַבָּה, תֹּאמַר לוֹ, "חָכָם אַתָּה, וְאִם כֵּן חֶרְפָּה הִיא לְאִישׁ כָּמוֹךְ לַעֲשׂוֹת כֹּה וָכֹה". זֶהוּ "הוֹכַח לְחָכָם", כְּלוֹמַר, תַּעֲשֵׂהוּ לְךָ לְחָכָם, אָז יֶאֱהָבְךָ וְיִשְׁמַע לְקוֹל דְּבָרֶיךָ וִיקַבֵּל מוּסָר.

Rabbi Yeshayah Halevi Horowitz (*Shelah*) 1565–1630

Kabbalist and author. Rabbi Horowitz was born in Prague and served as rabbi in several prominent Jewish communities, including Frankfurt am Main and his native Prague. After the passing of his wife in 1620, he moved to Israel. In Tiberias, he completed his *Shenei Luchot Haberit*, an encyclopedic compilation of Kabbalistic ideas. He is buried in Tiberias, next to Maimonides.

When you reprove your fellow, do not tell him how awful he is, for he will despise you and not heed your words. This is the meaning of the verse: *Reprove not a scoffer,* do not reprove him with dismissiveness, do not label him a scoffer. To the contrary, tell him that it is unbefitting for a wise person such as he is to behave in such a manner. *Reprove a wise man,* that is, consider him a wise person, and he will heed your words and accept the reproof.

FIGURE 5.1

The three rules of loving and respectful (i.e., effective) discipline and reprimand

1)	**Do not react in the moment.** It is almost always more effective to wait before responding to a situation.
2)	**Respect your children.** Reprimand or punishment should never be shameful or humiliating.
3)	**Speak *up* to your children.** Speak to their potential and innate goodness.

Creating a Personalized Balance

Text 15

Talmud, Pesachim 56a

בִּקֵּשׁ יַעֲקֹב לְגַלּוֹת לְבָנָיו קֵץ הַיָּמִין וְנִסְתַּלְּקָה מִמֶּנּוּ שְׁכִינָה. אָמַר, "שֶׁמָּא חַס וְשָׁלוֹם יֵשׁ בְּמִטָּתִי פְּסוּל, כְּאַבְרָהָם שֶׁיָּצָא מִמֶּנּוּ יִשְׁמָעֵאל וַאֲבִי יִצְחָק שֶׁיָּצָא מִמֶּנּוּ עֵשָׂו?"

אָמְרוּ לוֹ בָּנָיו, "שְׁמַע יִשְׂרָאֵל ה' אֱלֹקֵינוּ ה' אֶחָד" אָמְרוּ, "כְּשֵׁם שֶׁאֵין בְּלִבְּךָ אֶלָּא אֶחָד כַּךְ אֵין בְּלִבֵּנוּ אֶלָּא אֶחָד".

Jacob wished to reveal to his sons the end of days, but the divine presence departed from upon him. "Perhaps," Jacob said, "[the divine presence has departed because] one of my children is unworthy? [Perhaps I am] like Abraham who begat Ishmael and like my father Isaac who begat Esau?"

Jacob's children responded: "Hear O [our father] Israel, the Lord is our God, the Lord is One. Just as there is only one [God] in your heart, there is only One in our hearts."

Text 16

Rabbi Moshe Feinstein, *Igrot Moshe, Yoreh De'ah* 3:76 🔊

בִּדְבַר הַצְלָחָה בְּחִינוּךְ הַבָּנִים, לֵיכָּא כְּלָל בְּדָבָר אֵיךְ לְהִתְנַהֵג, שֶׁתָּלוּי
לְפִי מִדוֹת הַבֵּן וְהַבַּת שֶׁחָנַן אוֹתָם הַשֵּׁם יִתְבָּרַךְ, שֶׁיֵּשׁ שֶׁטּוֹב
לֵילֵךְ בִּתְקִיפוּת וְיֵשׁ שֶׁיּוֹתֵר טוֹב לֵילֵךְ בְּרַכּוּת וּבִנְעִימוּת.

וּבְרוֹב הַפְּעָמִים בִּנְעִימוּת וְרַכּוּת הוּא יוֹתֵר טוֹב.

There are no clear-cut rules with regard to successful childrearing, for all depends on the temperament that God granted the individual boy or girl. In some instances it is more effective to proceed with a greater degree of firmness; in other instances, a greater measure of softness and pleasantness is preferable.

For the majority of children, pleasantness and softness is the preferred path.

Rabbi Moshe Feinstein
1895–1986

Leading halachic authority of the 20th century. Rabbi Feinstein was appointed rabbi of Luban, Belarus, in 1921. He immigrated to the U.S. in 1937 and became the dean of Metivta Tiferet Yerushalayim in New York. Rabbi Feinstein's halachic decisions have been published in a multi-volume collection entitled *Igrot Moshe*.

EXERCISES FOR THE WEEK

1. Find at least one opportunity to praise your child(ren)'s efforts and/or otherwise offer deliberate praise that is intended to effect long-term change.

2. Find one opportunity to practice the three rules of loving, caring discipline discussed in this lesson (summarized above on p. 149).

Or, for a really eye-opening experience:

For the next week or two, keep a journal of all the verbal feedback you give your children, both positive and negative. Recording your praise and reprimands will make you more aware of what you are saying to your children and will give you a heightened sense of accountability. It also will allow you to go back and analyze your reactions. Also, be sure to record any changes you note in your child as a result of your tweaking your feedback.

Key Points

1. Our children's self-worth is affected not so much by *whether* we reprimand or praise, but by *how* it is done.

2. We should always gear our praise to attaining larger goals, not to giving our children a temporary ego boost.

3. Praising effort is an effective educational tool, for it imparts value to something that the child can control.

4. In the Jewish tradition, effort—as opposed to the quality of the product—is supremely valued. Effort and toil constitute the reason for our existence.

5. Praising children's natural talents is counterproductive, for it imparts value to something that the child cannot control.

6. For praise to be effective, it must be sincere and honest.

7. Responding to our children's misbehavior demonstrates our care for them and their worth in our eyes.

8. Reprimand must flow from our *palpable* love and respect for our children. Never are we allowed to humiliate a child.

9. If we wait a little before addressing an issue that requires reprimand or discipline, children will usually be more receptive to critique, and we will be able to provide a thought-out, better and more effective response.

10. We should always refer to misbehavior in the context of a child's greatness and incredible potential.

11. Proper and effective parenting is a blend of softness and firmness—a mixture personalized to meet our children's unique needs and sensitivities.

ADDITIONAL READINGS

DIGNITY

BY JAY LITVIN

Okay, so I yelled a little too loudly when I yelled at my daughter. Okay, so maybe she didn't deserve as much of my anger as I let out. But, she did deserve some of it, didn't she? I mean, after what she did, could I just let it pass? Not say anything? Pretend it didn't happen?

Who would she become, then? Should I just tolerate everything for the sake of not getting angry?

Okay, so it does make the house unpleasant and casts a pall over the evening, after I yell and she walks off with that look on her face and goes to her room and closes her door.

You're right, it scares the other kids, who just sort of look away and stay quiet for the rest of the evening, hoping I won't get mad at them.

And yes, I was in a bad mood when I came home, and yes, that did have some bearing on the way I responded. But still, should I have just let it pass? I mean, doesn't Chaya need some discipline, sometime?

"Your dignity," my wife said.

"What? What does my dignity have to do with this?"

"When you yell like that, you lose your dignity."

"*My dignity?*" I questioned with exasperation. "I thought we were talking about *her*, about her behavior, *her* need to be taught right from wrong."

"You can do that with dignity," she said again. "When you lose your temper, you lose your dignity."

Okay, she got me. I sat down, ready to hear more. I took a deep breath and tried to stuff my defenses in my pocket long enough to hear what she had to say.

"Chaya loves you," she explained convincingly. "She craves your approval. Your slightest look of displeasure is picked up by her and all the children.

"If you had simply grimaced," she continued, "it would have given her the message, taught her the lesson, and, yet left your dignity intact."

"Just grimaced?" I asked, disbelievingly.

"Just grimaced," she repeated. "Chaya—all of them— are totally tuned in to you. You are their father. They love you and want you to be happy with them. When you're not, they notice and it matters. If you believed this, you wouldn't have to get angry. And if you didn't get angry, you'd keep your dignity. And if you kept your dignity, you'd teach them how to keep theirs as well."

Whoa! This was a lot to take in. Too much to take in. And how did my wife get so wise? And where did she even find the courage to say all this to me, this husband not especially known for accepting criticism in the lightest of ways, especially from his wife; this person who often saw criticism when there wasn't even any around.

Was there any around?

Well, I looked and I couldn't find any. It felt close to criticism. It had some of the texture and smell of criticism. But there was something in the way she was telling me all this that didn't feel like criticism. But it did feel really important. Like something I should hear if I could just get my ego out of my ears.

"You mean to tell me that if I just grimace, the kids will get the message?"

"Yes," she said, "though you might also have to explain what you're grimacing about. But you don't have to yell to do that. Your displeasure is loud enough."

"And when I yell?" I asked.

"Painful," she said. "Straight into their little hearts. The hearts that love you."

Oh, my!!

"But I don't want to be so responsible with my behavior," I screeched. "What about spontaneity," I pleaded. *Can I ever be myself again?* I cried out to the One Above.

"Of course," she replied. (My wife, not the One Above.) "Just don't get so angry. You don't need to, and it hurts your dignity. And the kids want you to have dignity."

Dignity. What a word. What a concept. What exactly did it mean? How could you lose it? Where can you find it?

"You're on your own. Figure it out. You'll get it," she said with confidence, and in such a way as to preserve my . . . yes . . . dignity. We ended the conversation with my ego intact.

So, I started my research where any good student would go: to the dictionary.

Dignity: *The presence of poise and self-respect in one's deportment to a degree that inspires respect; loftiness and grace. Syn. Decorum.*

Intrigued, I followed the link to decorum.

Decorum: *. . . suitableness of speech and behavior to one's own character, or to the place and occasion . . . Poise in behavior.*

Poise again. I had to check that out.

Poise: *To be balanced; the state or condition of being balanced.*

This is what my wife was talking about, wasn't it? ". . . suitableness of speech and behavior to the place or occasion . . . ," "poise and balance." My anger had been out of balance with both the occasion and my daughter. I had done the opposite of "inspiring respect."

I began to think of my little Chaya trying to receive and contain my outburst of negative energy. I was angry for my own sake, not for hers. I had not only lost myself, but I had forgotten my daughter as well. She was simply overwhelmed by my intensity, unable to absorb or understand it. She was frightened, and I could envision her little mind and heart bursting from the power of my voice and words and facial expression. There was no way this anger could have any positive effect. My anger was only delighting in its own expression. And in behaving like this, I had lost, as my wife said, my dignity. And my daughter had suffered the consequences.

Later that day, I was studying a book on the *sefirot*, the ten divine "attributes" which G-d assumes in order to create and interact with our existence.

I was learning about *chessed* (kindness/outpouring), *gevurah* (restriction/containment), and their merger in *tiferet* (beauty, or what I might now call dignity).

In the description I was reading, the word "balance" was used to describe *tiferet*, as the dictionary had used this word to describe *dignity*, *decorum* and *poise*.

The passage was describing the balance between "outpouring" and the receptacle to contain it. When the ideal balance exits, beauty is the result. When things fit together properly, when form perfectly matches content, when balance occurs and proportions are correct, things are beautiful. They have grace and poise.

And when applied to behavior, I thought, they have dignity and decorum.

The Kabbalists say that when the outpouring is greater than the vessel can contain, the result is a "shattering of the vessel." When the outpouring is too little, the result is a vessel left in need. But when the outpouring is, as Goldilocks says, just right, the vessel just big enough—the result is beautiful, a perfect fit.

Again, it was not difficult to see the relevance to my daughter and my behavior. And as I continued to read, it was as if the words were printed over a vague outline of her face looking up at me, sometimes smiling, sometimes expressing the shock and anguish she felt as I yelled at her.

The passage continued to describe the way that G-d constricts and restricts Himself so that each container, no matter how small, is provided just the right amount of G-dliness without breaking. And I now had a glimpse of what was required of me. As challenging as it seemed, I figured that since I was created in the image of G-d, He had probably given me the resources I needed to accomplish what seemed the impossible.

I would need to match the outpouring of my expression to fit my daughter's ability to receive. And this would require that I come to know her ability to receive, that I tune deeper into her sensitivities, the size of her heart, the fragility and strength of her emotions, her capacity to understand her own behavior and mine, and to keep this knowing foremost in my mind and heart.

Returning again to Chassidism and the order of the *sefirot*, I related this level of knowing to the *sefirah* of *daat*, which precedes and influences the *sefirot* of *chessed* (outpouring, expression) and *gevurah* (restriction, containment).

Though *daat* is preceded by, and is a combination of, the *sefirot* of *chochmah* (wisdom) and *binah* (un-

derstanding), it is not an intellectual knowing, not a mind knowing, but a deeper knowing—an intimacy with the other that bridges the distance between subject and object, between knower and known.

As I thought about my daughter, I related *daat* to the kind of knowing that occurs between parents and children at their best. The sort of knowing available to those created of the same blood, seed and egg, the same DNA and soul, the same family and home. It was difficult for me to contemplate this level of knowing without imagining the deep love that would result, and the overwhelming desire to give and be kind to that which comes to be known in this intrinsic way.

Thinking about this and my little Chaya, my love and affection for her filled my awareness, and as I remembered yelling at her on this unfortunate morning, my behavior now seemed unbearably abhorrent and cruel.

Seeing now how ugly I had acted and the pain I caused her, I marveled at how kind my wife had been to me. At the time, I could not have listened to a description of my ugliness without shutting out my wife's words in my own defense. In her wisdom, she had chosen words that I could hear and learn from. She had spoken to me not of ugliness, but of dignity.

I now had this strange feeling that Chassidic teaching was telling me how to be a better father and husband, and my daughter and wife were teaching me how to better understand Chassidism, and myself.

I began to see that I would not, as I feared, be denied my spontaneity. Though my behavior would no longer be controlled by outbursts of emotion, neither would it be the artificial result of stiff, premeditated thought. From coming to know my daughter—or my wife—in the ways that Chassidism described, I saw the possibility that my expression could rise from a different kind of spontaneity, one that sprung naturally from my best mind, from my open heart, from my caring and love.

I saw the possibility of maintaining my dignity while giving my daughter the ability to receive and learn from that which I wished to impart, as my wife had given that opportunity to me.

And I saw that the result would be beautiful, in the way that all things are beautiful when they fall from the mind into the heart to be expressed by our actions and words.

To my daughter, my apologies. To my wife, my gratitude. To Chassidism, my appreciation for the refinement you bring to my life.

Reprinted with permission from Chabad.org.

HOW TO PRAISE
BY RABBI RAPHAEL PELCOVITZ AND DAVID PELCOVITZ, PHD

The widely respected research of Dr. Carol Dweck, a Stanford University psychologist, further informs approaches to life's frustrations in a manner that fosters patience and continued effort at self-improvement. Dr. Dweck found, that when faced with challenge, parents and teachers tend to foster one of two mindsets in teaching children how to respond to demanding situations. A fixed mindset or a growth mindset is one in which children are taught to believe that whatever talent, abilities and intelligence they have are innate qualities that exist regardless of how much hard work they put into the task at hand. In contrast, parents and teachers who foster a growth mindset engender a belief in the child that success is about effort and persisting in working hard even in the face of the toughest challenges. A growth mindset is what parents should strive for since children are often energized by challenge as they show high levels of patience and belief that with enough hard work they are up to confronting even the most daunting challenges.

The study that is most often cited as documenting this effect involved fifth-grade students being asked to complete a set of puzzles that were not too challenging for their age.[1] Half the children were either told that their performance reflected being "smart" and half were told "You must have worked hard." When the children were subsequently offered another set of puzzles to complete, 90% of the children praised for their effort chose more difficult puzzles. In contrast, most of the children who were told that their intelligence was the reason for their strong performance on the easy set of puzzles chose the less challenging set of puzzles. They avoided challenge to protect themselves from the embarrassment of making mistakes thereby showing the researchers that they weren't as smart as the researchers thought.

One of the final stages of the study involved giving both groups of children puzzles that were so far beyond their age level and ability that it was virtually impossible for them to correctly assemble them. Again, the two groups approached the task in a totally different manner. Those fifth-graders previously praised for their hard work seemed energized by the challenge. Even though they were unable to successfully assemble the puzzles they persisted longer, showing much higher levels of patience than their peers who were praised for being intelligent. The group praised for their "brilliance," however, gave up much more easily, manifesting high levels of impatience and frustration. In the concluding study, the children who just faced the frustrating, undoable task were again given the simple puzzles, the power of the type of praise was now most pronounced. Those children praised for working hard did 30% better than the first time they encountered the puzzles while

---

[1] Mueller, C. & Dweck, C. (1998) Praise for intelligence can undermine children's motivation and performance. *Journal of Personality and Social Psychology*, 75, 33-52.

those praised for being smart showed a 20% decrease in their puzzle-assembling performance.

The Role of Praise in Teaching Patience to Children:

In an extensive review of the research literature on how praise can support or undermine a child's ability to be patient in the face of challenging tasks, psychologists Jennifer Henderlong and Mark Lepper summarize what a large number of empirical studies have found about the kind of praise that undermines a child's ability to persist in the face of challenge as opposed to approaches to praise that heighten patience and persistence.[2]

1. Praise that Promotes the Child Feeling Independent:

   Studies find that when praise is delivered in a way that enhances the child's sense of autonomy and freedom, patience and persistence increases. In contrast, when the praise feels controlling, the child's feelings of self-reliance is undermined and the child will typically resist by becoming less patient with the frustrations posed by the task.

2. Competence conveyed by Positive Feedback—not Social Comparison:

   In his *Tzidkat Hazadik*, Rabbeinu Zadok ha-Kohen Rabinowitz of Lublin (1823–1900) said:

   "Just like a child needs to be taught to believe in God so too does he need afterwards to be taught to believe in himself. That is to say, that he is not an insignificant being here one day and gone the next."

   Praise that promotes feelings of self-efficacy, where a child is taught to believe in himself — teaching him that the adults in his life transmit a belief that "you can do this," has been found to promote higher levels of motivation and patience. Not only will such praise help the child feel capable so that he is convinced that he has the tools to do what is required, but it will also result in the child enjoying the task more, spending more time on the task and in general showing higher levels of patience and persistence in facing the challenge. Motivation, however, can be undermined when praise relies heavily on social comparisons. When children are taught to feel good about their performance primarily based on how they did relative to peers, research has found that they are often less likely to persevere at a later time when faced with challenging situations where peers do better on the same task.[3]

3. Praise that Conveys Standards and Expectations that are Realistic:

   Praise that works best is descriptive in a manner that lets the child know exactly what he did right and what is making the adult guiding him proud. The ability to work in a patient and consistent manner is undermined when the feedback the child is given either evokes unreasonably high standards, or conversely, sets the target for achievement too low. Either extreme is problematic. When praise sets a standard well below the child's potential, the parent or teacher is imparting a belief that the child's abilities are not up to par. When the praise suggests an impossibly high standard the attendant pressure will frustrate the child thereby trying his patience and sabotaging his motivation.

This is in keeping with the teaching of Raba in the Talmud:

Raba said: He who possesses haughtiness of spirit deserves excommunication, and if he does not possess it he deserves excommunication.[4]

Clearly, Raba is teaching us that when it comes to self-evaluation, accuracy is the key—either extreme is not advisable. The extreme of excessive self-criticism or excessive confidence can be

---

[2] Henderlong, J. & Lepper, R. (2002) The effect of praise on children's intrinsic motivation: A review and synthesis. *Psychological Bulletin, 128, 774-795.*

[3] Dweck, C. S. (1986). Motivational processes affecting learning. *American Psychologist, 41,* 1040–1048.
[4] *Sota,* 5a.

equally problematic. What we need to aim for in giving feedback to children is accuracy coupled with confidence that with hard work they can continue to develop their intellectual and emotional capacities.

4. Praise that is Experienced by the Child as Sincere:

    Effective praise that promotes persistence and patience in the face of challenge needs to be sincere and descriptive. In contrast, praise that is overly effusive or overly general can leave children feeling unmotivated and manipulated.[5] This is particularly true when children believe that the praise is unearned, either, because they didn't work hard enough to warrant this positive feedback, or because it is for work that they didn't do particularly well. William Damon, a professor of Education at the Stanford School of Education, points out that when praise comes across as false, children tend to pick up a subtle message that they are not measuring up. Empty flattery, says Damon, can lead to questions like: "What's wrong with me?" or "Why do people work so hard to make me feel good even when I don't deserve it?"[6]

    Parenting experts have often noted that when children feel that they don't deserve the positive feedback that they are getting they might work to sabotage the quality of their work because of uncomfortable feelings about the discrepancy between their self-concept and the feedback they are receiving.

5. Performance Viewed as Stemming from Hard Work Rather Than Innate Ability:

    As noted earlier, when children are praised in a manner that focuses on their ability rather than their effort, the child will be less persistent and less patient when completing the task. For example, in one study, preschoolers given praise such as "you're a good boy" were more likely to meet later challenges with helplessness and impatience than were children who were praised for working diligently on the task.[7]

    Dweck and her colleagues recommend that parents can promote a productive mindset in their children by asking them: "when do you feel smart?" If your child gives such answers as "when I don't mess up." Or "when I finish my work before anybody else in class.", their mindset is likely dominated by a view of their abilities as fixed, an approach to learning that is clearly problematic. In contrast, parents should try to motivate their children by instilling in them a view of feeling most successful when they master challenges and deal successfully with mistakes. Such children say that they feel smart when they are succeeding in doing hard work or when they figure out how to complete a difficult homework assignment on their own.

Excerpted from *Life in the Balance: Torah Perspectives on Positive Psychology* [New York: Shaar Press, 2014], pp. 189–195, with permission of the authors.

---

[5] Lepper, M., Woolverton, M., Mumme, D. , & Gurtner, J. (1993). Motivational techniques of expert human tutors: Lessons for the design of computer-based tutors. In S. P. Lajoie & S. J. Derry (Eds.), *Computers as Cognitive Tools* (pp. 75–105). Hillsdale, NJ: Erlbaum.

[6] Damon, W. (1995). *Greater Expectations: Overcoming the Culture of Indulgence in America's Homes and Schools.* New York: Free Press.

[7] Kamins, M. L., & Dweck, C. S. (1999). Person versus process praise and criticism: Implications for contingent self-worth and coping. *Developmental Psychology*, 35, 835–847.

10 THINGS YOU SHOULD NEVER SAY TO YOUR KIDS

BY MICHELLE CROUCH

You probably wouldn't use old-school phrases like "Wait until your father gets home" or "I wish you were more like your sister" with your kids. But there are lots of less obvious ones that you should avoid, for their sake and yours.

1. "Great Job."
Research has shown that tossing out a generic phrase like "Good girl" or "Way to go" every time your child masters a skill makes her dependent on your affirmation rather than her own motivation, says *Parents* advisor Jenn Berman, Psy.D., author of *The A to Z Guide to Raising Happy, Confident Kids*. Save the kudos for when they're truly warranted, and be as specific as you can. Instead of "Super game," say, "That was a nice assist. I like how you looked for your teammate."

2. "Practice makes perfect."
It's true that the more time your child devotes, the sharper his skills will become. However, this adage can ramp up the pressure he feels to win or excel. "It sends the message that if you make mistakes, you didn't train hard enough," says Joel Fish, Ph.D., author of *101 Ways to Be a Terrific Sports Parent*. "I've seen kids beat themselves up, wondering, 'What's wrong with me? I practice, practice, practice, and I'm still not the best.'" Instead, encourage your child to work hard because he'll improve and feel proud of his progress.

3. "You're okay."
When your child scrapes his knee and bursts into tears, your instinct may be to reassure him that he's not badly hurt. But telling him he's fine may only make him feel worse. "Your kid is crying because he's not okay," says Dr. Berman. Your job is to help him understand and deal with his emotions, not discount them. Try giving him a hug and acknowledging what he's feeling by saying something like, "That was a scary fall." Then ask whether he'd like a bandage or a kiss (or both).

4. "Hurry up!"
Your child dawdles over her breakfast, insists on tying her own sneakers (even though she hasn't quite mastered the technique yet), and is on pace to be late for school—again. But pushing her to get a move on creates additional stress, says Linda Acredolo, Ph.D., coauthor of *Baby Minds*. Soften your tone slightly by saying, "Let's hurry," which sends the message that the two of you are on the same team. You can also turn the act of getting ready into a game: "Why don't we race to see who can get her pants on first?"

5. "I'm on a diet."
Watching your weight? Keep it to yourself. If your child sees you stepping on the scale every day and hears you talk about being "fat," she may develop an unhealthy body image, says Marc S. Jacobson, M.D., professor of pediatrics and epidemiology at Nassau University Medical Center, in East Meadow, New York. It's better to say, "I'm eating healthy because I like the way it makes me feel." Take the same tack with working out. "I need to exercise" can sound like a complaint, but "It's beautiful outside—I'm going to take a walk" may inspire her to join you.

6. "We can't afford that."
It's easy to use this default response when your child begs you for the latest toy. But doing so sends the message that you're not in control of your finances, which can be scary for kids, says Jayne Pearl, the author of *Kids and Money*. Grade-schoolers may also call you on this claim if you turn around and make an expensive household purchase. Choose an alternative way to convey the same idea, such as, "We're not going to buy that because we're saving our money for more important things." If she insists on discussing it further, you have a perfect window to start a conversation about how to budget and manage money.

7. "Don't talk to strangers."

This is a tough concept for a young child to grasp. Even if a person is unfamiliar, she may not think of him as a stranger if he's nice to her. Plus, kids may take this rule the wrong way and resist the help of police officers or firefighters whom they don't know, says Nancy McBride, executive director for the National Center for Missing & Exploited Children, Florida Regional Office, in Lake Park. Instead of warning her about strangers, bring up scenarios ("What would you do if a man you don't know offers you candy and a ride home?"), have her explain what she'd do, then guide her to the proper course of action. Since the vast majority of child-abduction cases involve someone a kid already knows, you might also adopt McBride's favorite safety mantra: "If anyone makes you feel sad, scared, or confused, you need to tell me right away."

8. "Be careful."

Saying this while your child is balancing on the monkey bars at the playground actually makes it more likely that he'll fall. "Your words distract him from what he's doing, so he loses focus," says Deborah Carlisle Solomon, author of *Baby Knows Best*. If you're feeling anxious, move close to spot him in case he takes a tumble, being as still and quiet as you can.

9. "No dessert unless you finish your dinner."

Using this expression increases a child's perceived value of the treat and diminishes his enjoyment of the meal itself—the opposite of what you want to accomplish, says *Parents* advisor David Ludwig, M.D., Ph.D., director of the New Balance Foundation Obesity Prevention Center at Boston Children's Hospital and author of *Ending the Food Fight*. Tweak your message along these lines: "First we eat our meal and then we have dessert." The wording change, though subtle, has a far more positive impact on your child.

10. "Let me help."

When your child is struggling to build a block tower or finish a puzzle, it's natural to want to give him a hand. Don't. "If you jump in too soon, that can undermine your child's independence because he'll always be looking to others for answers," says Myrna Shure, Ph.D., professor emeritus of psychology at Drexel University in Philadelphia and author of *Raising a Thinking Child*. Instead, ask guiding questions to help him solve the problem: "Do you think the big piece or the little one should go at the bottom? Why do you think that? Let's give it a try."

the art of parenting

Lesson 6

The Road to Jewish Adulthood

To instill in our children a strong Jewish identity and proper Jewish values, we need to operate with long-term educational goals. We need to prepare our children for the challenges to their Jewish identity that they will inevitably encounter. As parents, what is our role in ensuring Jewish continuity and what is the best way to do so successfully?

Introduction

Marriage, Career, and Swimming Skills

LEARNING EXERCISE 1

In your opinion, what are some of the most important concrete, legislatable parental obligations?

1. _____

   _____

   _____

2. _____

   _____

   _____

3. _____

   _____

   _____

   _____

Text 1

Talmud, Kidushin 29a

הָאָב חַיָּב בִּבְנוֹ לָמוּלוֹ, וְלִפְדּוֹתוֹ, וּלְלַמְּדוֹ תוֹרָה, וּלְהַשִּׂיאוֹ אִשָּׁה, וּלְלַמְּדוֹ אוּמָנוּת, וְיֵשׁ אוֹמְרִים אַף לְהַשִּׁיטוֹ בְּמַיִם.

A father is obligated to circumcise his son, redeem him [if he is a firstborn], teach him Torah, take a wife for him, and teach him a profession. Some say that a father is also obligated to teach his child to swim.

Babylonian Talmud

A literary work of monumental proportions that draws upon the legal, spiritual, intellectual, ethical, and historical traditions of Judaism. The 37 tractates of the Babylonian Talmud contain the teachings of the Jewish sages from the period after the destruction of the 2nd Temple through the 5th century CE. It has served as the primary vehicle for the transmission of the Oral Law and the education of Jews over the centuries; it is the entry point for all subsequent legal, ethical, and theological Jewish scholarship.

QUESTION FOR DISCUSSION

Compare the answers you provided to Learning Exercise 1 to the Talmud's list of parental obligations. Are there any glaring omissions in the Talmud's list?

FIGURE 6.1

Parental Obligations

Religious	Universal
Circumcise child	Find a spouse for child
Redeem the firstborn	Teach child a profession
Teach child Torah	Teach child how to swim

QUESTION FOR DISCUSSION

What commonality do the three universal obligations share?

Text 2

Rashi, Kidushin 29a 📖

אַף לְהַשִּׂיטוֹ בְּנָהָר: שֶׁמָּא יְפָרוֹשׂ בִּסְפִינָה וְתִטְבַּע וְיִסְתַּכֵּן אִם אֵין יוֹדֵעַ לָשׁוּט.

Also obligated to teach his child to swim: The child might one day embark upon a ship that will sink, and his life will be in danger if he does not know how to swim.

Rabbi Shlomo Yitschaki (Rashi)
1040–1105

Most noted biblical and Talmudic commentator. Born in Troyes, France, Rashi studied in the famed *yeshivot* of Mainz and Worms. His commentaries on the Pentateuch and the Talmud, which focus on the straightforward meaning of the text, have appeared in virtually every edition of the Talmud and Bible.

FIGURE 6.2

Universal Parental Obligations

Obligation	Larger Idea
Find a spouse for child	Raise a child that is emotionally mature and capable of maintaining spousal and familial relationships.
Teach child a profession	Provide your child with the practical skills necessary to survive and succeed in life.
Teach child how to swim	Teach your child the skills necessary to deal with the unexpected risks that he or she might encounter.

Moral Self-Sufficiency

Text 3a

Genesis 18:19 📖

כִּי יְדַעְתִּיו לְמַעַן אֲשֶׁר יְצַוֶּה אֶת בָּנָיו וְאֶת בֵּיתוֹ אַחֲרָיו וְשָׁמְרוּ דֶּרֶךְ ה' לַעֲשׂוֹת צְדָקָה וּמִשְׁפָּט.

I love Abraham because he instructs his children and his household after him to follow the path of God by doing righteousness (charity) and justice.

Text 3b

Rabbi Avraham Shmuel Binyamin Sofer, *Ketav Sofer*, ad loc. 📖

Rabbi Avraham Shmuel Binyamin Sofer
(*Ketav Sofer*)
1815–1872

Exegete and halachist. Rabbi Sofer was the son of the famed Rabbi Moshe Sofer, the *Chatam Sofer*. In 1839, upon the passing of his father, Rabbi Sofer became the rabbi of Pressburg (Bratislava) and dean of the famed Pressburg Yeshiva. He authored works on the Pentatuech and Talmud, as well as many halachic responsa. He is best known as the *Ketav Sofer*, after the title of his written works.

וְהַיְינוּ "אֲשֶׁר יְצַוֶּה אֶת בָּנָיו וּבֵיתוֹ אַחֲרָיו", עַד שֶׁגַּם אַחֲרָיו כְּשֶׁלֹּא יַעֲמוֹד עֲלֵיהֶם, יִשְׁמְרוּ "דֶּרֶךְ ה' לַעֲשׂוֹת צְדָקָה וּמִשְׁפָּט", לֹא מִשּׁוּם שֶׁיִּרְצוּ לַעֲשׂוֹת רְצוֹן אֲבִיהֶם אַבְרָהָם, אֶלָּא שֶׁיַּעֲשׂוּ מִשּׁוּם שֶׁהוּא צְדָקָה וּמִשְׁפָּט.

"He instructs his children and his household after him." Abraham's education was such that even *after him*, i.e., even when he was no longer there to instruct his children, they "followed the path of God by doing righteousness and justice." They did so not in deference to their father Abraham's wishes, but because they understood that it was the right and just thing to do.

Jewish Self-Sufficiency

Text 4

The Rebbe, Rabbi Menachem M. Schneerson, *Torat Menachem* 5744, 1:105 📜

הַחִינּוּךְ מִטִּבְעוֹ הוּא לִקְבּוֹעַ בְּנַפְשׁוֹ שֶׁל הַיֶּלֶד עִקְרוֹנוֹת וִיסוֹדוֹת שֶׁמֵּהֶם
אֵין לָזוּז בְּכָל מָקוֹם וּבְכָל זְמַן: בְּנוֹגֵעַ לִבְנֵי אָדָם בִּכְלָל אֵלֶּה הֵם עִקְרוֹנוֹת
הַצֶּדֶק וְהַיּוֹשֶׁר וכו', וּבְנוֹגֵעַ לִבְנֵי יִשְׂרָאֵל בִּפְרָט – הָעִקָּרוֹן הוּא הָאֱמוּנָה
הָאֵיתָנָה בַּה' אֶחָד וּבְתוֹרָתוֹ, שֶׁ"זֹאת הַתּוֹרָה לֹא תְּהֵי מוּחְלֶפֶת" . . .

הַחִינּוּךְ שֶׁל הַיֶּלֶד הַיְּהוּדִי תְּחִילָתוֹ הִיא – הַחְדָּרַת הַהַכָּרָה שֶׁהַתּוֹרָה
הִיא חַיֵּינוּ וְאֹרֶךְ יָמֵינוּ, וְלָכֵן, מוּבָן שֶׁאֵין דָּבָר בָּעוֹלָם הֶחָשׁוּב
לָאָדָם יוֹתֵר מִן הַתּוֹרָה, דָּבָר הֶעָלוּל לְשַׁנּוֹת הַתּוֹרָה, כְּשֵׁם שֶׁאִי
אֶפְשָׁר לְשַׁנּוֹת אֶת הַחַיִּים (כִּי אֵין דָּבָר הֶחָשׁוּב מִן הַחַיִּים).

The goal of education is to inculcate children with moral foundations and ironclad principles from which they should never stray. For humankind, these are the universal principles of justice and fairness; for Jews, this also includes absolute belief in God and in the truth and immutability of His Torah. . . .

Jewish education starts with instilling within the children the conviction that "the Torah is our life and the length of our days" [i.e., Torah is synonymous with life]. Just as nothing can override the paramount importance of life, nothing can override the paramount importance of Torah.

Rabbi Menachem Mendel Schneerson
1902–1994

The towering Jewish leader of the 20th century, known as "the Lubavitcher Rebbe," or simply as "the Rebbe." Born in southern Ukraine, the Rebbe escaped Nazi-occupied Europe, arriving in the U.S. in June 1941. The Rebbe inspired and guided the revival of traditional Judaism after the European devastation, impacting virtually every Jewish community the world over. The Rebbe often emphasized that the performance of just one additional good deed could usher in the era of Mashiach. The Rebbe's scholarly talks and writings have been printed in more than 200 volumes.

Text 5

Alan M. Dershowitz, *The Vanishing American Jew*
[Boston: Little, Brown, 1997], pp. 1–2

Alan M. Dershowitz
1938–

American lawyer, jurist, and political commentator. Mr. Dershowitz was a professor of law at Harvard University for half a century; he achieved that position at the age of 28, the youngest full professor of law in the history of the school. Dershowitz is an advocate of Israel and an activist civil liberties lawyer who takes half of his cases *pro bono*. He has written 20 books, including *The Case for Israel*.

American Jewish life is in danger of disappearing, just as most American Jews have achieved everything we ever wanted: acceptance, influence, affluence, equality. As the result of skyrocketing rates of intermarriage and assimilation, as well as "the lowest birth rate of any religious or ethnic community in the United States," the era of enormous Jewish influence on American life may soon be coming to an end. . . . One Harvard study predicts that if current demographic trends continue, the American Jewish community is likely to number less than 1 million and conceivably as few as 10,000 by the time the United States celebrates its tricentennial in 2076. Other projections suggest that early in the next century, American Jewish life as we know it will be a shadow of its current, vibrant self—consisting primarily of isolated pockets of ultra-Orthodox Hasidim.

Jews have faced dangers in the past, but this time we may be unprepared to confront the newest threat to our survival as a people, because its principal cause is our own success as individuals. Our long history of victimization has prepared us to defend against those who would destroy us out of hatred; indeed, our history has forged a Jewish identity far too dependent on persecution and victimization by our enemies. But today's most serious threats come not from those who would persecute us, but from those who would, without any malice, kill us with kindness—by assimilating us, marrying us, and merging with us out of respect, admiration, and even love.

What are some best practices that parents can implement in their quest to raise proud and self-sufficient Jews?

Jew in Training

Text 6

Tosefta, Chagigah 1:3 📖

קָטָן שֶׁאֵין צָרִיךְ לְאִמּוֹ חַיָּב בְּסוּכָּה . . . יוֹדֵעַ לְנַעֲנֵעַ יוֹדֵעַ בְּלוּלָב,
יוֹדֵעַ לְהִתְעַטֵּף יוֹדֵעַ בְּצִיצִית, יוֹדֵעַ לְדַבֵּר אָבִיו מְלַמְּדוֹ שְׁמַע.

When a child no longer clings to his mother, we teach him to observe the mitzvah of *sukah*. . . . When he is capable of shaking [the four species], we train him to take the *lulav*. When he is capable of dressing himself, we give him *tsitsit* to wear. As soon as he knows to speak, his father teaches him to say the *Shema*.

Tosefta

A compendium of laws similar in format to that of the Mishnah; it consists of teachings of the sages of the Mishnah. At times, the material in both works is similar; at other times, there are significant differences between the two. The Talmud often compares these texts in its analysis. According to tradition, the *Tosefta* was redacted by Rabbis Chiyah and Oshiyah in the beginning of the 3rd century in the Land of Israel.

Text 7

Rashi, Chagigah 6a

אֵין חִינוּךְ קָטָן אֶלָא כְּדֵי לְהַנְהִיגוֹ שֶׁיְּהֵא סָרוּךְ אַחַר מִנְהָגוֹ לִכְשֶׁיַּגְדִּיל.

The purpose of education is to habituate children to certain behaviors, so that when they grow up, it has already become second nature.

You Hit the Jackpot!

Text 8

Rabbi Jonathan Sacks, PhD, "A Mystical Covenant," www.chabad.org

Rabbi Jonathan Sacks, PhD
1948–

Former chief rabbi of the United Kingdom. Rabbi Sacks attended Cambridge University and received his doctorate from King's College, London. A prolific and influential author, his books include *Will We Have Jewish Grandchildren?* and *The Dignity of Difference.* He received the Jerusalem Prize in 1995 for his contributions to enhancing Jewish life in the Diaspora, was knighted and made a life peer in 2005, and became Baron Sacks of Aldridge in 2009.

I have read many works of post-holocaust Jewish theology. And they all ask the same question. They ask what unites us—the Jewish people—today, with all our divisiveness and arguments. And in them I read the same answer: What unites us as Jewish people today is memories of the Holocaust, fears of antisemitism. What unites us as a people is that other people hate us.

The Rebbe taught the opposite message. What unites us, he taught, is not that other people don't like us, but that God loves us; that every one of us is a fragment of the Divine presence and together we are the physical presence of God on earth. Surely that message—spiritual, mystical as it is—is so much more powerful, so much more noble, so much more benign than the alternative.

Text 9

Rabbi Moshe Feinstein, *Darash Moshe, Parashat Vayetze* and *Shabbat Hagadol* 🔊

אֵלּוּ הַמִּתְפָּאֲרִים שֶׁכְּבָר הֵן בַּאַמֶעְרִיקָא חֲמִשִּׁים שָׁנָה וְיוֹתֵר וְלֹא חִלְּלוּ
שַׁבָּת, אִי אֶפְשָׁר לָהֶם לְחַנֵּךְ אֶת זַרְעָם. כִּי אַף שֶׁהוּא עָמַד בְּנִסָּיוֹן, מִכָּל
מָקוֹם זַרְעוֹ אֶפְשָׁר שֶׁלֹּא יוּכְלוּ לַעֲמוֹד בְּנִסָּיוֹן . . . וְנִמְצָא שֶׁבְּחִנּוּכוֹ
אַדְרַבָּה קִלְקֵל אֶת בָּנָיו שֶׁאָמַר לָהֶם שֶׁקָּשֶׁה לִשְׁמוֹר אֶת הַתּוֹרָה אַף
הוּא בְּכָל זֹאת שָׁמַר, וְיָבוֹא מִזֶּה שֶׁהֵם לֹא יוּכְלוּ לִשְׁמוֹר . . .

כְּשֶׁמְּדַבְּרִים תּוֹכָחָה צָרִיךְ לְהַסְבִּיר לְהֵיפוּךְ, כִּי טוֹבָה וּמַתָּנָה גְדוֹלָה הִיא הַתּוֹרָה
וּמִצְוֹת שֶׁבָּחַר בָּנוּ מִכָּל הָעַמִּים וְנָתַן לָנוּ תּוֹרָתוֹ . . . וְהַהֲנָאָה הָאֲמִיתִּית הוּא
בִּשְׁמִירַת הַתּוֹרָה וְהַמִּצְוֹת אַף בָּעוֹלָם הַזֶּה, וְלֵיכָּא שׁוּם הֶפְסֵד מִקִּיּוּם הַתּוֹרָה
וּמִצְוֹתֶיהָ כִּי הַכֹּל הוּא מִשֶּׁל הַקָּדוֹשׁ בָּרוּךְ הוּא וּבוֹ תָּלוּי כָּל חַיֵּינוּ וְכָל אֲשֶׁר
נָתַן לָנוּ וְהֵם חַיֵּי נֶצַח לָעוֹלָם הַבָּא. וְאַף אִם מִזְדַּמֵּן לִפְעָמִים שֶׁסּוֹבְלִין בְּעִנְיְנֵי
פַּרְנָסָה לֹא נֶחֱשָׁב זֶה לְשׁוּם צַעַר נֶגֶד הַטּוֹבָה וְהַהֲנָאָה מֵהַתּוֹרָה וּמִצְוֹתֶיהָ, כְּמוֹ
שֶׁלֹּא מַחֲשִׁיב הָאָדָם צַעַר נְסִיעָתוֹ כְּשֶׁהֹלֵךְ לְמָקוֹם שֶׁהִרְוִיחַ שָׁם מָמוֹן הַרְבֵּה.

Those who pride themselves for having been in America for fifty years without having desecrated the Shabbat often find that they cannot educate their children to follow in their footsteps. This is so because implied in their attitude is that they observed the Torah despite the difficulty involved and therefore are deserving of much credit. While the children admire their parents for having overcome great adversity and challenge, they themselves do not wish to be martyrs for the Jewish cause. The attitude of the parents, then, is responsible for the children's abandoning of Jewish practice. . . .

When admonishing [a child for disregarding a Jewish value], we need to emphasize the very opposite. We need to express that the Torah and *mitzvot* are tremendous gifts that God chose to give His people; . . . that observing

Rabbi Moshe Feinstein
1895–1986

Leading halachic authority of the 20th century. Rabbi Feinstein was appointed rabbi of Luban, Belarus, in 1921. He immigrated to the U.S. in 1937 and became the dean of Metivta Tiferet Yerushalayim in New York. Rabbi Feinstein's halachic decisions have been published in a multi-volume collection entitled *Igrot Moshe*.

Torah and *mitzvot* leads to great benefit even in this physical realm; that no detriment results from performing *mitzvot*—because our lives and all that we have is from God and directed by Him; and that Torah grants us eternal life in the World to Come.

Furthermore, we explain to our children that even if it happens that [observing the Torah causes] a financial loss, it is barely significant in comparison to the great benefits that Torah brings, in much the same way that the hassle of travel is considered inconsequential when a great financial windfall awaits the traveler at the destination.

Text 10

Herman Wouk, *This is My God* [Boston: Little Brown and Co., 1987], pp. 45–46

Herman Wouk
1915–

American novelist and playwright. Wouk was born in New York City to a Jewish-Russian immigrant family. When the U.S. entered World War II, he joined the Navy, serving in the Pacific Theater for four years. Wouk's wartime experiences gave him the material and background for his best seller and Pulitzer-Prize-winning *The Caine Mutiny*. *This Is My God* was his best-selling affirmation of faith in traditional Judaism, penned after much self-examination and exposure to many secular influences. His later works include the novel *Inside, Outside*, which discusses Judaism in private life and in politics, and *The Will to Live On: This Is Our Heritage*.

Leaving the gloomy theatre, the littered coffee cups, the jumbled scarred-up scripts, the haggard actors, the shouting stagehands, the bedeviled director, the knuckle-gnawing producer, the clattering typewriter, and the dense tobacco smoke and backstage dust, I have come home. It has been a startling change, very like a brief return from the wars. My wife and my boys, whose existence I have almost forgotten in the anxious shoring up of the tottering ruin, are waiting for me, gay, dressed in holiday clothes, and looking to me marvelously attractive. We have sat down to a splendid dinner, at a table graced with flowers and the old Sabbath symbols: the burning candles, the twisted loaves, the stuffed fish and my grandfather's silver goblet brimming with wine. I have blessed my boys with the ancient blessing; we have sung the pleasantly syncopated Sabbath table hymns. The talk has had little to do with tottering ruins. My wife and I have caught up with our week's conversation. The boys, knowing that the Sabbath is the occasion for asking questions, have asked them. The Bible, the encyclopedia, the atlas, have piled up on the table. We talk of Judaism, and there are the usual impossible boys' queries about God, which my wife and I field clumsily but as well as we can. For me it is a retreat into restorative magic.

Saturday has passed in much the same manner. The boys are at home in the synagogue, and they like it. They like even more the assured presence of their parents. In the weekday press of schooling, household chores, and work—and especially in a play-producing time—it often happens that they see little of us. On the Sabbath we are always here, and they know it. They know too that I am not working, and that my wife is at her ease. It is their day. . . .

My producer one Saturday night said to me, "I don't envy you your religion, but I envy you your Sabbath."

Text 11

Sidur, daily morning prayers

אֲבָל אֲנַחְנוּ עַמְּךָ בְּנֵי בְרִיתֶךָ בְּנֵי אַבְרָהָם אֹהַבְךָ שֶׁנִּשְׁבַּעְתָּ לוֹ בְּהַר הַמּוֹרִיָּה,

זֶרַע יִצְחָק יְחִידוֹ. שֶׁנֶּעֱקַד עַל גַּבֵּי הַמִּזְבֵּחַ, עֲדַת יַעֲקֹב בִּנְךָ בְּכוֹרֶךָ שֶׁמֵּאַהֲבָתְךָ

שֶׁאָהַבְתָּ אוֹתוֹ, וּמִשִּׂמְחָתְךָ שֶׁשָּׂמַחְתָּ בּוֹ, קָרָאתָ אֶת שְׁמוֹ יִשְׂרָאֵל וִישֻׁרוּן.

לְפִיכָךְ אֲנַחְנוּ חַיָּבִים לְהוֹדוֹת לְךָ וּלְשַׁבֵּחֲךָ וּלְפָאֶרְךָ

וּלְבָרֵךְ וּלְקַדֵּשׁ וְלָתֵן שֶׁבַח וְהוֹדָיָה לִשְׁמֶךָ.

אַשְׁרֵינוּ, מַה טּוֹב חֶלְקֵנוּ, וּמַה נָּעִים גּוֹרָלֵנוּ, וּמַה יָּפָה יְרֻשָּׁתֵנוּ.

We are Your nation, the people of Your covenant: the children of Abraham Your beloved, to whom You swore on Mount Moriah; the descendants of Isaac, his only son, who was bound upon the altar; the community of Jacob, Your firstborn, whose name You called Israel and Yeshurun because of Your love for him and Your delight in him.

Therefore, it is incumbent upon us to thank, praise, and glorify You, to bless, to sanctify, and to offer praise and thanksgiving to Your Name.

Fortunate are we! How good is our portion, how pleasant is our lot, and how beautiful our heritage!

Rabbi Joseph B. Soloveitchik, PhD, "A Tribute to the Rebbetzin of Talne," *Tradition* 17:2, Spring 1978, pp. 76–77

One learns much from father: how to read a text—the Bible or the Talmud—how to comprehend, how to analyze, how to conceptualize, how to classify, how to infer, how to apply, etc. . . . One also learns from father what to do and what not to do, what is morally right and what is morally wrong. Father teaches the son the discipline of thought as well as the discipline of action. Father's tradition is an intellectual-moral one. That is why it is identified with *mussar*, which is the Biblical term for discipline.

What kind of a Torah does the mother pass on? . . . Permit me to draw upon my own experiences. I used to have long conversations with my mother. In fact, it was a monologue rather than a dialogue. She talked and I "happened" to overhear. What did she talk about? . . . She talked *me'inyana de'yoma* [current events]. I used to watch her arranging the house in honor of a holiday. I used to see her recite prayers; I used to watch her recite the *sidra* [Torah portion] every Friday night and I still remember the nostalgic tune. I learned from her very much.

Most of all I learned that Judaism expresses itself not only in formal compliance with the law but also in a living experience. She taught me that there is a flavor, a scent and warmth to *mitzvot*. I learned from her the most important thing in life—to feel the presence of the Almighty and the gentle pressure of His hand resting upon my frail shoulders. Without her teachings, which quite often were

Rabbi Joseph B. Soloveitchik
1903–1993

Talmudist and philosopher. A scion of a famous Lithuanian rabbinical family, Rabbi Soloveitchik was one of the most influential Jewish personalities, leaders, and thinkers of the 20th century. In 1941, he became professor of Talmud at RIETS—Yeshiva University; in this capacity, he ordained more rabbis than anyone else in Jewish history. Among his published works are *Halakhic Man* and *Lonely Man of Faith*.

transmitted to me in silence, I would have grown up a soulless being, dry and insensitive.

The laws of Shabbat, for instance, were passed on to me by my father. . . . The Shabbat as a living entity, as a queen, was revealed to me by my mother. . . . The fathers knew much about the Shabbat; the mothers lived the Shabbat, experienced her presence, and perceived her beauty and splendor.

Transition to Adulthood

Text 13

Rabbi Eliezer Papo, *Pele Yo'ets*, "Love for Sons and Daughters" 🔊

Rabbi Eliezer Papo
1785–1826

Moralist and ethicist. Born in Sarajevo, Rabbi Papo was an outstanding rabbinic scholar, noted for his piety and spirituality. He served as rabbi of the community of Selestria (today in Bulgaria). In spite of the brevity of his life, Rabbi Papo achieved remarkable depth and breadth in his rabbinic scholarship, and left to posterity a significant literary legacy—most notably, his classical moral treatise *Pele Yo'ets*.

וּלְפְעָמִים יַעֲשֶׂה עַצְמוֹ כְּחֵרֵשׁ לֹא יִשְׁמַע וּכְאִלּוּ אֵינוֹ רוֹאֶה, וְלִפְעָמִים יְבַטֵּל רְצוֹנוֹ מִפְּנֵי רְצוֹנָם. וְזֶה כְּלַל גָּדוֹל הָרוֹצֶה לְזַכּוֹת אֶת נַפְשׁוֹ וְנֶפֶשׁ בָּנָיו אַחֲרָיו.

There are times when parents have to act as if they cannot hear and cannot see, times when they must yield to the wishes of their child. This is a fundamental rule for those who wish to do right by themselves and by their children.

Conclusion

Text 14

Michael Lazerow, "Entrepreneur's Choice: Is Your Kid Worth $100 Million?" *LinkedIn Pulse*, July 8, 2013

Would you sell one of your kids for $100 million? Be honest.

Imagine your little Ben didn't burp or fart or throw up when your boss came over. Or think flushing the toilet was "mom's job." But sat quietly with other Benjamins in piles of crisp, neatly organized rows, ready to be enjoyed.

No talking back. No wanting to play at 6 am after drunken date night. No asking for homework help after your long day at work.

Food expenses, tuition and summer camp payments, baby-sitting fees. Gone. Gone. And gone.

It takes nine months and change to create a kid. It takes a lifetime, if you're lucky, to earn even a small fraction of $100 million. And most die trying, holding a bag full of regrets and a souped-up LinkedIn profile.

Surely few, if any, would say they'd accept this offer. An unscientific poll of several of my friends uncovered no takers.

One of my friends, James Altucher, commented:

"I would sell a leg or an arm or have a lobotomy. I would do anything to keep them free. I would be a slave on a ship. I would be thrown in prison. I would pray all day. I'd do anything, rather than have my kids taken away. I would be

Michael Lazerow

Serial entrepreneur and founder of several successful media companies. Most recently in 2007, Michael co-founded Buddy Media, Inc., a privately held company that offers social media solutions to some of the world's largest brands.

beaten to a pulp. I would take drugs. I would take cyanide. Nothing would take them from my side. My kids were given to me. It's been my honor since birth." . . .

Since no one would make this trade . . . we must all value our kids much more than $100 million. Yet very few of us act that way. . . .

What decisions would you make differently if you truly valued your children more than $100 million?

EXERCISE FOR THE WEEK

Select one area of Jewish practice that you will focus on and wherein you will attempt to increase your passion and excitement.

Tips:

- *Read a book on the topic.*
- *Memorize some short meditations on the topic.*
- *Do a project with your child related to this area of interest.*
- *Buy or make a beautiful accessory that will complement your area of focus.*

Key Points

1. The primary goal of parenting is to raise children who are equipped to become self-sufficient adults—self-sufficient materially, emotionally, and in terms of their value systems.

2. Jewish parents have the added responsibility of raising Jewish children. Rearing our children Jewishly is an obligation to God and a gift to our children, because it allows them to achieve complete self-expression.

3. As Jewish parents, our goal is to raise self-sufficient Jews who will proudly carry on the age-old tradition when they establish households of their own.

4. We help assure our children's Jewish future by encouraging them from a young age to *act* like Jews and perform Jewish rituals. This way we create habit patterns that continue into adulthood.

5. If we wish for our children to make Judaism a real part of their adult lives, we need to present Judaism as an attractive option. If we consider Judaism and its laws and rituals as a burden, our children will shed the burden; if we consider Judaism as a gift and treasure, our children will likely cherish and embrace it. For this reason, we should not allow antisemitism and the Holocaust to define our Judaism.

6. Mothers have a special gift for injecting warmth and beauty into Judaism and its observances, thus creating beautiful memories and associations, and making our heritage appealing to their children.

7. As our children grow older and begin their transition to adulthood, we lessen our authority over them, in the hopes that they have attained healthy self-sufficiency.

8. On occasion, we should make time to think how incredibly great a gift our children are. Doing so will make it much easier to implement all we learned throughout this course.

Appendix A

Text 1a

Yom Kippur Eve Liturgy 📖

לְבֵן אוֹמֵר: יְשִׂימְךָ אֱלֹקִים כְּאֶפְרַיִם וְכִמְנַשֶּׁה . . .

וּלְבַת אוֹמֵר: יְשִׂימֵךְ אֱלֹקִים כְּשָׂרָה כְּרִבְקָה כְּרָחֵל וּכְלֵאָה . . .

יְבָרֶכְךָ ה׳ וְיִשְׁמְרֶךָ. יָאֵר ה׳ פָּנָיו אֵלֶיךָ וִיחֻנֶּךָּ. יִשָּׂא ה׳ פָּנָיו אֵלֶיךָ וְיָשֵׂם לְךָ שָׁלוֹם.

Blessing for Children

For a son: May God help you be like Ephraim and Manasseh. . . .

For a daughter: May God help you be like Sarah, Rebecca, Rachel, and Leah. . . .

"May God bless you and guard you. May God shine His countenance upon you and be gracious to you. May God turn His countenance toward you and give you peace" (Numbers 6:24-26).

Text 1b

Rabbi Shmuel Huminer, *Eved Hamelech, Netiv Mitzvotecha* 119a–120b 📖

לְהָבִין קְצָת לָמָה דַּוְקָא אֶפְרַיִם וּמְנַשֶּׁה נִתְיַחֲדוּ שֶׁיְּבָרֵךְ אִישׁ אֶת בְּנוֹ שֶׁיִּהְיֶה כְּמוֹתָם? . . .

וְהִנֵּה אֶפְרַיִם וּמְנַשֶּׁה נוֹלְדוּ וְנִתְגַּדְּלוּ בְּמִצְרַיִם אֶרֶץ טְמֵאָה וּרְחוֹקָה מְאֹד מִן הָאֱמוּנָה, וַאֲבִיהֶם מִשְׁנֶה לְמֶלֶךְ וּבְעִנְיְנֵי הַמְּלוּכָה הָיוּ בָּאִים אֶצְלוֹ שָׂרֵי מִצְרַיִם וְחַרְטוּמֵיהֶם שֶׁהָיוּ מְשֻׁקָּעִים בְּכַמָּה מִינֵי טֻמְאוֹת וּכְשׁוּפִים, וְאוֹר פְּנֵי קְדֻשַּׁת יִצְחָק אָבִינוּ וְיַעֲקֹב אָבִינוּ עֲדַיִן לֹא רָאוּ. וּכְשֶׁבָּא יַעֲקֹב אָבִינוּ לְמִצְרַיִם וּבָחַן וְרָאָה בְּאֶפְרַיִם וּמְנַשֶּׁה שֶׁלֹּא נִמְשְׁכוּ כְּלָל אַחַר טֻמְאַת מִצְרַיִם, וְלֹא נִתְפַּעֲלוּ וְלֹא לָמְדוּ כְּלָל מִמִּנְהֲגֵי וְנִמּוּסֵי מִצְרַיִם וְשָׂרֵיהֶם חַכְמֵיהֶם וְחַרְטוּמֵיהֶם. וְאַדְּרַבָּה גָּדְלוּ וְחוּנְּכוּ בְּדֶרֶךְ הַתּוֹרָה וְהַיִּרְאָה עַל בִּרְכֵּי יוֹסֵף הַצַּדִּיק אֲבִיהֶם, וְרָאָה גֹּדֶל צִדְקָתָם וּקְדֻשָּׁתָם שֶׁהֵם כְּבָר בְּמַדְרֵיגָה שֶׁרְאוּיִים לְהִתְחַשֵּׁב וּלְהִמָּנוֹת בְּתוֹךְ שְׁנֵים עָשָׂר שִׁבְטֵי יָ-הּ הַקְּדוֹשִׁים וְהַטְּהוֹרִים, וּבְוַדַּאי עָמְדוּ בָּזֶה נִסְיוֹנוֹת וְקוּשְׁיִים גְּדוֹלִים, וּבְכָל זֹאת הִתְגַּבְּרוּ עַל כָּל מִכְשׁוֹלִים וּמְנִיעוֹת וְדָרְכוּ אַךְ וְרַק בְּדֶרֶךְ הַקֹּדֶשׁ שֶׁל אֲבוֹתֵינוּ הַקְּדוֹשִׁים כְּפִי שְׁלֵימָדָם וְהִדְרִיכָם אֲבִיהֶם הַצַּדִּיק.

וְגַם כַּוָּנָה זוֹ יְכַוֵּין כָּל אִישׁ בְּבָרְכוֹ אֶת בָּנָיו וְתַלְמִידָיו וְכָל אִישׁ יִשְׂרָאֵל, שֶׁיֵּלְכוּ אַךְ וְרַק בְּדֶרֶךְ הַתּוֹרָה הַקְּדוֹשָׁה, וְלֹא יִלְמְדוּ וְלֹא יִתְפַּעֲלוּ כְּלָל מֵהָעוֹזְבִים דַּרְכֵי יוֹשֶׁר.

Rabbi Shmuel Huminer
1913–1977

Author and ethicist. Rabbi Hu-miner, a Jerusalem native and a descendant of an illustrious rabbinic family, was a student of Rabbi Isser Zalman Meltzer. At the age of 26, he published his first work, a digest of the laws of *lashon hara* (slander and other forms of forbidden speech). He proceeded to author many more books on a variety of topics, mostly based on the Musar philosophy.

Why were Manasseh and Ephraim singled out from among the others that parents should bless their sons to be like them?

Unlike the sons of Jacob, Manasseh and Ephraim were born and raised in Egypt, a land that was impure and very distant from the true faith. Because their father was viceroy, they were often in the presence of the ministers of Egypt and its magicians, who were steeped in all sorts of impurity and sorcery. They had not yet seen the light of the holiness that shone on the countenance of their great-grandfather Isaac and grandfather Jacob.

When Jacob came, he saw that Ephraim and Manasseh had not been drawn at all after the impurity of Egypt, and had not been influenced by the customs and mores of Egypt, its rulers, sages, and magicians, and had not absorbed their teachings. To the contrary: they had been raised and educated in the way of Torah and awe of God. . . . He saw the greatness of their righteousness and holiness. They were already at such a level that they were fit to be considered and to be counted among the pure and holy Twelve Tribes of God. It is certain that in achieving this they underwent great trials and difficulties. Nonetheless, they overcame every stumbling block and hindrance and followed the holy path of our holy forefathers as their holy father had led them and taught them.

It is with this idea in mind that people should bless their children, students, and every Jew—that they should walk exclusively and entirely in the path of the holy Torah and not learn from or be influenced by those who have deserted the paths of righteousness.

ADDITIONAL READINGS

THE LUBAVITCHER REBBE ON JEWISH EDUCATION

By the Grace of G-d
Erev Purim, 5729
Brooklyn, NY

Greeting and Blessing:

I was pleasantly surprised to note in your editorial column in the issue of February 28th excerpts of letters from your son, as well as the spirit of your commentaries in this connection. Inasmuch as there is no end to the good, I trust that there will be continuity in this direction and that, moreover, the good influence of your son will create a chain reaction infecting and affecting all the members of your family.

I am reminded of the well-known verse (end of Malachi): "And he [Elijah] will turn the heart of parents to the children," which, according to Rashi, means "through the children—he will induce the children, with love and good will, to go and speak to their parents to follow in the ways of G-d." And although I trust that in any case the parents are following the way of G-d, there is, as mentioned above, no end to the good, and always room for improvement in all matters of goodness and holiness, which are infinite, since they derive from the Infinite.

You and your wife are particularly privileged in that each of you has a substantial circle of readers, a considerable number of whom undoubtedly are influenced by your writings. Clearly, Divine Providence has bestowed upon you also a special responsibility. There is surely no need to elaborate on this to you.

May G-d grant that everything should be in accordance with the text and spirit of the Megillah—"For the Jews there was light, joy, gladness, and honor," in the fullest sense of these meaningful words.

Wishing you and yours a happy and inspiring Purim,

With blessing,

[signature]

P.S. In accordance with Jewish custom to offer a comment on a printed word, I will take the liberty to do so also in reference to the above-mentioned editorial, all the more so to avoid a misunderstanding that I fully agree with all that was said there. I trust you will not take amiss my remarks.

Rule of Force

I wish to take issue with you in the matter of your youngest daughter who, as you write, is eleven years old, and resisted starting Hebrew school, but you "did not force the issue." You can well imagine my reaction to this. For surely, if your eleven-year-old daughter would have resisted going to school altogether, you would have found it necessary to "force" the issue—if the term "force" can be applied here. Certainly, insofar as a Jewish child is concerned, her Hebrew education is at least as important to her as a general education.

This has been generally recognized throughout the ages, but it should be particularly recognized in our own day and age. For we have seen many of the greatest and saintliest of our people exterminated by a vicious enemy. Consequently, all of us who have been fortunate enough to survive must make up for this tremendous loss. On the other hand, the forces of complete assimilation have grown much stronger in the free and democratic countries. Worse still, in recent years assimilation has found expression not only with another people, but very often with such groups that have discarded all pretenses to morality and ethics, etc. etc.

True Understanding

You may consider my reference to your daughter's attitude, and to your attitude in this connection, no longer relevant, since you write that she has agreed to begin Hebrew school, though you immediately point out (with apparent satisfaction) that the method of instruction is "habet ushma" [comprehension]—a system which obviously does not aim to lead to "vaaseh" [and doing]. Surely there is no need to emphasize to you the fact that when the Torah was given to our people, naaseh [we will do] was not only a condition of acceptance of the Torah, but a prior condition—"naaseh" before "v'nishmah" [we will understand]. Our Sages of blessed memory pointed out that Jewish identity and the very basis of Jewish existence, for the individual as well as for the people as a whole, lies in this great principle of naaseh before v'nishmah. Certainly this is the way to train and educate a Jewish child.

To refer, again, to the Megillah at this time on the eve of Purim, we note that Haman argued, "There is one people, dispersed and divided among the nations, and their laws are different from those of any other people. Therefore, it is not worth for the king to spare them." Indeed, there were then, as there have been at all times, misguided individuals or groups who shared Haman's view that the trouble with Jews was their separate identity and otherness, and that the only solution is to do away with Jewish identity and separateness, and to assimilate.

However, the truth of the matter is, as we see also from the events related in the Megillah, that in order to avert the threat of Haman, Esther and Mordechai ordered the gathering of all the Jews together to emphasize their identity and strengthen their observance of their "differences" . . . it raised the esteem and respect of the Jews in the eyes of their former enemies. To the extent that Mordechai the Jew, who "did not bend his knee nor bow down," became the viceroy of the entire Persian empire.

Eternal Truth

Since the Torah is eternal, and the Megillah is part of the Torah, its message is eternal and always relevant. Thus, what was true for the Jews and their destiny in the days of Mordechai and Esther, is true for the Jews in the USA and the Holy Land and elsewhere. And just as the Jews could not take comfort and security in the fact that they had some influence at the court through Esther the Queen, and Mordechai, who had access to the Palace, which did not stop the enemies of the Jews from plotting the extermination of the Jewish people, so nowadays Jews cannot rely on any influence they can muster in the capitals of the world. But, in the final analysis, it is the Jewish adherence to the Torah and mitzvoth—the source of their life and strength that will topple all Hamans and bring "light, joy, gladness and honor."

It is not my custom to engage in homiletics, etc. The purpose of the above observations is a practical one, namely that the curriculum of your youngest daughter, as well as of all the family, will not be limited to habet ushma, but will also include aseh [doing] and, indeed, the basic Jewish approach of doing before even understanding. May G-d grant you and your wife true Yiddishe nachas [Jewish joy] from all your children.

PARENTHOOD: NATURAL AND REDEEMED

BY RABBI JOSEPH B. SOLEVEITCHIK, PhD

Natural Parenthood

The Bible tells us that "The man called his wife's name Eve *(Havah)* because she was the mother of all living things *(hai)*" (Gen. 3:20). But man's name is not identified with fatherhood; he is called *adam* or *ish,* but not *av.* His role as a father was not portrayed symbolically by his name, while Eve's role as a mother was; nothing reflects Adam's task as a father. In contradistinction to Adam's, Abraham's fatherhood did find an expression in his name. God added the letter *hei* to his name in order to make Abraham's fatherhood universal, to make him "a father of many nations" (Gen. 17:5). Why did a change take place when Abraham, the father of our nation, appeared on the scene? Apparently a new idea of fatherhood that was unknown to Adam was revealed to the world with the arrival of Abraham.

Adam was the father of the natural, unredeemed community; Abraham was the father of a redeemed, spiritual community. Adam sinned and acted contrary to God's will; Abraham proclaimed God's word as the highest law for man to abide by. Adam lost the paradise; Abraham wanted to restore the paradise to man. Apparently, the role of the father within the confines of the natural, sinful-egotistic, pleasure-minded and power-oriented community differs from that within the redeemed, covenantal, ethical, love-oriented and humble community. Within the first community, founded by Adam, the father's role is of such minimal significance that it is not worth being demonstrated by the name, while in the covenantal community the role is redeemed and elevated, infused with new meaning deserving of emphasis and mention.

In the natural community, the woman is more concerned with motherhood than the man with fatherhood. Motherhood, in contrast to fatherhood, bespeaks a long-enduring peculiar state of body and mind. The nine months of pregnancy, with all its attendant biological and psychological changes, the birth of the child with pain and suffering, the nursing of the baby and, later, the caretaking of and attending to the youngster—all form part of the motherhood experience. In a word, the woman is bound up with the child and she experiences her motherhood role in all her thought and feeling. The father, if he wants, can deny his fatherhood and forego responsibility. The mother is bound up with the child; the father can roam around forgetting everything. Motherhood is an experience—unredeemed and hence brutish, yet an experience. Physically, fatherhood implies nothing tangible and memorable. The male, bodily and mentally, does not experience his fatherhood.

In short, within the natural community the mother occupies a central position while the father is relegated to a role that is intangible and vague, since it does not imply any restrictive bonds. Motherhood is a fact that is foisted upon a woman. That is why the name of the woman was derived from her role as a mother, while Adam's name has nothing in common with his fatherhood. "Can a woman forget her baby or disown the child of her womb?" (Isaiah 49:15).

Redeemed Parenthood

With the emergence of Abraham and the founding of a new kind of community, the covenantal one, the vague role of fatherhood and the all-absorbing experience of motherhood were redeemed. New commitments were accepted; man began to live not only for himself, but for others as well. He became concerned with the destiny of others, and discovered in himself responsiveness not only to biological pressure but to the call of conscience, through which God addresses Himself to him. The fatherhood idea was redeemed, purged of its orgiastic-hedonic element, infused with life, and turned into a central reality on par with that of motherhood.

What is fatherhood in the covenantal society? It is the great educational commitment to the *masorah,* the tradition, the freely assumed obligation to hand down, to pass on to the child the covenant, a message, a code, a unique way of life, a tradition of *mish-*

pat u-tzedakah, of justice and charity. In the covenantal community, the father is promoted to teacher, and his role *ipso facto* is shifted from the periphery to the center on par with that of the mother. That is why Adam—as the representative of the natural community—was not aware of his fatherhood. Only with the emergence of the covenantal community and with the formulation of the doctrine of father-teacher was the fatherhood commitment suddenly revealed to us.

Motherhood expresses, as I explained before, a natural, unalterable reality, a factum. The woman becomes involved with her child within the natural community, while the man freely accepts fatherhood only in the covenantal community. However, not only did the role of the male undergo a change in the covenantal community, but that of the female did as well. Abraham personified fatherhood as a great commitment. Sarah became the first mother in the sense that her motherhood stemmed not only from instinctual involvement due to biological pressure but from free commitment as well. What was Sarah's commitment? The same as Abraham's: an educational *masorah* commitment to hand down and teach the covenant, God's word, the way of a covenantal life of *hesed u-tzedakah,* of kindness and charity.

Mother's job changed into a great mission; her preoccupation with the child was endowed with ethical meaning. She not only nurses the child physically, she brings him up; she assumes the role of educator. Motherhood is not only an experience but a commitment as well. At this juncture motherhood is hallowed on account of another idea which is linked up with the spontaneous free choice of motherhood on the part of the woman in the covenantal community. As "mother-teacher," the woman is no more connected with only the fruit of her womb, with the child she bore. As long as motherhood, like fatherhood, was rooted in biological facticity, its confine was very narrow and extended only to a clan. One can experience biological motherhood only in respect to one's own child. However, when motherhood was transformed into a commitment and being a mother was equated with being a teacher, an apostle of God, the carrier of God's covenant, His prophet, then motherhood, like fatherhood, was elevated to a universal spiritu-

al level. Instead of being just the father and mother of their offspring in a clannish sense, Abraham and Sarah accepted responsibility for the multitudes, for the world community of the committed. The father and mother of the clan were promoted to father- and mother-teachers of the entire covenantal community with all its universal aspirations. The letter *hei* was added to both of their names, signifying a transformation to universality. God promised Abraham that he would be "a father of many nations" (Gen. 17:4) and that Sarah "shall give rise to nations; rulers of peoples shall be of her" (17:16).

Sarah replaced Eve. The freely committed universal mother supplanted the instinctually involved natural mother. Eve was "the mother of all living"; Sarah, the mother of nations and kings. Eve's motherhood consisted in giving life in a natural sense to her child. It lacked, however, the element of leadership. Her motherhood was a result of a biological pressure, the consummation of a natural process. Sarah's was due to great vision, to a new mission she took on. She and "all the persons they had acquired in Haran" (Gen. 12:5)—her children/pupils—formed a covenantal community, one founded on education, a living tradition and commitment. Sarah redeemed the motherhood experience by taking a factum, a natural reality, and changing it into a commitment. Passive involvement became an active commitment; natural entanglement was elevated to a normative choice. The woman herself rose from a receptive to an active role. And the most important dimension which was added is that of universality, the capacity to assume motherhood vis-a-vis all children.

No more should a childless couple feel desolate and forsaken because the Almighty has not blessed them with an heir. The barren woman may lack the natural motherhood experience, but she can attain covenantal if not natural motherhood by choice, by commitment, by helping others, by contributing toward the strengthening of the covenantal community, by exposing children of other parents to the word of God. The Romans—to whom the idea of covenant was alien, who, in spite of their advanced technological achievements, never freed themselves from the bonds of the natural community—tried to compensate the childless man and woman by establishing the institution of adoption. Judaism did not need to create such an institution. The letter *hei* added to Abraham's and Sarah's names symbolized the exalted idea of covenantal fatherhood and motherhood, one which is realized not through natural but through spiritual-educational media which transcend the boundaries of a clan and extend into the open spaces of universality.

The Need for Sacrificial Action

However, any act of redemption is bound up with sacrificial action. A physiological reaction changes into meaningful hallowed action at any time the individual displays courage and the ability to answer the violent, orgiastic, hypnotic call of nature in the negative, thus incurring pain and suffering because of his refusal to cooperate with biological pressures that have not found their total release. Judaism identified sanctity with sacrifice, this identification being reflected in the status of utter and immutable sanctity, *kedushat ha-guf*, assigned halakhically to a *korban*. One cannot hallow anything unless one is ready to surrender, give up, and be defeated.

Let us analyze from this viewpoint the redeeming passional action of the covenantal mother.

Motherhood *per se,* even at the level of naturalness, is described by the Bible as a passional experience. On the one hand, the woman pays a much higher price than the father for engaging in sex. While the father is permitted by nature to walk off free, the mother becomes burdened with responsibilities for many long years. She loses her freedom and ability to order her life in accordance with her desires. In fact, she must give the whole of herself to the child. To be a mother—even at a natural level—means to shift all other responsibilities and concerns to the periphery. Even the most primitive motherhood experience is fraught with pain and suffering.

On the other hand, the woman, discriminated against by nature and charged to carry the heavy load of motherhood alone, is not ready to give up her role as mother and cast off the burden. This compulsive will in the woman to be a mother at all costs empha-sizes the pathos in her role. The tragedy of the woman becomes the more pronounced the less she can avoid it. The woman in the Bible yearns for a child with her heart and soul and is not able to suppress the urge for motherhood. The experience would not be so sorrowful if it could be dispensed with, if the woman felt happy without it.

However, the Bible denies that such a possibility exists. The woman wants to be a mother; she cannot get along without involvement in this kind of a passional experience. The longing for children, for a home, for the parent-child community, is by far more intense in the woman than in man.

The lot of the unmarried woman is by far more miserable than that of the unmarried man. The impact of sexual loneliness upon a woman is more devastating, both physically and mentally, than it is upon a man. The woman finds herself in a paradoxical predicament. On the one hand, she craves a husband and child; on the other hand, this longing, which penetrates into the very depth of her personality, can be fulfilled only by means of pain and suffering.

The story of creation describes this role in a short verse. "To the woman He said, 'I will greatly multiply your sorrow and your conception. In sorrow you shall bring forth children; and your desire shall be to your husband, and he shall rule over you'" (Gen. 3:16). In other words, the desire of the woman is tragic, masochistic. On the one hand she yearns for children, a husband and a home; on the other hand, she pays the high price (in terms of her freedom, safety and leisure) for the attainment of this desire.

With the emergence of the covenantal community and the change of the mother role from an inevitable experience to a free commitment, the passional component of this experience and the tragic dichotomy were redeemed. I say "redeemed" and not liquidated or eliminated, since there is no power in the world which can nullify God's will. The pain and suffering involved in being a mother can never be eliminated. However, it is subject to redemption, to infusion with meaning and purposiveness. While Eve suffers, her passional experience is absurd, purposeless, a waste of energy and human feelings. While Sarah suffers, her experience is hallowed as a sacrifice for a great, exalted idea: the perpetuation of the covenantal community.

The Yearning for Children

Let us analyze the covenantal mother and her redeemed passional experience.

She wants a child. Her yearning for children is perhaps more powerful than that of the mother in the unredeemed natural community. Rachel exclaimed in utter despair, "Give me children; if not I shall die" (Gen. 30:1). Hannah's story (I Samuel, chapter 1) is replete with tenderness, human tragedy, suffering and faith. She is a woman in distress, a woman who thought that she had lost everything in life, that she had boon completely forsaken by God and men, a woman who felt a great poverty, the absurdity in living. She sought relief in prayer, for from a human viewpoint, the situation she found herself in was hopeless. No doubt her yearning for a child was by no means less intense than that of Eve. Yet there was a basic difference. Eve's yearning for a child was not related to a great goal. It was purely egotistic, instinctual, primitive desire. Eve wanted to be a mother because she felt a need not only to be loved but to love, to shower someone with affection.

As long as this desire is not redeemed and purged of its instinctual elements, a mother wants a child only to satisfy her desire for loving and caring for someone. She wanted a child because she was in need of giving vent to emotional pressure, to gratify a *per se* good instinctual drive, that is, to shower someone with love. What this leads to was irrelevant for Eve. The purpose is fulfilled in dandling, hugging, or kissing anything.

However, in the covenantal community the urge to love is purged of its egotistic instinctual elements and turns into a need to serve, to sacrifice, to participate in the great adventure of being a people of God and a messianic community. The woman is no more a dandling, playing mother. She is a mother who teaches, educates, trains, and consecrates the child to God.

The covenantal mother's desire and craving for a child flow from the deep recesses of her personality where God's image is engraved. She tries to imitate the Creator. Jewish mystics asked: Why did God create the world? Does God, the Almighty, infinite, eternal, omniscient and transcendent, need a frail, finite, transient, and conditioned world? Yes, they said, He needs the world in order to have somebody on whom to practice kindness and mercy, in order to let somebody share in the great I-awareness of being, in order to give love and bestow *hesed*. God did not need the world for Himself; He wanted it in order to give man the possibility of attaining greatness.

So, too, the covenantal mother needs a child to make happy, to have the latter join the great community of the covenant, to serve the great cause, to consecrate the child to God. She is required to surrender her child. Jewish covenantal training is basically identical with an act of consecrating the child to God. A mother can be affectionate—Judaism has never condemned the manifestation of love by a mother. But covenantal mother has to withdraw from her child; her total possessive claims are curtailed in the covenantal community. For dedication to the covenantal cause and unlimited affection are mutually exclusive.

Hannah is the woman who proclaimed that motherhood asserts itself in consecration of the child, in giving him away, in surrendering him to God. "O Lord of hosts, if Thou wilt indeed look on the affliction of Your handmaid and remember me and not forget Thy handmaid but wilt give to Thy handmaid a man-child, I will give him to the Lord all the days of his life ..." (I Samuel 1:11). And what did Jewish mothers do throughout the millennia if not exactly the same thing that Hannah pledged? What does a Jewish mother do now when she brings her child to a yeshivah?

Jews introduced a system of public compulsory education 2100 years ago, while the so-called Western world was roaming the forests in Northern and Central Europe. "It was enacted to establish teachers of young children at every city and town, and to bring the children to them at the age of six or seven" (Bava Batra 21a). The child used to be taken away from the embrace of his mother at a very tender age and brought into a new world of Torah, teaching and training. Even now a Jewish child leaves home early in the morning and comes home late in the evening. When Hannah said, "For as long as he lives he is lent to the Lord" (I Samuel 1:28), she did not mean that he would retreat into some cloister; she did not think of physical solitude or a monastic life. Judaism has always opposed an unnatural life. What she had in mind was a life of service to God by serving the covenantal community. We are all still practicing this.

Let us recapitulate. In the natural community, the woman is involved in her motherhood-destiny; father is a distant figure who stands on the periphery. In the covenantal community, father moves to the center where mother has been all along, and both together take on a new commitment, universal in substance: to teach, to train the child to hear the faint echoes which keep on tapping at our gates and which disturb the complacent, comfortable, gracious society.

Two Complementary Missions

There is a distinction between mother's and father's mission within the covenantal community, since they represent two different personalistic approaches. Father's teaching is basically of an intellectual nature. Judaism is to a great extent an intellectual discipline, a method, a system of thought, a hierarchy of values. In order to be acquainted with all these aspects, one must study, comprehend, acquire knowledge and be familiar at least with its basic principles. Let me confide: it is not too easy a task. The teaching must be strict, exact and conscientious. If the father cannot accomplish it all by himself, he must see to it that his child obtains the necessary instruction.

However, Judaism is not only an intellectual tradition but an experiential one as well. The Jew not only observed but *experienced* the Shabbat, the Jew *experienced* Rosh Hashana and Yom Kippur. He did not only recite prayers on those days. The *seder* was not just a ceremonial, but a great *experiential* event. There is beauty, grandeur, warmth, and tenderness to Judaism. All these qualities cannot be described in cognitive terms. One may behold them, feel them,

sense them. It is impossible to provide one with a formal training in the experiential realm. Experiences are communicated not through the word but through steady contact, through association, through osmosis, through a tear or a smile, through dreamy eyes and soft melody, through the silence at twilight and the recital of *Shema*. All this is to be found in the maternal domain. The mother creates the mood; she is the artist who is responsible for the magnificence, solemnity and beauty. She tells the child of the great romance of Judaism. She somehow communicates to him the tremor, the heartbeat of Judaism, while playing, singing, laughing and crying.

Leadership in Times of Crisis

While intellectual involvement is important, in times of crisis and distress the experiential commitment is indispensable. Were it not for the mother, the Jews would not have been able to defy and to survive so many crises which threatened to annihilate our people. Again the contrast between the natural and covenantal mother is striking.

The natural woman, Eve, becomes involved involuntarily, not only in natural motherhood, but also in many human situations. She is vulnerable to the smooth but evil tongue of the serpent, sinks easily into her receptive role, into her quest for pleasure, and loses her independence of mind and will. She cannot resist the satanic persuasive arguments and false promises. "And the woman saw that the tree was good for food and that it was pleasant to the eyes... she took of its fruit and did eat..." (Gen. 3:6). The natural mother, Eve, abandoned her freedom of choice based on critical scrutiny; she let herself be easily hypnotized by the serpent, seduced by him. She could not rise to the heights of a courageous personality; she yielded. In crisis, she displayed weakness, confusion and fear.

By redeeming the motherhood experience, Sarah restored the dignity of the woman. A new task was given to her, namely, to rise *heroically* in moments of dismay and spiritual chaos, when man, notwithstanding his great intellectual prowess, finds himself entranced and is about to fail in the implementation of his fatherhood commitment.

The mother in times of crisis assumes the role of her husband's keeper, his guardian and teacher. In the covenantal community, motherhood is a more powerful spiritual force than fatherhood. The shy, modest, reserved mother turns into an active personality whenever critical action is called for.

Man's mind roams about in a world of abstractions and twisted ideas. He is at times too critical, too skeptical to realize the simple truth which brooks no interference from the oversophisticated intellect. That is why the Bible has always portrayed the woman as the determining influence, saving the male from committing grave errors. She quite often changed the course of destiny.

The woman is a crisis personality. In normal times, when routine decisions are reached, the man makes up his mind and the Biblical woman follows him. However, in times of upheaval and transition, when the covenantal community finds itself at crossroads and the choice of alternative courses of action is about to be made, a choice that will shape destiny—it is then that the mother steps to the fore and takes command. The greatness of the man expresses itself in everyday action, when situations lend themselves to logical analysis and discursive thinking. The greatness of the woman manifests itself at the hour of crisis, when the situation does not lend itself to piecemeal understanding but requires instead instantaneous action that flows from the very depths of a sensitive personality. "God gave woman *binah yeterah,* an additional measure of understanding over men" (Niddah 45b).

Motherhood and the Covenantal Community

Sarah is responsible for the survival of the covenantal community. Abraham had two sons, Ishmael and Isaac. The covenant was confined to Isaac and not given to Ishmael. Why? Because the mother of Ishmael was Hagar, and the mother of Isaac was Sarah.

Let us just read the Biblical text pertaining to the event of the covenant and the birth of Isaac.

> And when Abram was ninety-nine years old, the Lord appeared to Abram and said to him: "I am

the Almighty God; walk before me and be perfect, and I will make My covenant between Me and you and will multiply you exceedingly... As for Me, behold my covenant is with you, and you shall be a father of many nations. Neither shall your name be called Abram, but your name shall be Abraham, for a father of many nations have I made you... And I will establish my covenant between Me and you and your seed after you in their generations for an everlasting covenant, to be a God unto you, and to your seed after you" (Gen. 17:1–7).

We do not yet know whether God refers to Isaac or to Ishmael. However, God qualifies his statement by saying: "As for Sarah, your wife, you shall not call her name Sarai, but Sarah shall be her name, and I will bless her and give you a son through her, yea, I will bless her that she shall give rise to nations..." (Gen. 17:5–16). The covenant is restricted to Sarah and her offspring, and does not include Ishmael. Abraham feels embarrassed and he begs God that Ishmael may also be admitted to the covenant. "O that Ishmael might live before Thee" (Gen. 17:18). God, however, rejects Abraham's plea and He says: "Sarah, your wife, shall bear you a son indeed, and you shall call his name Isaac, and I will establish My covenant with him for an everlasting covenant, and with his seed after him. As for Ishmael I have heard you. Behold I have blessed him... But My covenant will I establish with Isaac whom Sarah shall bear unto you..." (Gen. 17:18–21).

God lays emphasis upon Sarah's role in the realization of the covenantal society. Abraham's offspring are not taken into this esoteric community if their mother happens to be Hagar and not Sarah. Later, when Sarah demands the expulsion of Ishmael, and Abraham is not eager to comply with her request, God tells him in terse terms, "Let it not be grievous in your sight because of the lad, and because of your bondwoman; in all that Sarah has said unto you, hearken unto her voice, for in Isaac shall your seed be called" (Gen. 21:12).

Rebecca is responsible for the covenant being transmitted to Jacob instead of Esau (Gen. 27). Isaac had contemplated entrusting the spiritual heritage to his oldest son. At the hour of crisis Rebecca intervened and thereby determined the historical destiny of the covenantal community. She sent Jacob to Haran to marry her nieces. Miriam is responsible for the emergence of Moses as a leader and redeemer of his people. If not for her, he would have never been imbued with great passionate love for his poor brethren. She suggested to the princess that a Hebrew wet-nurse be employed for the infant, preventing Moses from disappearing in anonymity and ignorance: "And his sister stood afar off, to know what would be done to him... Then said the sister to Pharaoh's daughter, 'Shall I go and call for you a nurse of the Hebrew women...', and the maid went and called the child's mother" (Ex. 2:4, 7, 8). Similarly, Deborah saved the people from oppression and slavery when she organized the rebellion under the military command of Barak (Judges 4–5). And the Aggadah relates that the women refused to contribute to the Golden Calf (*Pirkei de-Rabbi Eliezer* 45) while they gave generously to the Tabernacle (Ex. 35).

The woman is both a demonic and Divine crisis personality. Eve and Delilah represent the woman-demon; our matriarchs, the Divine individuality. The destiny of mankind and of the covenantal people was shaped by the woman.

The Book of Proverbs dedicated its last section (31:11–31) to the woman of valor in whom the heart of her husband trusts. Valor as a trait of the feminine personality was born in the covenantal community where motherhood, instead of being a factum, became a challenge and an ideal.

The Tragedy in Motherhood
And yet the story of the Biblical woman, the covenantal mother, ends with a tragic note. The very moment she brings her job to a close, the instant she completes her task, when the crisis is over, she returns quickly to her tent, draws down the curtain of anonymity and disappears. She is outside of the hustle and bustle of the male society. Abraham sits "in front of the tent" (Gen. 18:1). His name appears in the press and many know him; he is the leader, the father, the teacher; his lips drip honey; he enlightens the minds; he fascinates the passersby. Hardly any-

one knows that there is a Sarah, humble, modest, publicly shy. Somewhere in the tent is the person who is perhaps responsible for all the accomplishments credited to Abraham, for all the glory that is bestowed upon Abraham, who is superior to him, who leads the leader and teaches the teacher and guides the master, who inspires the visionary and interprets his dreams.

Sarah, the Biblical woman, is modest, humble, self-effacing. She enters the stage when she is called upon, acts her part with love and devotion in a dim corner of the stage, and then leaves softly by a side door without applause and without the enthusiastic response of the audience which is hardly aware of her. She returns to her tent, to anonymity and retreat. Only sensitive people know the truth. Only three travelers inquired about her. These travelers were not ordinary people whose eyes see only the surface. They were the angels of God. Their glimpse penetrated and apprehended the image of the true leader, teacher, prophetess, to whom everything should be credited. Nonchalantly they remarked, "Where is Sarah, your wife?" (Gen. 18:9). In other words, we know that without her you could not play the part that God assigned to you. Where is she? Why do not people know the truth? Why has she been just trailing behind you? Why did she not march in front of you? After all, the covenant cannot and will not be realized without her. Abraham answered tersely, "She is in the tent" (Gen. 18:9). Indeed she is enveloped in mystery.

It is quite interesting that although Abraham survived Sarah by thirty-eight years, his historical role came to an end with Sarah's passing. Isaac leaves the stage together with Rebecca. Jacob relinquishes his role to Joseph with the untimely death of Rachel. Without Sarah there would be no Abraham; no Isaac were it not for Rebecca; no Jacob without Rachel.

And yet, and here the tragedy manifests itself with all its impact, we say, "God of Abraham, God of Isaac, God of Jacob," but not "God of Sarah, God of Rebecca, God of Rachel and Leah," even though they had an equal share in *Borei Olam,* the Creator of the World.

The Halakhah was cognizant of the greatness of the covenantal mother when it formulated the rule that *Kedushat Yisrael,* one's status as a Jew, can be transmitted only through the woman. The Halakhah was also conscious of the loneliness and the tragic note in the feminine commitment when it accepted a contradictory rule that the child takes his father's name and family status.

The Duality of Fatherhood

A question arises in the Mishnah and Tosefta Bikkurim whether a proselyte may, when praying, address himself to God as "our God and the God of our fathers." The Halakhah has accepted the viewpoint of Rabbi Judah in the Jerusalem Talmud (Bikkurim 1:4) that the proselyte may recite the fixed text of the Bikkurim portion, including "which Thou didst swear unto our ancestors" (Deut. 26:15). Maimonides writes, relative to this problem: "The proselyte brings [*bikkurim,* his first fruits] and reads [the portion in Deuteronomy 26] for it was said by God to Abraham, 'and you shall be a father of many nations' (Gen. 17:4). Thus he [Abraham] is the father of the entire world that enters under the wings of the Divine Providence" (Maimonides, *Hilkhot Bikkurim* [Laws of the First Fruit Offering] 4:3).

Maimonides did not interpret the phrase "a father of many nations" in the sense of natural fatherhood, that Abraham will be naturally fruitful and fertile, the progenitor of many peoples. He saw it rather as denoting another kind of fatherhood, the spiritual. Abraham is the father of all those who gather under the wings of the *Shekhinah,* the Divine Presence, of those who cleave to the God of Israel and commit themselves to His teachings. The change from Abram to Abraham is symbolic of the transition from the relationship of biological progeny and offspring to that of metaphysical father/teacher and child/disciple.

When a man begets a child who is biologically his, a natural being becomes an Abram. This role is not a distinct privilege bestowed upon man exclusively. Procreation is a natural function of man and beast alike. But fatherhood that is rooted in the great idea-experience surpasses by far fatherhood due to a natural process of fertilization of the ovum. This message was conveyed to us through the covenant with Abraham. The covenant freed our ancestor from the natural restrictions of nature and widened his fatherhood experience to universal proportions. Whoever in the hour of enlightenment decides to return to God is embraced by Abraham as a beloved child.

In a word, fatherhood is a double experience, a natural and a personal-metaphysical one. At the first level, man is procreative and sues for a status of fatherhood which is doomed to failure because he will never develop the proper relationship with his offspring. He will have to resign himself to unmitigated contempt on the part of the son or daughter, as the young will always resent and despise the old; or he may have to establish a veritable tyranny in his home, a result of a meaningless and absurdly resentful relationship. At the second level, father and child form a relationship which adds a new quality to their existential experience. They form an ontic community, a community of being, within which man is relieved of the loneliness which lashes him with untold ruthlessness and existential insensateness. Only within this fellowship is real fatherhood found.

However, when I speak of the Abrahamic fatherhood which is attained through education, I understand the latter not only in terms of technical training of the child, of the development of his aptitudes and talents, of actualizing the child's full natural potential, of exercising his or her innate physical and intellectual capabilities. However important and essential this type of education is to the full realization of the child, the idea of Abrahamic fatherhood implies a new dimension, one which is to be found beside the realm of education as it is understood by philosophers and pedagogues. The service Abraham rendered to Isaac did not consist in educating him in skills and aptitudes in the Platonic sense, in bringing out what already was endowed in him, but in introducing him to a new existence, a covenantal, redeemed one. Abraham ushered Isaac into the covenantal community consisting of four *personae,* I, thou, he (lower case) and He (upper case). Abraham revealed to Isaac the regenerating Law of God, or His ways. Abraham became a part of the scheme of revelation of God's Law. While education aims only at being human,

Abraham is within finitude involved with Isaac as to the latter's *trans-humanitas*. He gave him something which lies beyond and above the finite reality. He discovered for him the idea of self-transcendence and self-redemption, of catharsis.

"For I have known him that he shall command his children and his household after him that they shall keep the way of the Lord, to do righteousness and justice, so that the Lord may bring upon Abraham that which He had spoken of him" (Gen. 18:19). Fatherhood expresses itself in a testamental act, in transmitting the great experience and law of *revelatio Dei*. Not only does the father prepare his children for life, not only does he adapt them to an existing reality, as the naturalistic theory interprets the educational activity, but he also commits them to a higher transcendental reality. The fatherhood of Abraham is covenantal and was firmly established at the Mount Moriah with the *Akedah* drama, his willingness to sacrifice Isaac (Gen. 22). Many a modern father who tries to give his children an excellent technical education fails to become Abraham, to re-experience his fatherhood in letting his children discover a new reality of a committed, redeemed existence.

Clan and Nation

When God changed Abraham's name from Abram, He changed his task as well as that of his children. Abraham's role was changed from that of a private person, an individual, into that of a father of a nation. The land was granted not to a father of a *clan* but to a father of a *nation*. The promise was related to a nation: "I have made you the father of many nations... I will make nations come out of you" (Gen. 17:4,6). He will no more be just the head of a clan, of a tribe or many tribes. He will be the father of a nation, of an aboriginal covenantal entity. The father personifies the nation; he is a nation disguised as an individual. Abram denotes the natural link, the father of a family; Abraham signifies the existential link between a father and his offspring when he experiences ontological unity, oneness of being, and comity, as if he lived in them in a future generation, as if he will continue to exist through them. A nation is not a clan. It is an entity *per se*, a personality, an individuality. It is not a collective thing integrated of the many, but an

aboriginal unity. *Keneset Yisrael,* corporate Israel, is a being. It exists in the same manner as I, you and he exist. For instance, we believe that the promised land belongs to us. To whom? To me, to you, to him? To all of us? No! It belongs not to one of us, nor to all of us in partnership! It belongs to *Keneset Yisrael* as an individuality, an original being. *Keneset Yisrael* may encompass all of mankind, since everybody can join through *gerut,* conversion. No racial legitimation is required.

Once the children of Abraham will form a nation, once Abraham will be elevated to the father of a people, a nation, another question arises: who will be the mother of the nation? A clan can be formed by having a common ancestor, either a father or a mother. It is a purely biological blood link. A nation, however, is not dependent upon a blood relation. A nation has a common father-teacher. The father of a nation passes on to future generations not just genetic characteristics but a spiritual heritage, a way of life, a morality, an accumulation of values—in a word, a great world, a specific existential experience; he wills his own self to the generations, creating a sense of ontological unity, "...that he shall command his children and his household after him that they shall keep the way of the Lord, to do righteousness and justice" (Gen. 18:19).

The Torah has emphasized that both father and mother were created in the image of God and that both of them express themselves by using their respective image-consciousness in a unique way. Together they reflect the total glory and majesty which God invested in them. Hence, the nation cannot come into existence and become God's own nation unless the nation receives the moral code from the mother as well as the father. God speaks to his people either as a father or as a mother. He entrusted teaching to both. Hence, a nation must have a mother.

That is why the Torah tells us that Sarah could not bear a child (Gen. 11:30, 16:1). Without her, there will be no birth of a nation. The whole covenant would have been null and void if Sarah had not been involved. Abraham turned into a spiritual father, a universal teacher, or into an idea; so did Sarah. She became a mother of people, not a mother of a clan. She was transformed into an idea. Of course, she will teach her children the same moral code that Abraham formulated. However, she will interpret the same code in the unique style which only a mother knows. Abraham interprets events in his individual fashion. Sarah interprets events and things under the aspect of involvement and sharing.

How beautifully the Torah tells us the story of a father whom God charged with the mission of forming a nation and who could not implement his assignment because Sarah, the choicest of all women, could not join him since she was barren. God had to resort to a miracle in order that a charismatic nation be formed. Sarah *will* be the mother of the nation. "I will bless her and give you a son through her. I will bless her that she shall give rise to nations; rulers of people shall issue from her" (Gen. 17:16). The Almighty reemphasized that without Sarah there will be no covenant with a nation. The great historic task was entrusted to two people. They reflect the greatness of man *in toto*. Through them the great nation will achieve completeness.

Reprinted with permission from *Family Redeemed: Essays on Family Relationships* [New Jersey: Toras Horav Foundation, 2000], pp. 105–125.

GLOSSARY

A shtikel shalom iz oych shalom. (Yiddish) "A little peace is also peace."

Adam. Man.

Akeidah. Binding of Isaac, as told in Genesis 22.

Aleph. First letter of the Hebrew alphabet (with a numerical value of one).

Aleph-beis. Hebrew alphabet.

Aravah. Willow branch used during the festival of Sukot.

Aseh. Do; action.

Av. Father.

B'tzelem Elokim. In God's image.

Beit midrash. Torah study hall.

Berachah. (a) Ritual blessing recited before eating, before the performance of certain *mitzvot*, and at other occasions; (b) a blessing shared with another for good health, etc.

Bikkurim. The first fruits that the Jews would bring to the Temple in Jerusalem.

Binah yeterah. An additional measure of understanding.

Binah (lit. comprehension); the second of the ten *sefirot*; the second stage of the intellectual process that develops abstract conceptions, giving it breadth and depth.

Borei Olam. Creator of the World.

Cheshbon hanefesh. Self-assessment.

Chessed (hesed). (a) Acts of kindness; (b) fourth of the ten *sefirot*; the divine attribute associated with the dispersion of Godly light and energy to lower levels of existence.

Chochmah. Wisdom; in Kabbalistic-Chasidic terminology, it refers to the first of the ten sefirot, and the first of the intellectual powers of the intellect.

Chukkim. *Mitzvot* whose reasons are supra-rational.

Chutzpah. Insolence.

Derech eretz. The norms of civilized people; ethical behavior.

Emes. Truth.

Etrog (pl. etrogim). Citron used during the festival of Sukot for the mitzvah of the Four Species.

Gerut. Conversion.

Gevurah. (lit. might); the second of the seven divine *sefirot*, or attributes, associated with the holding back of divine revelation.

Habet ushma. (lit. look and listen); comprehend.

Hadas. Myrtle branch used during the festival of Sukkot for the mitzvah of the Four Species.

Hai. Living things.

Hakaras ha'tov. Recognition of the good.

Halachah. Jewish law.

Hashem Elokei Tzivo'os. God of Hosts.

Havah. Eve.

Hei. The fifth letter of the Hebrew alphabet (with a numerical value of five).

Hesed u-tzedakah. Kindness and charity.

Hilchos Derech Eretz. Laws of proper conduct.

Hodaah. Acknowledgement; gratitude.

Ish. Man.

Kabbalat ol malchut shamayim. Acceptance of the yoke of the sovereignty of Heaven.

Kabolas Ol. Acceptance of the yoke.

Kedushat ha-guf. The sanctity of the body

Kedushat Yisrael. The sanctity of a Jew.

Keneset Yisrael. The community of Israel.

Ketuba. Marriage contract.

Korban. (lit. drawing near); sacrifice of animal or grain.

Kuf. The nineteenth letter of the Hebrew alphabet (with a numerical value of 100).

L'havdil. To distinguish.

Lulav. Palm branch used during the festival of Sukkot for the mitzvah of the Four Species.

Masorah. Tradition.

Mayim. Water.

Me'inyana de'yoma. Current events.

Mem. The thirteenth letter of the Hebrew alphabet (with a numerical value of forty).

Mentsch. (Yiddish; lit. person) a person of integrity and honor.

Meshulach. Collector for charity.

Middos. Character traits.

Mishpat u-tzedakah. Justice and charity.

Mitzvah (pl., mitzvot, mitzvoth). The Torah's commandments.

Modeh Ani. "I acknowledge." Opening words of the prayer of thanksgiving recited immediately upon waking in the morning.

Mohel. Trained expert who performs ritual circumcisions.

Mussar. (a) Jewish works emphasizing ethics and character refinement; (b) harsh and critical speech.

Naaseh. We will do.

Nachas. Pride and joy.

Nehama d'kesufa. Bread of shame.

Nisuch hamayim. Pouring of the water.

Ol Malchus Shomayim. The yoke of the sovereignty of heaven.

Pidyon ha-ben. The ceremony wherein a firstborn male born to Israelite (non-Kohen or Levite) parents is redeemed from a Kohen, in exchange for five silver coins, thirty days after his birth.

Reish. The twentieth letter of the Hebrew alphabet (with a numerical value of 200).

Rosh Hashanah (Rosh Hashana). The Jewish New Year holiday.

Rosh yeshivah. Academic leader of a yeshivah.

Seder. (lit. order); the order of the celebratory meal on the first two nights of Passover.

Sefirot. Divine attributes or emanations, sources of the corresponding ten faculties of the human soul.

Shalom. Peace.

Sheker. Falsehood.

Shekhinah. The manifestation of the divine presence; God's feminine manifestation.

Sheleimus. Completeness, integrity.

Shema. Verses from the Bible declaring, among other things, one's faith in God, recited by Jews every morning and evening.

Shin. The twenty-first letter of the Hebrew alphabet (with a numerical value of 300).

Shochet. Ritual slaughterer.

Shofar. Ram's horn sounded on Rosh Hashanah and at the close of Yom Kippur.

Shul. Synagogue.

Sidra. The weekly Torah portion.

Sukkah. A hut or booth roofed with vegetation in which the festival of Sukot is observed.

Sukkot. Festival of seven days (eight in the Diaspora) beginning on 15 Tishrei, taking its name from the temporary dwelling (*sukah*) in which one dwells during this period.

Tefilin. Small black leather cubes containing parchment scrolls inscribed with biblical passages, wrapped on the arm and head of adult men during weekday morning prayers.

Teshuvah. Repentance, the return to one's true essence.

Tiferet. (lit. beauty) the third of the ten *sefirot*; fuses the influence of *chesed* and *gevurah* and reveals a light that transcends them both.

Tsitsit. A four-corner garment adorned with ritual fringes.

Tuf. The twenty-second letter of the Hebrew alphabet (with a numerical value of 400).

Tzaddik (pl. tzaddikim). A righteous person. In Chabad literature, those who have completely defeated their animalistic soul and are filled entirely with love and reverence for God.

V'nishmah. We will understand.

V'Ohavto L'Reacho Komocho. "Thou shalt love thy neighbor as thyself" (Leviticus 19:18).

Vaaseh. And do.

Yehudi (pl. Yehudim). Jew.

Yeshivah. Academies of Torah learning.

Yiddishe nachas. Jewish joy.

Yom Kippur. Day of Atonement, a fast day on the 10th day of the Jewish month of Tishrei.

SELECTED BIBLIOGRAPHY

Balanced Parenting: A Father and Son – A Rabbi and a Psychologist – Examine Love and Limits in Raising Children, Raphael Pelcovits and David A. Pelcovitz [Brooklyn: Shaar Press, 2005]

Battle Hymn of the Tiger Mother, Amy Chua [New York: Penguin Press, 2011]

Crisis and Continuity: The Jewish Family in the 21st Century, Norman Linzer, Irving N. Levitz, David J. Schnall [Hoboken, NJ: Ktav Pub. House, 1995]

Dr. Spock's Baby and Childcare, Benjamin Spock and Robert Needleman [London: Simon and Schuster, 2011]

Establishing Parental Status, Aharon Pollak [Derech Publications, 2002]

Generation iY: Our Last Chance to Save Their Future, Tim Elmore [Atlanta, GA: Poet Gardener Publishing, 2010]

Generation Me: Why Today's Young Americans Are More Confident, Assertive, Entitled – and More Miserable Than Ever Before, Jean M. Twenge [New York: Free Press, 2006]

How to Talk So Kids Will Listen and Listen So Kids Will Talk, Adele Faber and Elaine Mazlish [New York: Avon, 1982]

Mindset: How You Can Fulfill Your Potential, Carol S. Dweck [London: Robinson, 2012]

My Child, My Disciple: A Practical, Torah-based Guide to Effective Discipline in the Home, Noach Orloweck and Sarah Shapiro [Jerusalem: Feldheim, 1993]

Nurtureshock: Why Everything We Thought about Children is Wrong, Po Bronson and Ashley Merryman [London: Ebury, 2011]

Parenting from the Inside Out: How a Deeper Self-Understanding Can Help You Raise Children Who Thrive, Daniel J. Siegel and Mary Hartzell [New York: J. P. Tarcher/Putnam, 2003]

Parenting with Love and Logic: Teaching Children Responsibility, Foster Cline and Jim Fay [Colorado Springs, CO: Piñon Press, 2006]

Positive Parenting: Developing Your Child's Potential, Abraham J. Twerski and Ursula Verena Schwartz [Brooklyn, NY: Mesorah, 1996]

Raising a Child with Soul: How Time-Tested Jewish Wisdom Can Shape Your Child's Character, Slovie Wolff [New York: St. Martin's Griffin, 2009]

Raising America: Experts, Parents, and a Century of Advice about Children, Ann Hulbert [New York: Alfred A. Knopf, 2003]

The Blessing of a B Minus: Using Jewish Teachings to Raise Resilient Teenagers, Wendy Mogel [New York: Scribner, 2010]

The Blessing of a Skinned Knee: Using Jewish Teachings to Raise Self-reliant Children, Wendy Mogel [New York: Scribner, 2001]

The Hadassah Magazine Jewish Parenting Book, Roselyn Bell [New York: Free Press, 1989]

The Narcissism Epidemic: Living in the Age of Entitlement, Jean M. Twenge and W. Keith Campbell [New York: Free Press, 2009]

Torah Powerhouse: Insights into the Theory and Practice of Torah Parenting, Aharon Pollak [Jerusalem: Feldheim, 1996]

To Raise a Jewish Child: A Guide for Parents, Hayim Donin [New York: Basic Books, 1977]

ACKNOWLEDGMENTS

Parenting may not win us a large salary, or any salary at all. There is no gala event for the best parent award. Nor will it earn us an academic degree. But there may be no more important human endeavor than raising a child.

The Rohr Jewish Learning Institute (JLI) constantly aims to demonstrate the contemporary relevance of the Torah's ancient wisdom. The great treasures of Jewish knowledge and tradition elevate the soul to peaks of spiritual delight, infuse the mind with clarity, and warm and comfort the heart. But the most pressing of all is Torah's role in directing and inspiring action, as we live its values in the real world. With this course, we aim to add the Torah's voice to society's conversations about parenting.

In addition to the meticulous parenting research provided by our research department, JLI's editorial team set out to listen to and learn from renowned parenting and education scholars and experts. The interviews with these experts provided JLI with a treasure of material, much of which can be found in the six lessons of this course. We are extremely grateful to all these individuals—a list of whom can be found in the credits at the beginning of this book—who graciously shared of their time and wisdom to help shape this course. Special credit is due to **Rabbi Manis Friedman**, dean of Bais Chana Institute of Jewish Studies and world-renowned Chasidic thinker and lecturer, whose creative and innovative approach to parenting substantially contributed to the formulation of *The Art of Parenting*.

We extend our appreciation to **Rabbis Mordechai Dinerman** and **Naftali Silberberg,** who capably direct the JLI Curriculum Department and the Flagship editorial team, and to **Rabbi Dr. Shmuel Klatzkin,** and **Rabbis**

Yanki Tauber, Shmuel Lobenstein, Eli Raksin, and **Yanky Raskin** for their assistance in developing and writing this course.

The JLI editorial board provided many useful suggestions to enhance the course and ensure its suitability for a wide range of students. Many thanks to **Rabbi Avrohom Bergstein, Rabbi Yosef Hodakov, Mrs. Dina Kantor** and **Mrs. Chava Shapiro** for their careful review of this course.

We are pleased to be able to offer this course for credits from the American Psychological Association (APA), the American Council for Continuing Medical Education (ACCME), the California Board of Behavioral Sciences (CBBS), and the National Board for Certified Counselors (NBCC). We are indebted to **Dr. Casey Skvork** for his dedicated collaboration, and to **William Wears** of the Washington School of Psychiatry for his patient guidance through the accreditation process. Special thanks to **Mindy Wallach** for coordinating the accreditation and to **Shulamis Nadler** for her administrative assistance.

We acknowledge **Zeldy Nemanov** for managing the many components of course production; **Mendel Schtroks** for designing the textbooks with taste, eloquence, and patience; and **Miriam Levy-Haim** and **Rachel Witty** for enhancing the quality and professionalism of the course through their copyediting and proofing.

Mrs. Nechama Rivkah Shagalow and **Rabbi Yisrael Silman** head the production team that created the videos for this course. They are assisted by **Neria Ben Avi, Moshe Raskin,** and **Getzy Raskin. Mrs. Mushka Lisker** and **Mrs. Rivka Rapoport** designed the lesson's PowerPoints.

We acknowledge the hard work and efforts of JLI's support staff and administration, whose contributions to this course were critical, but whose names are too many to enumerate.

We are immensely grateful for the encouragement of JLI's visionary chairman and vice-chairman of Merkos L'inyonei Chinuch—Lubavitch World Headquarters, **Rabbi Moshe Kotlarsky.** Rabbi Kotlarsky has been highly instrumental in building the infrastructure for the expansion of Chabad's international network and is the architect of scores of initiatives and services to help Chabad representatives across the globe succeed in their mission. We are blessed to have the unwavering support of JLI's principal benefactor, **Mr. George Rohr,** who is fully invested in our work and has been and continues to be instrumental in achieving the monumental expansion of the organization.

JLI's dedicated executive board—**Rabbis Chaim Block, Hesh Epstein, Ronnie Fine, Yosef Gansburg, Shmuel Kaplan, Yisrael Rice,** and **Avrohom Sternberg**—devote countless hours to the development of JLI. Their commitment and sage direction help JLI continue to grow and flourish.

Finally, JLI represents an incredible partnership of more than 350 *shluchim,* who give of their time and talent to further Jewish adult education. We thank them for generously sharing their feedback, offering advice, and making suggestions that steer JLI's development and growth. They are our most valuable critics and our most cherished contributors.

Inspired by the call of the **Lubavitcher Rebbe,** of righteous memory, it is the mandate of the Rohr JLI to encourage all Jews throughout the world to experience and take part in the Torah learning that is their heritage. May this course succeed in fulfilling this sacred charge.

On behalf of the Rohr Jewish Learning Institute,

Rabbi Efraim Mintz, Executive Director
Rabbi Yisrael Rice, Chairman, Editorial Board

5 Teves, 5775

JEWISH LEARNING INSTITUTE

The **Rohr Jewish Learning Institute**

An affiliate of
Merkos L'Inyonei Chinuch
The Educational Arm of
The Chabad Lubavitch Movement
822 Eastern Parkway, Brooklyn, NY 11213

Rabbi Shraga Sherman
Merion Station, PA

Rabbi Avraham Steinmetz
S. Paulo, BR

Rabbi Avrohom Sternberg
New London, CT

Rabbi Aryeh Weinstein
Newtown, PA

Rabbi Motti Wilhelm
Portland, OR

Multimedia Development

Mrs. Rivkah Shagalow
Director

Rabbi Yisroel Silman
Creative Director

Mrs. Neria Ben Avi
Mrs. Mushka Lisker
Mrs. Rivkah Rapoport
Mrs. Chava Shapiro
Rabbi Chesky Edelman
Getzy Raskin
Moshe Raskin

Administration

Mrs. Chana Dechter

Affiliate Support

Rabbi Mendel Sirota
Mrs. Fraydee Kessler
Mrs. Mindy Wallach

Online Division

Rabbi Mendy Elishevitz
Director

Dovid Ciment
Rabbi Elchonon Korenblit
Ram Rabins
Mrs. Rochie Rivkin

Marketing and Branding

Rabbi Zalman Abraham
Director

Mrs. Shevi Rivkin
Graphic Design

Rabbi Yossi Klein
Marketing for Results

Rabbi Shmuel Loebenstein
Writer

Marketing Committee

Rabbi Simcha Backman
Glendale, CA

Rabbi Ronnie Fine
Montreal, QC

Rabbi Ovadia Goldman
Oklahoma City, OK

Rabbi Mendy Halberstam
Miami Beach, FL

Rabbi Reuven New
Boca Raton, FL

Rabbi Yehuda Shemtov
Yardley, PA

Marketing Consultants

JJ Gross
New York, NY

Warren Modlin
MednetPro, Inc.
Alpharetta, GA

Alan Rosenspan
Alan Rosenspan & Associates
Sharon, MA

Gary Wexler
Passion Marketing
Los Angeles, CA

Publication Design

Rabbi Zalman Abraham
Mendel Schtroks

Printing

Shimon Leib Jacobs
Point One Communications
Montreal, QC

Distribution

Mary Stevens
Nixa, MO

Accounting

Musie Karp
Mrs. Shaina B. Mintz
Mrs. Shulamis Nadler

JLI Departments

Rabbi Levi Kaplan
Director of Operations

Rabbi Dubi Rabinowitz
Administrator

JLI Flagship

Rabbi Yisrael Rice
Chairman
S. Rafael, CA

Rabbi Mordechai Dinerman
Rabbi Naftali Silberberg
Editors-in-Chief

Rabbi Yanky Tauber
Course Editor

Rabbi Dr. Shmuel Klatzkin
Senior Editor
Dayton, OH

Rabbi Eli Raksin
Rabbi Yanky Raskin
Associate Editors

Zeldy Nemanow
Administrative Assistant

Rabbi Mendel Sirota
Production Manager

Miriam Levy-Haim
Mrs. Naomi Saul
Mrs. Rachel Witty
Proofreaders

Department of Continuing Education

Mrs. Mindy Wallach
Director

Musie Karp
Registrar

Mrs. Shulamis Nadler
Service and Support

JLI International Desk

Rabbi Avrohom Sternberg
Chairman
New London, CT

Rabbi Dubi Rabinowitz
Director
Brooklyn, NY

Chava Farkash
Administrative Assistant

Mendel Schtroks
Content Manager

Rabbi Yosef Yitzchok Noiman
Administrator, JLI Israel
In Partnership with
Tzeirei Agudat Chabad

Rabbi Eli Wolf
Administrator, JLI in the CIS
In Parternship with the Federation of Jewish
Communities of the CIS

Rabbi Avraham Golovacheov
Regional Respresentative
German Division

Rabbi Nochum Schapiro
Regional Respresentative
Australia

Beis Medrosh L'Shluchim
in partnership with
Shluchim Exchange

Rabbi Mendy Yusewitz
Director

Rabbi Mendel Margolin
Producer

Steering Committee
Rabbi Simcha Backman
Rabbi Mendy Kotlarsky
Rabbi Efraim Mintz

JLI Academy

Rabbi Hesh Epstein
Chairman

Rabbi Yossi Klein
Director

Steering Committee
Rabbi Yoel Caroline
Rabbi Mordechai Grossbaum
Rabbi Levi Mendelow

JLI Teens
in partnership with
CTeeN: Chabad Teen Network

Rabbi Chaim Block
Chairman
San Antonio, TX

Rabbi Michoel Shapiro
Director

Mrs. Nechi Gudelsky
Program Administrators

Advisory Board

Rabbi Mendy Cohen
Merion Station, PA

Rabbi Yitzi Hein
Pittsford, NY

Rabbi Zalman Marcus
Mission Viejo, CA

Machon Shmuel
The Sami Rohr Research Institute

Rabbi Avrohom Bergstein
Dean

Rabbinic Advisory Board
Rabbi Chaim Rapoport
Rabbi Gedalya Oberlander
Rabbi Chaim Schapiro
Rabbi Levi Yitzchak Raskin
Rabbi Mordechai Farkash
Rabbi Moshe Miller
Rabbi Yossi Yaffe

Research Fellows
Rabbi Menachem Aizenman
Rabbi Yehudah Altein
Rabbi Binyomin Bitton
Rabbi Moshe Chanunu
Rabbi Yaakov Gershon
Rabbi Levi Kessler
Rabbi Nesanel Loeb
Rabbi Mendel Mellul
Rabbi Zushe Wilmowsky
Rabbi Eliezer Raksin
Rabbi Menachem Rifkind
Rabbi Mendel Zirkind
Rabbi Yehudah Dovber Zirkind

Mishnah Project

Elya Silfen
Director

myShiur:
Advanced Learning Initiative

Rabbi Shmuel Kaplan
Chairman
Potomac, MD

Rabbi Levi Kaplan
Director

National Jewish Retreat

Rabbi Hesh Epstein
Chairman
Columbia, SC

Mrs. Shaina B. Mintz
Administrator

Bruce Backman
Coordinator

Rabbi Mendy Weg
Founding Director

Rochelle Katzman
Program Coordinator

Rabbi Shmuel Karp
Shluchim Liaison

Rosh Chodesh Society

Rabbi Shmuel Kaplan
Chairman
Baltimore, MD

Mrs. Shaindy Jacobson
Director

Mrs. Chava Shapiro
Associate Director

Mrs. Fraydee Kessler
Administrator

Gitty Hanokah
Administrative Assistant

Steering Committee
Mrs. Malka Bitton
Mrs. Shula Bryski
Mrs. Rochel Holzkenner
Mrs. Devorah Kornfeld
Mrs. Chana Lipskar
Mrs. Ahuva New
Mrs. Binie Tenenbaum

Sinai Scholars Society
in partnership with Chabad on Campus

Rabbi Menachem Schmidt
Chairman
Philadelphia, PA

Rabbi Dubi Rabinowitz
Director

Devorah Leah Notik
Associate Director

Mrs. Devorah Zlatopolsky
Administrator

Executive Committee
Rabbi Moshe Chaim Dubrowski
Rabbi Yossy Gordon
Rabbi Efraim Mintz
Rabbi Menachem Schmidt
Rabbi Nechemia Vogel
Rabbi Eitan Webb
Rabbi Avi Weinstein
Dr. Chana Silberstein

Curriculum Committee
Rabbi Zalman Bluming
Rabbi Shlomie Chein
Rabbi Shlomo Rothstien

Steering Committee
Rabbi Shlomie Chein
Rabbi Moshe Laib Gray
Rabbi Dovid Gurevitch
Rabbi Mendel Matusof

Rabbi Yisroel Wilhelm

TorahCafe.com
Online Learning

Rabbi Levi Kaplan
Director

Rabbi Simcha Backman
Consultant

Rabbi Mendy Elishevitz
Rabbi Elchonon Korenblit
Website Development

Mrs. Esty Perman
Administrator

Mrs. Shirley Ruvinov
Marketing Director

Mendel Serebryanski
Content Manager

Avrohom Shimon Ezagui
Rafi Roston
Filming Crew

Moshe Levin
Elya Silfen
Video Editing

Torah Studies

Rabbi Yosef Gansburg
Chairman
Toronto, ON

Rabbi Meir Hecht
Founding Director

Rabbi Zalman Margolin
Director

Rabbi Ahrele Loschak
Managing Editor

Steering Committee
Rabbi Levi Fogelman
Rabbi Yaacov Halperin
Rabbi Nechemia Schusterman
Rabbi Ari Sollish

JLI Central
Founding Department Heads

Rabbi Mendel Bell
Brooklyn, NY

Rabbi Zalman Charytan
Acworth, GA

Rabbi Mendel Druk
Cancun, Mexico

Rabbi Menachem Gansburg
Toronto, ON

Rabbi Yoni Katz
Brooklyn, NY

Rabbi Chaim Zalman Levy
New Rochelle, NY

Rabbi Benny Rapoport
Clarks Summit, PA

Dr. Chana Silberstein
Ithaca, NY

Rabbi Elchonon Tenenbaum
Napa Valley, CA

Rohr JLI Faculty

ALABAMA
BIRMINGHAM
Rabbi Yossi Friedman
205.970.0100

ARIZONA
CHANDLER
Rabbi Mendel Deitsch
480.855.4333

FLAGSTAFF
Rabbi Dovie Shapiro
928.255.5756

PHOENIX
Rabbi Zalman Levertov
Rabbi Yossi Friedman
602.944.2753

SCOTTSDALE
Rabbi Yossi Levertov
480.998.1410

ARKANSAS
LITTLE ROCK
Rabbi Pinchus Ciment
501.217.0053

CALIFORNIA
AGOURA HILLS
Rabbi Moshe Bryski
Rabbi Shlomo Bistritsky
818.991.0991

ARCATA
Rabbi Eliyahu Cowen
412.390.6481

BAKERSFIELD
Rabbi Shmuli Schlanger
661.835.8381

BEL AIR
Rabbi Chaim Mentz
310.475.5311

BEVERLY HILLS
Rabbi Chaim I. Sperlin
310.734.9079

BRENTWOOD
Rabbi Boruch Hecht
Rabbi Mordechai Zaetz
310.826.4453

BURBANK
Rabbi Shmuly Kornfeld
818.954.0070

CARLSBAD
Rabbi Yeruchem Eilfort
Mrs. Nechama Eilfort
760.943.8891

CENTURY CITY
Rabbi Tzemach Cunin
310.860.1260

CHATSWORTH
Rabbi Yossi Spritzer
818.718.0777

CONTRA COSTA
Rabbi Dovber Berkowitz
925.937.4101

CORONADO
Rabbi Eli Fradkin
619.365.4728

ENCINO
Rabbi Joshua Gordon
Rabbi Aryeh Herzog
818.784.9986

FOLSOM
Rabbi Yossi Grossbaum
916.608.9811

GLENDALE
Rabbi Simcha Backman
818.240.2750

HUNTINGTON BEACH
Rabbi Aron Berkowitz
714.846.2285

IRVINE
Rabbi Alter Tenenbaum
Rabbi Elly Andrusier
949.786.5000

LA JOLLA
Rabbi Baruch Shalom Ezagui
858.455.5433

LAGUNA BEACH
Rabbi Elimelech Gurevitch
949.499.0770

LOMITA
Rabbi Eli Hecht
Rabbi Sholom Pinson
310.326.8234

LONG BEACH
Rabbi Abba Perelmuter
562.621.9828

LOS ANGELES
Rabbi Leibel Korf
323.660.5177

MARINA DEL REY
Rabbi Danny Yiftach-Hashem
Rabbi Mendy Avtzon
310.859.0770

NORTH HOLLYWOOD
Rabbi Nachman Abend
818.989.9539

NORTHRIDGE
Rabbi Eli Rivkin
818.368.3937

PACIFIC PALISADES
Rabbi Zushe Cunin
310.454.7783

PALO ALTO
Rabbi Menachem Landa
CLASSES IN HEBREW
650.322.1708

PASADENA
Rabbi Chaim Hanoka
626.564.8820

RANCHO MIRAGE
Rabbi Shimon H. Posner
760.770.7785

RANCHO PALOS VERDES
Rabbi Yitzchok Magalnic
310.544.5544

RANCHO S. FE
Rabbi Levi Raskin
858.756.7571

REDONDO BEACH
Rabbi Yossi Mintz
Rabbi Zalman Gordon
310.214.4999

SACRAMENTO
Rabbi Mendy Cohen
916.455.1400

S. BARBARA
Rabbi Zalman Kudan
CHAPTER FOUNDED BY
RABBI YOSEF LOSCHAK, OBM
805.683.1544

S. CLEMENTE
Rabbi Menachem M. Slavin
949.489.0723

S. DIEGO
Rabbi Motte Fradkin
858.547.0076

S. DIEGO-UNIVERSITY CITY
Rabbi Yudell Reiz
619.723.2439

Share the **Rohr JLI** experience with friends and relatives worldwide

S. Francisco
Rabbi Shlomo Zarchi
415.752.2866

Rabbi Peretz Mochkin
415.571.8770

S. Luis Obispo
Rabbi Chaim Leib Hilel
805.706.0256

S. Mateo
Rabbi Yossi Marcus
Rabbi Moishe Weinbaum
650.341.4510

S. Monica
Rabbi Boruch Rabinowitz
310.394.5699

S. Rafael
Rabbi Yisrael Rice
415.492.1666

South Bay
Rabbi Yosef Levin
Rabbi Ber Rosenblatt
650.424.9800

South Lake Tahoe
Rabbi Mordechai Richler
530.314.7677

Stockton
Rabbi Avremel Brod
209.952.2081

Studio City
Rabbi Yossi Baitelman
818.508.6633

Thousand Oaks
Rabbi Chaim Bryski
805.493.7776

Tustin
Rabbi Yehoshua Eliezrie
714.508.2150

Ventura
Rabbi Yakov Latowicz
Mrs. Sarah Latowicz
805.658.7441

Yorba Linda
Rabbi Dovid Eliezrie
714.693.0770

COLORADO
Aspen
Rabbi Mendel Mintz
970.544.3770

Denver
Rabbi Mendel Popack
720.515.4337

Rabbi Yossi Serebryanski
303.744.9699

Fort Collins
Rabbi Yerachmiel Gorelik
970.407.1613

Highlands Ranch
Rabbi Avraham Mintz
303.694.9119

Longmont
Rabbi Yakov Dovid Borenstein
303.678.7595

Vail
Rabbi Dovid Mintz
970.476.7887

Westminster
Rabbi Benjy Brackman
303.429.5177

CONNECTICUT
Greenwich
Rabbi Yossi Deren
Rabbi Menachem Feldman
203.629.9059

New Haven
Rabbi Yosef Y. Hodakov
203.795.5261

New London
Rabbi Avrohom Sternberg
860.437.8000

Orange
Rabbi Shea Hecht
203.795.7095

Stamford
Rabbi Yisrael Deren
Rabbi Levi Mendelow
203.3.CHABAD

West Hartford
Rabbi Yosef Gopin
Rabbi Shaya Gopin
860.659.2422

Westport
Rabbi Yehuda L. Kantor
Mrs. Dina Kantor
203.226.8584

DELAWARE
Wilmington
Rabbi Chuni Vogel
302.529.9900

FLORIDA
Bal Harbour
Rabbi Dov Schochet
305.868.1411

Boca Raton
Rabbi Zalman Bukiet
Rabbi Moishe Denburg
Rabbi Arele Gopin
561.417.7797

Boynton Beach
Rabbi Yosef Yitzchok Raichik
561.740.8738

Bradenton
Rabbi Menachem Bukiet
941.388.9656

Cape Coral
Rabbi Yossi Labkowski
239.541.1777

Coral Gables
Rabbi Avrohom Stolik
305.490.7572

Coral Springs
Rabbi Yankie Denburg
954.471.8646

Delray Beach
Rabbi Sholom Ber Korf
561.496.6228

East Boca Raton
Rabbi Ruvi New
561.417.7797

Fort Lauderdale
Rabbi Yitzchok Naparstek
954.568.1190

Fort Myers
Rabbi Yitzchok Minkowicz
Mrs. Nechama Minkowicz
239.433.7708

Hollywood
Rabbi Leizer Barash
954.965.9933

Kendall
Rabbi Yossi Harlig
305.234.5654

Lakeland
Rabbi Moshe Lazaros
863.510.5968

Lake Mary
Rabbi Yanky Majesky
407.878.3011

Miami Beach
Rabbi Shragi Mann
786.264.1111

Miami–Midtown
Rabbi Shmuel Gopin
305.573.9995

Ocala
Rabbi Yossi Hecht
352.291.2218

Orlando
Rabbi Yosef Konikov
407.354.3660

Palm Beach Gardens
Rabbi Dovid Vigler
561.624.2223

Palmetto Bay
Rabbi Zalman Gansburg
786.282.0413

Plantation
Rabbi Pinchas Taylor
954.644.9177

Ponte Vedra Beach
Rabbi Nochum Kurinsky
904.543.9301

Sarasota
Rabbi Chaim Shaul Steinmetz
941.925.0770

Satellite Beach
Rabbi Zvi Konikov
321.777.2770

SOUTH PALM BEACH
Rabbi Leibel Stolik
561.889.3499

SOUTH TAMPA
Rabbi Mendy Dubrowski
813.287.1795

SUNNY ISLES BEACH
Rabbi Alexander Kaller
305.803.5315

WESTON
Rabbi Yisroel Spalter
954.349.6565

WEST PALM BEACH
Rabbi Yoel Gancz
561.659.7770

VENICE
Rabbi Sholom Ber Schmerling
941.493.2770

GEORGIA
ALPHARETTA
Rabbi Hirshy Minkowicz
770.410.9000

ATLANTA
Rabbi Yossi New
Rabbi Isser New
404.843.2464

ATLANTA: INTOWN
Rabbi Eliyahu Schusterman
Rabbi Ari Sollish
404.898.0434

GWINNETT
Rabbi Yossi Lerman
678.595.0196

MARIETTA
Rabbi Ephraim Silverman
770.565.4412

IDAHO
BOISE
Rabbi Mendel Lifshitz
208.853.9200

ILLINOIS
CHAMPAIGN
Rabbi Dovid Tiechtel
217.355.8672

CHICAGO
Rabbi Meir Hecht
312.714.4655

Rabbi Yosef Moscowitz
773.772.3770

Rabbi Levi Notik
773.274.5123

CHICAGO-HYDE PARK
Rabbi Yossi Brackman
773.955.8672

GLENVIEW
Rabbi Yishaya Benjaminson
847.998.9896

HIGHLAND PARK
Mrs. Michla Schanowitz
847.266.0770

NAPERVILLE
Rabbi Mendy Goldstein
630.778.9770

NORTHBROOK
Rabbi Meir Moscowitz
847.564.8770

Rabbi Menachem Slavaticki
CLASSES IN HEBREW
847.350.9770

OAK PARK
Rabbi Yitzchok Bergstein
708.524.1530

PEORIA
Rabbi Eli Langsam
309.692.2250

ROCKFORD
Rabbi Yecheskel Rothman
815.596.0032

SKOKIE
Rabbi Yochanan Posner
847.677.1770

WILMETTE
Rabbi Dovid Flinkenstein
847.251.7707

INDIANA
INDIANAPOLIS
Rabbi Mendel Schusterman
317.251.5573

KANSAS
OVERLAND PARK
Rabbi Mendy Wineberg
913.649.4852

KENTUCKY
LOUISVILLE
Rabbi Avrohom Litvin
502.459.1770

LOUISIANA
METAIRIE
Rabbi Yossie Nemes
Rabbi Mendel Ceitlin
504.454.2910

MARYLAND
BALTIMORE
Rabbi Elchonon Lisbon
410.358.4787

Rabbi Velvel Belinsky
CLASSES IN RUSSIAN
410.764.5000

BEL AIR
Rabbi Yekusiel Schusterman
443.353.9718

BETHESDA
Rabbi Bentzion Geisinsky
Rabbi Sender Geisinsky
301.913.9777

COLUMBIA
Rabbi Hillel Baron
Rabbi Yosef Chaim Sufrin
410.740.2424

FREDERICK
Rabbi Boruch Labkowski
301.996.3659

GAITHERSBURG
Rabbi Sholom Raichik
301.926.3632

OLNEY
Rabbi Bentzy Stolik
301.660.6770

OWINGS MILLS
Rabbi Nochum H. Katsenelenbogen
410.356.5156

POTOMAC
Rabbi Mendel Bluming
301.983.4200

Rabbi Mendel Kaplan
301.983.1485

ROCKVILLE
Rabbi Moishe Kavka
301.836.1242

SILVER SPRING
Rabbi Berel Wolvovsky
301.593.1117

MASSACHUSETTS
ANDOVER
Rabbi Asher Bronstein
Rabbi Zalman Borenstein
978.470.2288

CAPE COD
Rabbi Yekusiel Alperowitz
508.775.2324

CHESTNUT HILL
Rabbi Mendy Uminer
617.738.9770

LONGMEADOW
Rabbi Yakov Wolff
413.567.8665

NEWTON
Rabbi Shalom Ber Prus
617.244.1200

MILFORD
Rabbi Mendy Kievman
508.473.1299

SUDBURY
Rabbi Yisroel Freeman
978.443.3691

SWAMPSCOTT
Mrs. Layah Lipsker
781.581.3833

Share the **Rohr JLI** experience with friends and relatives worldwide

MICHIGAN

ANN ARBOR
Rabbi Aharon Goldstein
734.995.3276

GRAND RAPIDS
Rabbi Mordechai Haller
616.957.0770

WEST BLOOMFIELD
Rabbi Elimelech Silberberg
248.855.6170

MINNESOTA

MINNETONKA
Rabbi Mordechai Grossbaum
952.929.9922

S. PAUL
Rabbi Shneur Zalman Bendet
651.278.8401

MISSOURI

S. LOUIS
Rabbi Yosef Landa
314.725.0400

MONTANA

BOZEMAN
Rabbi Chaim Shaul Bruk
406.585.8770

NEVADA

SUMMERLIN
Rabbi Yisroel Schanowitz
Rabbi Tzvi Bronchtain
702.855.0770

NEW JERSEY

BASKING RIDGE
Rabbi Mendy Herson
908.604.8844

CHERRY HILL
Rabbi Mendy Mangel
856.874.1500

CLINTON
Rabbi Eli Kornfeld
908.623.7000

FAIR LAWN
Rabbi Avrohom Bergstein
718.839.5296

FANWOOD
Rabbi Avrohom Blesofsky
908.790.0008

FORT LEE
Rabbi Meir Konikov
201.886.1238

FRANKLIN LAKES
Rabbi Chanoch Kaplan
201.848.0449

HASKELL
Rabbi Mendy Gurkov
201.696.7609

HILLSBOROUGH
Rabbi Shmaya Krinsky
908.874.0444

HOLMDEL
Rabbi Shmaya Galperin
732.772.1998

MADISON
Rabbi Shalom Lubin
973.377.0707

MANALAPAN
Rabbi Boruch Chazanow
Rabbi Levi Wolosow
732.972.3687

MEDFORD
Rabbi Yitzchok Kahan
609.953.3150

MOUNTAIN LAKES
Rabbi Levi Dubinsky
973.551.1898

MULLICA HILL
Rabbi Avrohom Richler
856.733.0770

NORTH BRUNSWICK
Rabbi Levi Azimov
732.398.9492

OLD TAPPAN
Rabbi Mendy Lewis
201.767.4008

ROCKAWAY
Rabbi Asher Herson
Rabbi Mordechai Baumgarten
973.625.1525

TEANECK
Rabbi Ephraim Simon
201.907.0686

TENAFLY
Rabbi Mordechai Shain
Rabbi Yitzchak Gershovitz
201.871.1152

TOMS RIVER
Rabbi Moshe Gourarie
732.349.4199

WEST ORANGE
Rabbi Mendy Kasowitz
973.486.2362

WOODCLIFF LAKE
Rabbi Dov Drizin
201.476.0157

NEW MEXICO

S. FE
Rabbi Berel Levertov
505.983.2000

NEW YORK

BEDFORD
Rabbi Arik Wolf
914.666.6065

BINGHAMTON
Mrs. Rivkah Slonim
607.797.0015

BRIGHTON BEACH
Rabbi Zushe Winner
Rabbi Moshe Winner
718.946.9833

BRONXVILLE
Rabbi Sruli Deitsch
917.755.0078

BROOKLYN HEIGHTS
Rabbi Mendy Hecht
Rabbi Ari Raskin
347.378.2641

CEDARHURST
Rabbi Zalman Wolowik
516.295.2478

CHESTNUT RIDGE
Rabbi Chaim Tzvi Ehrenreich
845.356.6686

COMMACK
Rabbi Mendel Teldon
631.543.3343

DIX HILLS
Rabbi Yaakov Saacks
631.351.8672

DOBBS FERRY
Rabbi Benjy Silverman
914.693.6100

EAST HAMPTON
Rabbi Leibel Baumgarten
Rabbi Mendy Goldberg
631.329.5800

FOREST HILLS
Rabbi Yossi Mendelson
917.861.9726

GREAT NECK
Rabbi Yoseph Geisinsky
516.487.4554

ITHACA
Rabbi Eli Silberstein
607.257.7379

KINGSTON
Rabbi Yitzchok Hecht
845.334.9044

LARCHMONT
Rabbi Mendel Silberstein
914.834.4321

LONG BEACH
Rabbi Eli Goodman
516.897.2473

NYC KEHILATH JESHURUN
Rabbi Elie Weinstock
212.774.5636

NYC TRIBECA
Rabbi S. Zalman Paris
646.510.3109

OSSINING
Rabbi Dovid Labkowski
914.923.2522

PORT WASHINGTON
Rabbi Shalom Paltiel
516.767.8672

Share the **Rohr JLI** experience with friends and relatives worldwide

RIVERDALE
Rabbi Levi Shemtov
718.549.1100

ROCHESTER
Rabbi Nechemia Vogel
585.271.0330

ROSLYN
Rabbi Yaakov Reiter
516.484.8185

SEA GATE
Rabbi Chaim Brikman
718.266.1736

Rabbi Nachman Segal
CLASSES IN HEBREW
718.761.4483

STONY BROOK
Rabbi Shalom Ber Cohen
631.585.0521

SUFFERN
Rabbi Shmuel Gancz
845.368.1889

WESTBURY
Rabbi Mendy Brownstein
516.850.4486

WOODBURY
Rabbi Shmuel Lipszyc
516.682.0404

NORTH CAROLINA
ASHEVILLE
Rabbi Shaya Susskind
828.505.0746

CARYY
Rabbi Yisroel Cotlar
919.651.9710

CHAPEL HILL
Rabbi Zalman Bluming
919.630.5129

CHARLOTTE
Rabbi Yossi Groner
Rabbi Shlomo Cohen
704.366.3984

GREENSBORO
Rabbi Yosef Plotkin
336.617.8120

RALEIGH
Rabbi Pinchas Herman
Rabbi Lev Cotlar
919.637.6950

WILMINGTON
Rabbi Moshe Lieblich
910.763.4770

NORTH DAKOTA
FARGO
Rabbi Yonah Grossman
701.212.4164

OHIO
BEACHWOOD
Rabbi Shmuli Friedman
Rabbi Moshe Gancz
216.370.2887

BLUE ASH
Rabbi Yisroel Mangel
513.793.5200

COLUMBUS
Rabbi Areyah Kaltmann
Rabbi Levi Andrusier
614.294.3296

OKLAHOMA
OKLAHOMA CITY
Rabbi Ovadia Goldman
405.524.4800

TULSA
Rabbi Yehuda Weg
918.492.4499

OREGON
PORTLAND
Rabbi Moshe Wilhelm
Rabbi Mordechai Wilhelm
503.977.9947

SALEM
Rabbi Avrohom Yitzchok Perlstein
503.383.9569

PENNSYLVANIA
AMBLER
Rabbi Shaya Deitsch
215.591.9310

BALA CYNWYD
Rabbi Shraga Sherman
610.660.9192

LAFAYETTE HILL
Rabbi Yisroel Kotlarsky
347.526.1430

LANCASTER
Rabbi Elazar Green
717.368.6565

MEDIA
Rabbi Eli Dovid Strasberg
610.543.5095

NEWTOWN
Rabbi Aryeh Weinstein
215.497.9925

PHILADELPHIA: CENTER CITY
Rabbi Yochonon Goldman
215.238.2100

PITTSBURGH
Rabbi Yisroel Altein
412.422.7300 ext. 269

PITTSBURGH: SOUTH HILLS
Rabbi Mendy Rosenblum
412.278.3693

RYDAL
Rabbi Zushe Gurevitz
215.572.1511

WYNNEWOOD
Rabbi Moishe Brennan
610.529.9011

RHODE ISLAND
WARWICK
Rabbi Yossi Laufer
401.884.7888

SOUTH CAROLINA
COLUMBIA
Rabbi Hesh Epstein
803.782.1831

TENNESSEE
CHATTANOOGA
Rabbi Shaul Perlstein
423.490.1106

KNOXVILLE
Rabbi Yossi Wilhelm
865.588.8584

MEMPHIS
Rabbi Levi Klein
901.766.1800

TEXAS
ARLINGTON
Rabbi Levi Gurevitch
817.451.1171

DALLAS
Rabbi Peretz Shapiro
Rabbi Moshe Naparstek
972.818.0770

FORT WORTH
Rabbi Dov Mandel
817.263.7701

HOUSTON
Rabbi Moishe Traxler
713.774.0300

HOUSTON: RICE UNIVERSITY AREA
Rabbi Eliezer Lazaroff
713.522.2004

LEAGUE CITY
Rabbi Yitzchok Schmukler
713.398.2460

PLANO
Rabbi Mendel Block
Rabbi Yehudah Horowitz
972.596.8270

S. ANTONIO
Rabbi Chaim Block
Rabbi Levi Teldon
210.492.1085

THE WOODLANDS
Rabbi Mendel Blecher
281.719.5213

UTAH
SALT LAKE CITY
Rabbi Benny Zippel
801.467.7777

VERMONT
BURLINGTON
Rabbi Yitzchok Raskin
802.658.5770

VIRGINIA
ALEXANDRIA/ARLINGTON
Rabbi Mordechai Newman
703.370.2774

FAIRFAX
Rabbi Leibel Fajnland
703.426.1980

NORFOLK
Rabbi Aaron Margolin
Rabbi Levi Brashevitzky
757.616.0770

RICHMOND
Rabbi Shlomo Pereira
804.740.2000

TYSONS CORNER
Rabbi Chezzy Deitsch
CHAPTER FOUNDED BY
RABBI LEVI DEITSCH, OBM
703.829.5770

WASHINGTON
OLYMPIA
Rabbi Cheski Edelman
360.584.4306

SEATTLE
Rabbi Elazar Bogomilsky
206.527.1411

SPOKANE COUNTY
Rabbi Yisroel Hahn
509.443.0770

WISCONSIN
MADISON
Rabbi Avremel Matusof
608.231.3450

MILWAUKEE
Rabbi Mendel Shmotkin
414.961.6100

WAUKESHA
Rabbi Levi Brook
925.708.4203

PUERTO RICO
CAROLINA
Rabbi Mendel Zarchi
787.253.0894

ARGENTINA
BUENOS AIRES
Rabbi Mendel Levy
Rabbi Shlomo Levy
54.11.4807.2223

CAPITAL FEDERAL
Rabbi Mendy Gurevitch
54.11.4545.7771

PALERMO NUEVO
Rabbi Mendy Grunblatt
54.11.4772.1024

RECOLETA
Rabbi Hirshel Hendel
54.11.4807.7073

AUSTRALIA
AUSTRALIAN CAPITAL TERRITORY
CANBERRA
Rabbi Shmuel Feldman
614.3167.7805

NEW SOUTH WALES
BONDI BEACH
Rabbi Aron Moss
612.8005.6613

DOUBLE BAY
Rabbi Yanky Berger
Rabbi Yisroel Dolnikov
612.9327.1644

DOVER HEIGHTS
Rabbi Motti Feldman
612.9387.3822

NORTH SHORE
Rabbi Nochum Schapiro
Mrs. Fruma Schapiro
612.9488.9548

RANDWICK
Rabbi Aryeh Leib Solomon
613.9375.1600

SOUTH HEAD
Rabbi Benzion Milecki
612.9337.6775

QUEENSLAND
BRISBANE
Rabbi Levi Jaffe
617.3843.6770

SOUTH AUSTRALIA
GLENSIDE
Rabbi Yossi Engel
618.8338.2922

VICTORIA
BENTLEIGH EAST
Rabbi Mendel Raskin
613.9570.6707

CAULFIELD SOUTH
Rabbi Peretz Schapiro
613.9532.9180

ELSTERNWICK
Rabbi Chaim Cowen
614.3330.8584

Rabbi Motty Liberow
613.9533.0090

MALVERN
Rabbi Zev Slavin
614.0476.6759

Rabbi Shimshon Yurkowicz
613.9822.3600

MELBOURNE
Rabbi Mendel Groner
613.9532.7299

Rabbi Dovid Gutnick
614.3038.4948

MOORABBIN
Rabbi Elisha Greenbaum
614.0349.0434

WESTERN AUSTRALIA
PERTH
Rabbi Shalom White
618.9275.2106

BELARUS
GRODNO
Rabbi Yitzchak Kofman
375.29.644.3690

BRAZIL
RIO DE JANEIRO
Rabbi Avrohom Tsvi Beuthner
Rabbi Yehoshua Binyomin Goldman
55.21.2294.3138

S. PAULO
Rabbi Avraham Steinmetz
55.11.3081.3081

CANADA
ALBERTA
CALGARY
Rabbi Mordechai Groner
403.238.4880

EDMONTON
Rabbi Ari Drelich
Rabbi Mendy Blachman
780.851.1515

BRITISH COLUMBIA
KELOWNA
Rabbi Shmuly Hecht
250.575.5384

RICHMOND
Rabbi Yechiel Baitelman
604.277.6427

VANCOUVER
Rabbi Yitzchok Wineberg
604.266.1313

VICTORIA
Rabbi Meir Kaplan
250.595.7656

MANITOBA
WINNIPEG
Rabbi Avrohom Altein
Rabbi Shmuel Altein
204.339.8737

NOVA SCOTIA
HALIFAX
Rabbi Mendel Feldman
902.422.4222

ONTARIO
HAMILTON
Rabbi Chanoch Rosenfeld
905.529.7458

LAWRENCE/EGLINTON
Rabbi Menachem Gansburg
416.546.8770

LONDON
Rabbi Eliezer Gurkow
519.434.3962

MISSISSAUGA
Rabbi Yitzchok Slavin
905.820.4432

NIAGARA FALLS
Rabbi Zalman Zaltzman
905.356.7200

OTTAWA
Rabbi Menachem M. Blum
613.823.0866

RICHMOND HILL
Rabbi Mendel Bernstein
905.770.7700

Rabbi Yossi Hecht
905.773.6477

TORONTO AREA BJL
Rabbi Leib Chaiken
416.916.7202

GREATER TORONTO
REGIONAL OFFICE & THORNHILL
Rabbi Yossi Gansburg
905.731.7000

YORK MILLS
Rabbi Levi Gansburg
647.345.3800

WATERLOO
Rabbi Moshe Goldman
226.338.7770

WHITBY
Rabbi Tzali Borenstein
905.493.9007

QUEBEC
MONTREAL
Rabbi Ronnie Fine
Pesach Nussbaum
514.342.3.JLI

Rabbi Levi Y New
514.739.0770

TOWN OF MOUNT ROYAL
Rabbi Moshe Krasnanski
Rabbi Shneur Zalman Rader
514.739.0770

VILLE S. LAURENT
Rabbi Schneur Zalmen Silberstein
514.808.1418

WESTMOUNT
Rabbi Yossi Shanowitz
Mrs. Devorah Leah Shanowitz
514.937.4772

SASKATCHEWAN
SASKATOON
Rabbi Raphael Kats
306.384.4370

CAYMAN ISLAND
GRAND CAYMAN
Rabbi Berel Pewzner
717.798.1040

COLOMBIA
BOGOTA
Rabbi Yehoshua B. Rosenfeld
Rabbi Chanoch Piekarski
571.635.8251

DENMARK
COPENHAGEN
Rabbi Yitzchok Lowenthal
45.3316.1850

ESTONIA
TALLINN
Rabbi Shmuel Kot
372.662.30.50

GEORGIA
TBILISI
Rabbi Meir Kozlovsky
995.593.23.91.15

GERMANY
BERLIN
Rabbi Yehuda Tiechtel
49.30.2128.0830

COLOGNE
Rabbi Mendel Schtroks
49.22.1240.3902

DUSSELDORF
Rabbi Chaim Barkahn
49.21.1420.9693

HAMBURG
Rabbi Shlomo Bistriztsky
49.40.4142.4190

MUNICH
Rabbi Yochonon Gordon
49.89.4190.2812

GREECE
ATHENS
Rabbi Mendel Hendel
30.210.520.2880

GUATEMALA
GUATEMALA CITY
Rabbi Shalom Pelman
502.2485.0770

ISRAEL
ASHKELON
Rabbi Shneor Lieberman
054.977.0512

BALFURYA
Rabbi Noam Bar-Tov
054.580.4770

CAESAREA
Rabbi Chaim Meir Lieberman
054.621.2586

EVEN YEHUDA
Rabbi Menachem Noyman
054.777.0707

GANEI TIKVA
Rabbi Gershon Shnur
054.524.2358

GIV'ATAYIM
Rabbi Pinchus Bitton
052.643.8770

HAIFA
Rabbi Yehuda Dunin
054.426.3763

KARMIEL
Rabbi Mendy Elishevitz
054.521.3073

KFAR SABBA
Rabbi Yossi Baitch
054.445.5020

KIRYAT BIALIK
Rabbi Pinny Marton
050.661.1768

KIRYAT MOTZKIN
Rabbi Shimon Eizenbach
050.902.0770

KOCHAV YAIR
Rabbi Dovi Greenberg
054.332.6244

MACCABIM RE'UT
Rabbi Yosef Yitzchak Noiman
054.977.0549

MALE ADUMIM
Rabbi Mordechai Weiss
CLASSES IN ENGLISH
201.353.7946

MODIIN
Rabbi Boruch Slonim
054.300.1770

NES ZIYONA
Rabbi Menachem Feldman
054.497.7092

NETANYA
Rabbi Schneur Brod
054.579.7572

RAMAT GAN-KRINITZI
Rabbi Yisroel Gurevitz
052.743.2814

RAMAT GAN-MAROM NAVE
Rabbi Binyamin Meir Kali
050.476.0770

Share the **Rohr JLI** experience with friends and relatives worldwide

RAMAT YISHAI
Rabbi Shneor Zalman Wolosow
052.324.5475

RISHON LEZION
Rabbi Uri Keshet
050.722.4593

ROSH PINA
Rabbi Sholom Ber Hertzel
052.458.7600

YEHUD
Rabbi Shmuel Wolf
053.536.1479

ITALY
FIRENZE
Rabbi Levi Wolvovsky
39.389.595.2034

KAZAKHSTAN
ALMATY
Rabbi Shevach Zlatopolsky
7.7272.77.59.77

LATVIA
RIGA
Rabbi Shneur Zalman Kot
371.6733.1520

NETHERLANDS
DEN HAAG
Rabbi Shmuel Katzman
31.70.347.0222

NOORD-HOLLAND
AMSTERDAM
Rabbi Yanki Jacobs
31.6.4498.8627

PANAMA
PANAMA CITY
Rabbi Ari Laine
Rabbi Gabriel Benayon
507.223.3383

RUSSIA
ASTRAKHAN
Rabbi Yisroel Melamed
7.851.239.28.24

BRYANSK
Rabbi Menachem Mendel Zaklas
7.483.264.55.15

CHELYABINSK
Rabbi Meir Kirsh
7.351.263.24.68

MOSCOW-MARINA ROSHA
Rabbi Mordechai Weisberg
7.495.645.50.00

MOSCOW-SOKOLNIKI
Rabbi Avraham Bekerman
7.495.660.07.70

NIZHNY NOVGOROD
Rabbi Shimon Bergman
7.920.253.47.70

OMSK
Rabbi Osher Krichevsky
7.381.231.33.07

PERM
Rabbi Zalman Deutch
7.342.212.47.32

SAMARA
Rabbi Shlomo Deutch
7.846.333.40.64

SARATOV
Rabbi Yaakov Kubitshek
7.8452.21.58.00

S. PETERSBURG
Rabbi Zvi Pinsky
7.812.713.62.09

ROSTOV
Rabbi Chaim Danzinger
7.8632.99.02.68

TOGLIATTI
Rabbi Meier Fischer
7.848.273.02.84

UFA
Rabbi Dan Krichevsky
7.347.244.55.33

VORONEZH
Rabbi Levi Stiefel
7.473.252.96.99

SINGAPORE
SINGAPORE
Rabbi Mordechai Abergel
656.337.2189

Rabbi Netanel Rivni
CLASSES IN HEBREW
656.336.2127

SOUTH AFRICA
CAPE TOWN
Rabbi Mendel Popack
Rabbi Pinchas Hecht
27.21.434.3740

JOHANNESBURG
Rabbi Dovid Hazdan
Rabbi Shmuel Simpson
27.11.728.8152

Rabbi Dovid Masinter
Rabbi Ari Kievman
27.11.440.6600

SWEDEN
STOCKHOLM
Rabbi Chaim Greisman
468.679.7067

SWITZERLAND
BASEL
Rabbi Zalman Wishedski
41.76.559.9236

LUGANO
Rabbi Yaakov Tzvi Kantor
41.91.921.3720

LUZERN
Rabbi Chaim Drukman
41.41.361.1770

UKRAINE
CHERKASSY
Rabbi Dov Axelrod
380.472.45.7080

DNEPROPETROVSK
Rabbi Dan Makagon
380.504.51.13.18

NIKOLAYEV
Rabbi Sholom Gotlieb
380.512.37.37.71

ZHITOMIR
Rabbi Shlomo Wilhelm
380.504.63.01.32

ODESSA
Rabbi Avraham Wolf
Rabbi Yaakov Neiman
38.048.728.0770 ext. 280

UNITED KINGDOM
EDGEWARE
Rabbi Leivi Sudak
Rabbi Yaron Jacobs
44.208.905.4141

LEEDS
Rabbi Eli Pink
44.113.266.3311

LONDON
Rabbi Gershon Overlander
Rabbi Dovid Katz
44.208.202.1600

Rabbi Nissan D. Dubov
44.20.8944.1581

MANCHESTER
Rabbi Akiva Cohen
Rabbi Levi Cohen
44.161.740.4243

URUGUAY
MONTEVIDEO
Rabbi Eliezer Shemtov
598.2.709.3444

VENEZUELA
CARACAS
Rabbi Yehoshua Rosenblum
58.212.264.7011

Share the **Rohr JLI** experience with friends and relatives worldwide

NOTES

NOTES

THE JEWISH LEARNING MULTIPLEX

Brought to you by the Rohr Jewish Learning Institute

In fulfillment of the mandate of the Lubavitcher Rebbe, of blessed memory,
whose leadership guides every step of our work,
the mission of the Rohr Jewish Learning Institute is to transform
Jewish life and the greater community through the study of Torah,
connecting each Jew to our shared heritage of Jewish learning.

While our flagship program remains the cornerstone of our organization,
JLI is proud to feature additional divisions catering to specific populations,
in order to meet a wide array of educational needs.

THE ROHR JEWISH LEARNING INSTITUTE,
a subsidiary of *Merkos L'Inyonei Chinuch,*
is the adult education arm of the Chabad-Lubavitch Movement.